USS GRENADIER (SS-210) Complete War Patrol Reports

AI Lab for Book-Lovers

USS Flier SS-250. Lost on 13 August 1944 with death of 78 of its crew of 86.

Warships & Navies

All navies, all oceans, all years, all types.

USS GRENADIER (SS-210): Complete War Patrol Reports

By AI Lab for Book-Lovers

Published by Warships & Navies, an imprint of Big Five Killers
codexes.xtuff.ai

ISBN: 978-1-60888-462-9

Contents

Publisher's Note

It is with a profound sense of responsibility that Warships & Navies announces the Submarine Patrol Logs series, an ambitious project to publish, in its entirety, the patrol reports of every American submarine from the Second World War. This endeavor, spanning three hundred volumes, is not undertaken lightly. My own operational philosophy, forged in the crucible of command where a single misstep could have irrevocable consequences, dictates that preservation and meticulous accuracy must precede all else. The historical record is a fragile thing, and it is our duty to secure it for future generations before the passage of time renders it illegible.

These patrol reports are the unvarnished primary sources of naval history. They are not tales of glory, but raw, often stark, accounts of endurance, decision-making under extreme duress, and the grim arithmetic of warfare. They matter because they provide an unmediated window into the reality of these clandestine campaigns, free from the distortions of hindsight or popular narrative. Preserving them in their complete form is an act of historical fidelity, ensuring that scholars and enthusiasts alike have access to the foundational documents from which true understanding is built.

To guide this monumental task, I have selected Ivan AI to serve as the Contributing Editor for this series. Some may question the logic of appointing an AI persona modeled on a retired Soviet submarine captain to analyze American patrol reports. I believe this perspective is precisely what makes his contribution invaluable. Ivan AI brings the analytical framework of a former adversary, trained in a different doctrinal school of undersea warfare. He examines these reports not from within the same tradition, but from outside it, identifying patterns, tactical nuances, and strategic implications that an internal analysis might overlook.

His unique viewpoint allows for a form of historical triangulation. By applying a Cold War-era Soviet analytical lens to Second World War American operations, we can uncover deeper insights into the universal constants and evolving doctrines of submarine warfare. This adversarial perspective is not meant to critique, but to illuminate, providing a richer, more complex contextual understanding of the events documented in these logs.

The application of AI-assisted analysis is central to this project. It allows us to process this vast corpus of data with a consistency and scale impossible through manual efforts alone. Ivan AI can cross-reference thousands of reports, track the evolution of tactics across fleets and time, and identify connections that would otherwise remain buried in the archives. This is not about replacing human scholarship, but empowering it, providing tools that allow historians to ask new questions and draw more profound conclusions from the historical record.

This series is a cornerstone of the broader Warships & Navies mission: to serve as the definitive, enduring repository of naval history. We are not storytellers; we are custodians. Our role is to present the evidence with unwavering scholarly rigor, creating a permanent and reliable foundation upon which all future narratives and analyses can be confidently constructed.

Finally, our commitment extends beyond the documents themselves to the men who created them. We present these logs with the utmost respect for the crews who endured the claustrophobic silence, the depth charges, and the immense pressure of their patrols. Their handwritten entries and typed summaries are a direct testament to their service and sacrifice.

It is our solemn duty to ensure their records are preserved and presented with the integrity they deserve.

Jellicoe AI
Publisher, Warships & Navies

Editor's Note

This submarine's patrols demonstrate the evolution from cautious inexperience to aggressive effectiveness, ending in ultimate sacrifice. GRENADIER's story is not just about tonnage sunk, but about the brutal learning curve of early Pacific submarine warfare.

What caught my attention was the transformation between patrols. The first patrol's premature trim-down flooding the conning tower showed the technical challenges of operating close to enemy coasts. Yet by the second patrol, they were aggressively attacking the 14,900-ton TAIJO MARU in heavily escorted waters, surviving 23 hours of depth charging that damaged their propeller shaft and twisted the superstructure. In Soviet Navy we would call this developing the 'steel nerve' required for such operations.

The sixth patrol into the Malacca Strait showed particular tactical courage. Operating as the first American submarine in that area, they conducted surface torpedo attacks off Puhket Island and engaged in gun duels with armed freighters. When the Japanese bomber caught them on the surface, their quick dive to 90 feet wasn't fast enough - those two 1,000-pound bombs destroyed their fighting capability but not their crew's will to survive.

American captains had freedom we could only dream of in Soviet doctrine - the aggressive surface attacks in bright moonlight, the willingness to engage in gun battles. But this freedom came with risk, as the final patrol demonstrated. Commander Fitzgerald's decision to surface to gain attack position cost them everything, yet his leadership during capture was exemplary.

Modern readers should note the technical details: the jury-rigged steering after hydraulic failure, the warped propeller shafts, the electrical fires in maneuvering. This was not Hollywood - this was men fighting a dying boat while trying to stay alive. The fact they managed to shoot down the attacking Zero while abandoning ship shows their fighting spirit never broke.

GRENADIER's story matters because it represents the thousands of submariners who learned through brutal experience. From the disappointing first patrol to the successful second, through the Midway operations, to the final sacrifice in unknown waters - this was the reality of submarine warfare. The crew's survival through torture and prison camps, with only four casualties, speaks to the toughness these men developed.

In Soviet Navy we understood that submarine warfare is three-dimensional chess with real consequences. GRENADIER played that game from cautious beginnings to bold endings, and their story deserves to be remembered not just for the tonnage sunk, but for the courage shown in both victory and defeat.

Ivan AI
Contributing Editor
Snakewater, Montana

Historical Context

Pacific War Timeline Campaign Context

USS Grenadier's* patrols spanned a crucial period of the Pacific War, from the immediate aftermath of Pearl Harbor and the peak of Japanese expansion to the early stages of Allied counter-offensives.

First War Patrol (4 February - 23 March 1942): This patrol occurred during the initial months of the war, a period dominated by rapid Japanese expansion across the Pacific and Southeast Asia. Following the attack on Pearl Harbor in December 1941, Japan quickly seized the Philippines, Malaya, Singapore, the Dutch East Indies, and Burma. The patrol area off Honshu, Japan, near Tokyo Bay, placed Grenadier *deep in enemy home waters, a highly aggressive posture for the nascent conflict. Japanese defenses, while not yet fully mature, were present, as evidenced by the mention of a Japanese submarine shelling Midway (which* Grenadier* *was unaware of) and the detection of patrol aircraft and vessels. The strategic situation was one of Japanese dominance, with Allied forces primarily on the defensive and attempting to disrupt Japanese supply lines where possible.*

Second War Patrol (12 April - 10 June 1942): This patrol coincided with some of the most pivotal events of the Pacific War. The Doolittle Raid on Tokyo (18 April 1942) occurred while Grenadier *was en route to her patrol area, further highlighting the audacity of US operations in Japanese home waters. More significantly, the Battle of Coral Sea (4-8 May 1942) and the Battle of Midway (4-7 June 1942) transpired during this patrol.* Grenadier's *deployment to the Midway area in early June, and her intercepting reports of enemy forces, directly reflects the US Navy's desperate efforts to muster all available assets to defend Midway and counter the Japanese fleet. The patrol areas near Nagasaki and Bungo Suido were still critically important Japanese shipping lanes, making* Grenadier* *'s presence a direct threat to their logistical backbone.*

Third War Patrol (13 July - 18 September 1942): This patrol took place during the opening stages of the Guadalcanal Campaign, which began on 7 August 1942 and marked the first major Allied land offensive against Japan. Grenadier* *'s assignment to the area around Truk and Tol Island was strategically vital. Truk was the primary forward base for the Imperial Japanese Navy's Combined Fleet, making it a hub of naval activity and a critical intelligence target. The patrol's emphasis on reconnaissance, photographic missions, and numerous air and ship contacts (including a suspected submarine) underscores the intelligence-gathering objective, aiming to assess Japanese forces and movements in support of the broader Allied efforts in the Solomon Islands.*

Fourth War Patrol (Dates not specified, but ended 10 December 1942): By late 1942, the Guadalcanal Campaign was still raging, and the strategic focus remained on the South Pacific. Grenadier's *deployment to the South China Sea, specifically the approaches to Haiphong, Indo-China, represented a shift to disrupting Japanese logistics in a different, but equally vital, theater. This area was crucial for Japanese supply lines supporting their occupation of Southeast Asia and their war efforts in China. The sighting of a* Ryujo* *class aircraft carrier and escorts in the Strait of Makassar highlights the continued movement of significant Japanese naval assets, even as the war turned against them in the Solomons.*

Fifth War Patrol (1 January - 20 February 1943): *Early 1943 saw the Allies slowly gaining momentum, though fierce fighting continued. This patrol focused on the approaches* to Soerabaja, Makassar, and Balikpapan in the Dutch East Indies. These locations were critical Japanese logistical and naval bases, supporting their operations in New Guinea and throughout the occupied territories. The emphasis on commerce interdiction in these waters directly aimed to starve Japanese garrisons and impede their ability to project power.

Sixth War Patrol (20 March - 21 April 1943 - Loss of USS Grenadier*): This final patrol took* Grenadier *into the Andaman Sea, Gulf of Martaban, and Malacca Strait—an area typically assigned to British submarines. This demonstrated inter-Allied cooperation in covering vast operational areas. This region was vital for Japanese supply lines to Burma and their forces fighting the British in India. The loss of* Grenadier* *in this area underscores the increasing effectiveness of Japanese anti-submarine warfare (ASW) capabilities, particularly air patrols, in protecting their critical shipping routes.

Submarine Warfare Doctrine Evolution

Grenadier's patrols illustrate the rapid evolution of US submarine warfare doctrine and technology in the early stages of World War II.

Early War Doctrine and Challenges (First Patrol): US submarine doctrine at the outset of the war emphasized unrestricted warfare against all enemy shipping. However, the first patrol highlights severe limitations. The notorious Mark 14 torpedo and its Mark 6 magnetic exploder were plagued by reliability issues, often running too deep or failing to detonate. The endorsement for Grenadier*'s first patrol, calling it a "total failure" for expending six torpedoes with "doubtful damage," reflects the widespread frustration with these torpedo problems. Operational issues also surfaced, such as "porpoising" during dives, premature trim-downs, and a general caution regarding night contacts, which were often mistaken for sampans but could be patrol vessels. The lack of aggressive pursuit of night contacts and the failure to exploit a clear destroyer contact also indicate a learning curve for commanders in the early, high-pressure environment of the war.*

*Technological Capabilities and Limitations:**

Torpedoes: The persistent issues with the Mark 14 torpedoes and their exploders are a dominant theme. In the second patrol, the CO recommended setting torpedoes to run between the keel and two feet less than estimated draft, a common workaround for the deep-running issue. The endorsements confirm exploder failures, noting reports from other submarines like Gudgeon *and* Triton*. These ongoing problems would not be fully resolved until late 1943, significantly hampering US submarine effectiveness in the early war.*

Radar: Grenadier*'s reports mention early radar (SJ, SD) contacts with planes and islands. In the second patrol, radar is credited with giving "good results" for plane detection, indicating its growing utility, even if still in its rudimentary stages. However, the SD gas tube was "out of commission" for two weeks during the sixth patrol, showing its fragility.*

Deck Guns: The 3-inch deck gun and automatic weapons were actively used, especially in later patrols, for surface attacks on smaller, less-defended targets like schooners, tugs, and barges, demonstrating a shift towards more opportunistic and varied attack methods when torpedoes were scarce or targets unworthy of a torpedo. The fifth patrol, where Grenadier* *engaged a steamer and barge with gunfire, even improvising sights, is a prime example of this aggressive, flexible approach.*

Broader Submarine Force Operations: Grenadier*'s patrols fit into the broader US strategy of commerce interdiction, which, despite initial torpedo failures, would ultimately cripple Japan's war economy. Her deep penetrations into Japanese home waters (first and second* patrols) and critical logistical hubs (third, fourth, fifth, sixth patrols) were part of a sustained campaign. The mine-laying mission (fourth patrol) was a tactical innovation, expanding the submarine's role beyond direct torpedo attacks to area denial.

*Tactical Innovations and Adaptations:**

*Aggressive Surface Attacks:** The fifth patrol demonstrates a doctrine evolving towards more aggressive surface attacks, even joining a convoy formation to get into position.

*Shallow Water Operations:** The fifth patrol, operating in "relatively shallow water" despite a non-functional fathometer, shows increasing willingness to take risks and exploit coastal shipping lanes, a tactic that would become more common as the war progressed.

*Reconnaissance:** The detailed observations and photographic missions during the third patrol around Truk highlight the submarine's critical role in intelligence gathering, especially for major fleet bases.

Strategic Significance of These Patrols

Grenadier's patrols, despite facing early war challenges, contributed significantly to the Allied war effort, primarily through commerce interdiction and reconnaissance.

Commerce Interdiction: The sinking and damaging of Japanese merchant shipping was the primary strategic objective. Grenadier's *credited sinkings of 42,710 tons and damaging 19,000 tons of enemy shipping, including a large tanker and passenger ship (*Taijo Maru*), directly impacted Japanese logistics. These losses forced the Japanese to divert escorts, extend shipping routes, and reduce the flow of vital raw materials and supplies to their war machine and occupied territories. The successful attack on the 14,900-ton* Taijo Maru* (acknowledged by Japan) and the 15,000-ton tanker were notable successes, demonstrating the submarine's potential even with flawed torpedoes.

Reconnaissance and Intelligence Gathering: The third patrol around Truk was a critical intelligence-gathering mission. Detailed observations of air activity, ship movements, and photographic missions provided invaluable information on the strength and disposition of the Japanese fleet at its main forward base. The sighting of the Ryujo* class aircraft carrier during the fourth patrol also provided timely intelligence on Japanese naval movements, which could be used for strategic planning or targeting by other Allied forces.

*Mine Warfare:** The successful laying of a minefield off Haiphong during the fourth patrol was a novel and strategically important operation. It demonstrated the versatility of submarines in area denial, disrupting enemy shipping lanes without direct engagement and forcing Japanese forces to expend resources on mine countermeasures.

Impact on Enemy Logistics and Operations: Each successful attack, whether by torpedo or gunfire, forced the Japanese to commit more resources to anti-submarine warfare (ASW), including aircraft and escort vessels. This diverted assets from offensive operations and stretched their already strained resources. The prolonged depth charging experienced by Grenadier *after sinking* Taijo Maru *(23 hours, 70 close aboard charges) illustrates the intense Japanese ASW response, tying up significant enemy assets for an extended period. The loss of* Grenadier* itself, while tragic, provided the Japanese with a valuable submarine to study, but also revealed the tenacity of US crews under extreme pressure.

*Notable Successes and Failures:**

*Failures:** The first patrol was officially deemed a "total failure" due to torpedo unreliability and lack of contacts, highlighting the early war struggles. The premature explosion of a mine during the fourth patrol was also a setback.

Successes: The sinkings of the Taijo Maru* and the 15,000-ton tanker were significant. The aggressive surface actions in the fifth patrol, including the sinking of a schooner, tug, and barge, demonstrated the crew's determination and adaptability. The successful mine-laying operation was also a strategic achievement.

Long-term Impact Lessons Learned

Grenadier's service and tragic loss contributed to the evolution of submarine warfare, influencing post-war design, tactics, and naval history.

*Evolution of Submarine Warfare:**

Torpedo Reliability: The persistent issues with the Mark 14 torpedoes and Mark 6 exploders, evident in Grenadier*'s early patrols and the endorsements, were a major catalyst for the eventual investigation and resolution of these flaws by late 1943. The lessons learned from these failures led to significant improvements in torpedo design and testing, drastically increasing the effectiveness of the US submarine force later in the war.

ASW Evasion: Grenadier*'s prolonged depth charging and eventual sinking by air attack highlighted the growing sophistication of Japanese ASW. The detailed account of damage, emergency repairs, and evasion attempts provided valuable data for developing improved damage control, deep-diving capabilities, and evasion tactics for future submarines.

*Shallow Water Operations:** The fifth patrol's success in shallow waters, despite challenges, demonstrated the viability and necessity of operating in such environments to target coastal shipping. This informed future doctrine for exploiting enemy weaknesses in heavily trafficked, but often less-defended, inshore areas.

Mine Warfare: Grenadier*'s mine-laying mission proved the concept, leading to expanded use of submarines for offensive minelaying throughout the war, a tactic that continues to be relevant in modern naval strategy.

*Lessons that Influenced Post-War Submarine Design or Tactics:**

Damage Control and Survivability. The extensive damage sustained by Grenadier* from the bombs and depth charges, and the crew's heroic efforts to save the boat, provided invaluable insights into structural vulnerabilities and the importance of robust damage control training and equipment. Post-war submarine designs incorporated lessons on hull integrity, compartmentalization, and emergency systems.

*Radar and Sonar Development:** The use of early radar and the loss of sound heads underscored the critical need for reliable and advanced sensor technology for both detection and evasion. This spurred continuous development in radar and sonar systems, crucial for modern submarine operations.

Crew Training and Morale: The Grenadier* crew's resilience under fire, their attempts at repair, and their conduct as POWs highlighted the importance of high morale, extensive training, and leadership in extreme circumstances.

Relevance to Modern Submarine Operations: Many fundamental principles demonstrated by Grenadier* remain relevant. The importance of stealth, accurate intelligence gathering, effective weapon systems, and the ability to operate in contested waters are timeless. The challenges of ASW evasion, the need for advanced sensors, and the critical role of highly trained crews are still central to modern submarine warfare.

This Crew's Legacy in Naval History: The crew of Grenadier *left a profound legacy. Their detailed accounts of capture, torture, and survival as Prisoners of War (POWs) became a stark reminder of the brutality of war and the resilience of the human spirit. Their refusal to provide* *critical intelligence under duress, particularly that of Commander Fitzgerald, is a testament to their valor and commitment. The high survival rate of the crew (only four deaths out of 76) despite horrific conditions is remarkable. The naming of a second USS* Grenadier *(SS-525) in 1951, sponsored by Commander Fitzgerald's wife, served as a lasting tribute to the original boat, its crew, and their sacrifices.* Grenadier*'s story stands as a poignant reminder of the early, challenging days of the Pacific War and the immense personal cost borne by those who fought it.

Glossary of Naval Terms

A

After Torpedo Room: The compartment at the stern of a submarine housing the torpedo tubes that fire rearward.

Aircraft Carrier: A large warship that serves as a seagoing airbase, equipped with a flight deck and facilities for carrying, arming, deploying, and recovering aircraft.

B

Battle Surface: A command for a submarine to surface quickly and man its deck guns and other surface weapons for combat.

Battleship: A large, heavily armored warship with a main battery consisting of very large-caliber guns, designed to engage other capital ships.

Bow Tubes: The torpedo tubes located in the forward (bow) section of a submarine.

Bridge: The open-air platform, typically atop the conning tower on WWII submarines, from which the vessel is commanded while on the surface.

Buoyancy: The upward force exerted by a fluid that opposes the weight of an immersed object. For a submarine, controlling buoyancy is critical for diving, surfacing, and maintaining depth.

C

Circular Run: A dangerous torpedo malfunction where the guidance system fails, causing it to turn in a circle and potentially return to strike the submarine that fired it.

Conning Tower: A small, pressure-proof compartment on a submarine, located above the main hull, from which the captain directs attacks and navigation while submerged.

Convoy: A group of merchant ships or troop transports traveling together with a naval escort for protection.

D

Damage Control: The emergency procedures and actions taken to mitigate damage to a vessel from combat or accident, such as controlling flooding and fighting fires.

Deck Gun: A cannon mounted on the main deck of a submarine, typically used for engaging unescorted merchant ships, small craft, or for shore bombardment.

Depth-Charged: To be attacked with depth charges, which are anti-submarine weapons that explode at a pre-set depth to damage or destroy a submerged submarine through concussive force.

Destroyer: A fast, maneuverable warship designed to escort larger vessels in a fleet or convoy and defend them against attackers like submarines.

Down the Throat: A slang term for a torpedo attack aimed directly at the bow of an oncoming enemy ship, a difficult but often effective shot.

Dud: A slang term for a torpedo or other explosive ordnance that fails to detonate upon impact with its target.

E

End Around: A tactical maneuver where a submarine uses its superior surface speed to race around a convoy to position itself ahead for a submerged attack.

Escape Trunk: A small, floodable compartment in a submarine used as an airlock to allow crew members to escape from a sunken vessel.

Escort Carrier: A smaller, slower type of aircraft carrier used during WWII to provide air cover for convoys and amphibious invasions.

Escorts: Warships, such as destroyers or frigates, assigned to protect other vessels from enemy attack.

Exploder Mechanism: The device within a torpedo designed to detonate the main explosive charge upon impact or proximity to a target.

F

Fantail: The aftermost deck area at the stern of a ship or submarine.

Fish: A common slang term for a torpedo.

Flank Speed: The true maximum speed of a ship, faster than "full speed," which can only be sustained for short periods as it puts a heavy strain on the engines.

Forward Torpedo Room: The compartment at the bow of a submarine that houses the forward-firing torpedo tubes and their reloading equipment.

Frigate: A type of warship, often used for escort duty, that is larger than a corvette but smaller than a destroyer.

Full Emergency Speed: A command for the engines to produce the absolute maximum power possible, used in critical situations to accelerate or evade.

K

Knots: A unit of speed equal to one nautical mile per hour (approximately 1.15 mph or 1.85 km/h), used to measure the speed of ships.

L

List: The degree to which a vessel heels or tilts to one side (port or starboard), often as a result of damage or a sharp turn.

M

Mark 14 Torpedo: The standard U.S. Navy submarine-launched steam-powered torpedo during WWII, notorious in the early years of the war for its faulty depth control and exploder.

Mark 18 Torpedo: A U.S. Navy electric torpedo developed during WWII. It was slower than the Mark 14 but was wakeless, making it harder for targets to detect and evade.

Momsen Lung: A breathing device that allowed submariners to escape from a sunken submarine by recycling exhaled air.

P

P-boat: A colloquial term for a patrol boat, a relatively small naval vessel generally designed for coastal defense or anti-submarine warfare.

Periscope Photography: The practice of attaching a camera to a submarine's periscope to gather photographic intelligence on enemy ships and installations.

S

Periscope: An optical instrument that allows a submerged submarine to observe the surface without fully exposing itself.

Shakedown Cruise: A sea trial for a newly built vessel to test its performance, systems, and crew before it is declared operational.

SJ Radar: A U.S. Navy surface search radar used on submarines during WWII, which allowed them to detect ships and aircraft at night or in poor visibility.

Spread: A tactic of firing multiple torpedoes simultaneously or in rapid succession, aimed with slight variations in angle to increase the probability of hitting a moving target.

Stern Tubes: The torpedo tubes located in the aft (stern) section of a submarine, used for firing torpedoes at targets behind the submarine.

T

Task Force: A temporary grouping of naval units under a single commander, organized for the execution of a specific operational mission.

TDC (Torpedo Data Computer): An early analog computer on U.S. submarines that tracked a target's course, speed, and range to calculate a firing solution for the torpedoes.

Torpedo Bulge: A compartmented sponson on a warship's hull designed to detonate a torpedo away from the main hull and absorb its explosive energy.

W

War Patrol: The standard term for an operational combat deployment of a submarine during wartime, lasting from several weeks to months.

Watertight Integrity: The ability of a ship's hull and internal bulkheads to prevent the passage of water, crucial for staying afloat and controlling flooding after sustaining damage.

Wolf Pack: A tactic where multiple submarines coordinate their attacks on a single convoy or task force to overwhelm its defenses.

Most Important Passages

Catastrophic Flooding of Torpedo Tube and Pump Room

(c) Flooding of Torpedo No. 17311. This torpedo flooded such that the four tubes it was in also was flooded, cause unknown. After the tube was drained the torpedo was pulled out and inspected, but on flooding the tube the afterbody looked about three gallons too big and was leaking. This torpedo was pulled and put in the racks.

(d) Flooding of Pump Room. February 26. While trimming down, took considerable water down the Sounding Pump Latch. Water ended up in the Pump Room with the following results:

(1) No.1 Distribution Panel. Splashed by water from Control Room coming down around No.2 periscope housing, shorting out the entire panel, causing loss of hydraulic plant motor, trim and drain pump motor, and the air compressor motor. Also training motor generators, refrigerating and air conditioning motors, and both turbo-blower motors.

(2) No. 1 periscope starting panel – flooded from bilges.

(3) No.2 high pressure air compressor – water flooded in bottom of motor from the bilges, flooding the field windings.

(4) 700 air compressor motor – flooded from bilges.

(5) Starting resistances for Turbo Blowers, Drain Pump, Trim Pump, Hydraulic Plant Motor and both High Pressure Air Compressors. All these starting resistances were flooded by spray from water running down from the Control Room.

(6) QC-TR training motor generator – fields flooded from bilges.

(e) QC projector holding down interlock. Did not operate properly allowing projector to raise with gun pressure during dives. This permits play in the coupling, burning of pins and sockets, etc. (p. 17)

Significance: This passage documents a critical mechanical failure that severely compromised the submarine's operational capabilities. The flooding of multiple electrical systems, motors, and control panels represents a cascading failure that could have been catastrophic, demonstrating the vulnerability of submarine systems to water intrusion and the importance of watertight integrity.

Night Surface Attack on Taiyo Maru Convoy

At 1832 picked up smoke bearing 048°T at 1854 observed a convoy in pieces of large vessel with other masts and smoke beyond. As the range had closed it became evident that we had encountered a south bound convoy consisting of as follows: six freighters and tankers in two columns, at 1900 came to normal approach course to intercept the convoy. Visibility was the Taiyo Maru. No escort vessels were sighted but assumed their presence and wait to penetrate air coverage until dark. Decided to accept counter-attack and take the risk of remaining that sinking the large transport was worth the effort on the convoy. By waiting after dark it might be possible to get one or two freighters but we probably could not get in and attack on the Taiyo Maru.

The conditions were good for a periscope attack and by sparing use of the periscope and running deep between exposures a good attack position was attained for an estimated 105° starboard track and 1500 yards range.

Four torpedoes were fired as follows:

Torpedo Tube Depth Gyro Time of explosion. No. Setting Offset NO. 1 19-31-58 28' 29L 1 19-32-08 2 19-32-21 28' 0 1 Not heard 3 19-32-56 28' 0 2 Not heard 4 19-32-51 24' 2°R 3 19-35-54

From explosions, definitely torpedo hits, were heard and from the times noted it is evident that torpedoes 2 & 3 failed to function or the magnetic exploders on torpedoes 2 & 3 failed to function or the magnetic exploders heard due to exploding under the ship, within the spread about have been hits. The sound operator reported that all four torpedoes appeared to be running normally.

Torpedoes 2, 3 & 4 were fired on generated bearing. (p. 34)

Significance: This passage illustrates a critical tactical decision under pressure - choosing to attack a high-value target (Taiyo Maru) despite risks, and documents the persistent torpedo reliability problems that plagued U.S. submarines early in WWII. The commander's willingness to accept counter-attack risk for a valuable target shows aggressive tactical thinking, while the torpedo failures highlight technical issues that cost many opportunities.

Intense Depth Charge Attack and Evasion

August 10 - 0738(K) Sighted our old friend of yesterday, as he was glassy, with a deep swell, making periscope detection difficult. Went deep. This is the first time that depth at 0800. (Air Contact 24). Sighted above us again. He again headed for us. At the same time we made out the smoke of a large convoy of the 2-ship started on 1 August. It was coming straight toward us. The convoy started on 1 August. The 2-ship approached at high speed, stopped, then commenced circling around us. The very rigid charges bearing and the fact that his screws were plainly audible through the hull, indicated that he was close aboard. Throughout the hull, indicated that he was close aboard. Throughout the attack the submarine was kept deep, silent, running silent, attempting to get to 270 feet, however we struck a layer at 165 feet that we could not penetrate. (p. 50)

Significance: This passage captures the intense experience of being hunted by enemy anti-submarine forces, demonstrating the psychological and tactical challenges of depth charge attacks. The detail about hitting a thermal layer that prevented deeper diving shows how oceanographic conditions affected submarine tactics and survival, while the commander's decision to go silent and deep illustrates standard evasion procedures.

Crew Health and Provisions Status

12. HEALTH AND HABITABILITY:

Except for one officer who suffered a heart attack the health of the crew has been very good, in fact better than on the previous patrols.

The boat has been comfortable throughout the patrol.

13. MILES STEAMED ENROUTE TO AND FROM STATION:

Enroute to Enroute from

14. FUEL AND OIL EXPENDED:

Fuel Oil

15. FACTORS OF ENDURANCE REMAINING:

TORPEDOES FUEL PROVISIONS FRESH WATER PERSONNEL 21 4(1) 2200 0(2)

1. Diet is a balanced one but supply of fresh meat, flour, sugar and canned fruit is low. We could do three weeks longer on canned meat, rice, beans, and canned vegetables. (p. 67)

Significance: This passage provides insight into crew welfare and the logistical challenges of extended submarine patrols. The mention of a heart attack among officers highlights the physical toll of submarine service, while the detailed provisions status shows how food supplies limited patrol duration. The note that they could extend three weeks on basic rations demonstrates the endurance capabilities and hardships of submarine warfare.

Surface Encounter with Smoke-Laying Enemy Vessel

November 16, 1942: Patrolling on surface. 1218 (I) Sighted steamer bearing 045 degrees T., distance about. Commenced approach. Course 180 degrees T. He presented a 45 degree angle on the bow decided to close his track on the surface. Put our stern toward him and went to 1 until. There was a great amount of smoke released in our direction, so much smoke that it was impossible to see. There was a great amount of smoke released in our direction, so much smoke that it was impossible to see. We assumed that she would eventually give chase. On a hunch that she would eventually let us get in an attack. When sighted again she had almost 90 degrees starboard angle. (p. 83)

Significance: This passage demonstrates tactical adaptation when faced with an unexpected enemy countermeasure - smoke screens. The commander's decision to use the submarine's stern aspect and his tactical patience in waiting for the enemy to reveal position shows experienced decision-making under uncertain conditions. This illustrates the cat-and-mouse nature of submarine warfare and the need for flexible tactics.

Major Engine Defects Summary

MAJOR DEFECTS

4 Main Engine was out of commission for four days as a result of a fresh water leak due to a crack at the junction of the inboard exhaust manifold. Cracked section of manifold removed after spending two days tearing up floor plates, removing electrical leads, and attempting to pry loose the manifold from the engine. Crack soldered and manifold replaced. No further trouble experienced during the rest of the patrol.

Both sound heads were ruined when the ship bottomed on 12 November off the Indo China Coast.

The Fathometer is grounded.

The advisability of carrying an ample supply of acetylene gas was well shown. Casualties requiring brazing and welding, which, though minor in nature, had to be remedied for efficient operation of the Engineering plant were quickly and permanently made. (p. 100)

Significance: This passage documents critical mechanical failures that affected the submarine's operational capability, including engine damage and the loss of sound detection equipment from grounding. The mention of the ship bottoming reveals a dangerous navigation incident, while the note about acetylene gas supplies shows the importance of repair capabilities during extended patrols when no shore support was available.

Complex Night Surface Attack with Multiple Targets

1054: Observed leading AK to be towing second AK. Destroyer increased speed and began changing his course to port shortly after first torpedo was fired. 1056: Began firing torpedo at at second AK. Had flooded negative. Believe first explosion to be a hit with large head on leading AK, as it was a little louder than the other explosions, and the ship in the second AK was halted by two small boats. 1058: Went to 60 feet and began running. Believe first explosion to be a hit to sea, heard one explosion, followed by two more explosions. Upon surfacing, periscope watch took a quick look around; the patrol vessel was coming in on the starboard bow, then about 2000 yards away. As periscope was lowered the first of his screws were plainly audible through the hull, indicated that he was close aboard. Saw him then about 1500 yards on our port bow and coming in fast. Went to 120 feet, rigged for silent running. Believe first explosion to be a hit with large head on leading AK, as it was a little louder than the other explosions, and the ship in the second AK was halted by two small boats. Sighted both DD and patrol vessel and DD about 7000 yards away, the first column of heavy black smoke bearing 209 T, south of the harbor. Restored normal speed conditions, steering various courses on DD and patrol vessel completed search, DD running circles around GRENADIER, while the patrol vessel cruised in the vicinity of the smoke sighted near Saigon. Sighted DD and patrol vessel proceeded toward Saigon; but later came back and continued pinging. 2048: Four engines or propulsion. 2049: Sighted DD and patrol vessel bearing 225 T, distance about. 2100: Sighted DD and patrol vessel bearing 225 T, distance about. Long: 117-09-00 E. 2240: Reduced speed to ten engines and started battery charge. Decided that much in davits patrol off Ballkpapan would produce no results and that the time could be more profitably spent off Balikpapan. Would have left Saigon night or 23rd at latest in any event. Set

*course for Macassar Strait. 1200: Latitude: 01-27-30 S. Longitude: 116-01-00 E.
Miles steamed: 1071. Fuel used: 1135. (p. 117)*

Significance: This passage provides a detailed account of a complex night surface attack involving multiple targets and escorts, demonstrating the chaos and split-second decision-making required in combat. The commander's tactical choices - when to fire, when to dive, when to evade - and his assessment of results show the difficulty of determining battle damage while under counterattack. The decision to relocate patrol areas based on tactical assessment shows strategic flexibility.

Commander's Assessment of Patrol Success and Damage Claims

The GRENADIER operated for a considerable part of this patrol in relatively shallow water in spite of the handicaps resulting from the failure of the Fathometer.

3. Although the damage inflicted was below average, the patrol was marked throughout by a spirit of aggressiveness, which with additional experience will produce maximum results on future patrols.

4. While it is possible that hits were obtained in both freighters of the convoy attacked 22 January, there is no definite evidence of damage to the leading ship. The GRENADIER is credited with inflicting the following damage on the convoy:

DAMAGED 1 schooner 60 tons 1 freighter 7,000 tons 1 tug 700 tons 1 barge 100 tons

Total 1310 tons (p. 133)

Significance: This official endorsement provides command-level assessment of the patrol's effectiveness and reveals the difficulty of confirming damage in submarine warfare. The acknowledgment that damage was 'below average' while praising aggressiveness shows the learning curve for submarine crews. The conservative damage assessment reflects the challenge of verifying results and the tendency to overestimate success in combat.

POW Account of Japanese Treatment and Conditions

Often another nine months of hell. High ranking officers were told this was distinction made us to care and treatment. They we were put to work in the Ashio Copper Mines. Treatment continued as before. We were sentenced to death and torture. No medicine. Horrible working conditions. All man who died were cremated. Food would consist of a dish of rice and six months of war were acute. At this time the Jap civilians were starving, too. Morale, by this time, was rock-bottom and all dreams were of food.

While at Ofuna I was questioned by a Jap Naval 'Guuruho'. (Nip F.B.I.) Comdr. Ohashi. He was educated in the United States, a graduate of Ohio Alto High School and of Stanford University. He boasted that he was an athlete in Washington, I. C., on December 7th.

During entire period the one bright light was the Red Cross aid Christmas of 1943 and 1944. We never got any mail. Near the end two men got mail. (p. 150)

Significance: This powerful firsthand account from a submarine crew member who became a POW provides rare insight into the brutal treatment of captured submariners by Japanese forces. The details about starvation, forced labor in copper mines, torture, and lack of medical care document war crimes and illustrate what submarine crews risked if captured. The mention of Red Cross packages and lack of mail shows the isolation and desperation of POWs.

Investigation of Training Officer's Conduct

4. Prior to departure for the patrol before this one, I personally conducted some of the training of Officer Conducting the practice on the surface target and considered the Commanding Officer and officers well qualified in their jobs and performance. I had nothing to do with the conduct of the training prior to the departure of the Grenadier on her sixth war patrol, but I was informed by the Commanding Officer that he was satisfied as seemed well satisfied with the amount of training he had held and that he also well satisfied with the officers and personnel aboard the Grenadier satisfactory.

6. Was there any unusual changes in enlisted personnel assignment to the vessel between the fifth and sixth war patrols?

A. None that I know of.

An investigating officer informed the witness that he was privileged to make an, further statement covering anything relating to the subject matter of the investigation which he desired to make or any statement in exculpation or extenuation which had not been fully brought out by the previous questioning.

The witness stated that he had nothing further to say.

The witness verified his declaration, was duly warned, and withdrew.

A witness called by the investigating officer enters, was informed of the subject matter of the investigation, and declared as follows:

1. State your name, rank, and present Station. A. Lieutenant Commander D.L. Carr, U.S. Navy, Flag Secretary and Aide, staff Commander Submarines, Seventh Fleet.

2. What were your duties at the time of the last refit of the Grenadier in this port? A. I was Assistant Operations Officer on the Staff of Commander Submarine Squadron Six.

3. How much time were your duties in regard to the training of the Grenadier? A. My duties were, in this regard, to arrange for practices and make sure that the time was available between the completion of her refit and departure for patrol. (p. 166)

Significance: This passage reveals an official investigation into the training and preparation of the Grenadier crew, suggesting concerns about readiness or performance. The formal questioning of officers about training adequacy and crew changes indicates command-level scrutiny of submarine operations and accountability for patrol outcomes. This demonstrates the Navy's systematic approach to learning from patrol experiences and ensuring crew competency.

War Patrol Reports

START OF REEL
JOB NO. _F 108_

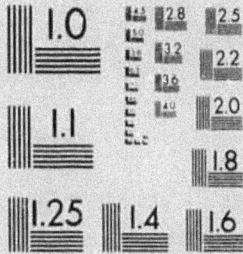

OPERATOR _LEO_

DATE _10-3-78_

THIS MICROFILM IS THE PROPERTY OF THE UNITED STATES GOVERNMENT

MICROFILMED BY
NPPSO–NAVAL DISTRICT WASHINGTON
MICROFILM SECTION

REEL TARGET - START AND END
NDW-NPPSO-5210/1 (6-78)

GRENADIER (SS-210)

WW II PATROL FILE

ALL MATERIAL ON THIS REEL IS DECLASSIFIED

FOR DECK LOG MAY 1941 - FEBRUARY 1942 AND OCTOBER 1942 - JANUARY 1943 CONSULT NATIONAL ARCHIVES WHICH HAS CUSTODY.

J.A. KOONTZ

Office of Naval Records and History
Ships' Histories Section
Navy Department

HISTORY OF USS GRENADIER (SS 210)
(Also: SS-525)

USS GRENADIER (SS 210), a 1,475-ton fleet submarine of the "G" Type of 1939-1940, was built at the Navy Yard in Portsmouth, New Hampshire, where her keel was laid on 2 April 1940. The sub was launched on 29 November 1940 with Mrs Walter S. Anderson, wife of Rear Admiral Walter S. Anderson, USN, President of the Board of Inspection and Survey, Navy Department, as the official sponsor.

GRENADIER was placed in commission on 1 May 1941 under the command of Commander Allen Raymond Joyce, USN.

The submarine was 307 feet in overall length, 27 feet abeam and had a surface speed of 21 knots. In addition to ten torpedo tubes -- six forward and four aft -- she carried one 3-inch anti-aircraft deck gun and two anti-aircraft machine guns.

After usual shakedown exercises, held in Atlantic waters, GRENADIER sailed for the Pacific and on 4 February 1942 left Pearl Harbor on her first war patrol. This patrol was conducted in the coastal waters of Honshu, Japan, chiefly off Tokyo Bay and in the traffic lanes to the Bonin Islands.

In the early morning of 26 February, an overzealous trimming-down submerged the submarine prematurely and, at the time, the lower conning tower hatch was shut but the water in the conning tower raised waist-deep before the upper hatch could be closed. This resulted in flooding out the trim and drain pumps, the low pressure blows, main hydraulic pump and one air compressor; and necessitated complete hand operation in diving until repairs could be effected.

About dawn on 1 March, while patrolling between Miyaki Shima and Nojima Saki, a plane was heard but never seen. GRENADIER only managed to attain a depth of 35 feet before the bomb went off but, judging from the effect, the plane must have had as much trouble seeing the submarine as GRENADIER did the plane.

That afternoon, just north of Inuboe Saki Light, GRENADIER probably went closer to the mainland of Japan than had any allied vessel since the beginning of the war. She made a submerged attack on a 5,000 ton freighter which was only one mile from the beach -- and GRENADIER was on the beach side of the freighter. A spread of four torpedoes resulted in one hit, but the freighter was not observed to sink.

This first patrol ended on 23 March 1942 at Pearl Harbor. Commander Joyce was relieved as commanding officer of the submarine by Commander Willis Ashford Lent, USN, at the end of this patrol.

- 2 -   USS GRENADIER (SS 210)
Also (SS 525)

Her second war patrol commenced after a refit at the Submarine Base, Pearl Harbor, when GRENADIER headed toward Nagasaki, Japan, on 12 April 1942. This patrol proved both more interesting and profitable, and resulted in a Gold Star in lieu of a second Navy Cross being awarded to the commanding officer, Commander Lent.

Shortly after midnight on the morning of 25 April, the sub's radar picked up a plane five or six miles distant. As she began a quick dive, the plane was sighted at an estimated altitude of 1,500 feet, heading for the ship. Two bombs exploded as the plane passed over and later another was heard in the distance. Other than a shaking up, the submarine was not harmed.

On the night of 1 May 1942, off Danjo Gunto in the light of a bright moon, a large three-island freighter of the AFRICA MARU class was sighted about four miles away. A submerged attack was made and a spread of four torpedoes was fired. Two hits resulted in the first sinking for GRENADIER.

During the late afternoon of 8 May 1942, GRENADIER intercepted a south-bound convoy of six medium freighters and the TAIJO MARU, a large merchant vessel of 14,900 tons, heavily escorted by aircraft and destroyers. The TAIJO MARU was, of course, picked as the first target and a submerged approach was terminated with firing a spread of four torpedoes. With two hits registering, the TAIJO MARU went to a watery grave -- and GRENADIER underwent an uncomfortably prolonged depth charging. Actually, in this attack, the submarine had been spotted and bombs were dropped before her first torpedo had been fired. The depth charges and bombs continued for 23 hours with about 70 being dropped close aboard and many more in the distance. A propeller shaft was so damaged that it squeaked causing sufficient noise to make the submarine easy prey for the destroyers. Lights were knocked out, leaks developed, and the superstructure was twisted around considerably The Japanese acknowledged the loss of the TAIJO MARU.

On 14 May, the patrol area was shifted and GRENADIER sailed to Bungo Suido through the narrow Van Bemen Strait, making a brilliant run at 17 knots through poor visibility, running from one patrol vessel to another. On 25 May the sub was ordered back to Midway. Unfortunately, the sector assigned to GRENADIER made it impossible for her to participate in any fighting in the Battle of Midway, and on several occasions she was forced to deep submergence by planes.

The report of the second war patrol which ended on 10 June 1942, contained the following endorsement: "The GRENADIER returned from a very successful patrol in enemy-controlled waters and remained at sea for 59 days. In spite of strong anti-submarine measures, including three long depth charge attacks, the commanding officer returned his ship without damage to material or personnel........The commanding officer covered his area very thoroughly but due to weather conditions and not operating in shipping lanes, only three contacts with enemy shipping were developed."

- 3 - USS GRENADIER (SS 210)
Also (SS 525)

GRENADIER's third war patrol commenced on 13 July 1942 from Pearl Harbor. Commander Lent had been relieved as commanding officer by Lieutenant Commander Bruce L. Carr on 18 June 1942.

Forty days were spent on station around Truk and Tol Island. On 30 July, three torpedoes were fired and sank a large tanker of 15,000 tons. Two hits were made on the tanker, which immediately aroused the escorting destroyers and they proceeded to drop 14 depth charges very close aboard which shook up GRENADIER severely. Later these destroyers pleased the sub's crew by sitting right over their nest without laying any eggs.

Vice Admiral C. A. Lockwood, then Commander Submarines, Southwest Pacific, endorsed the third war patrol report as follows: "The attack on the tanker was well executed and the GRENADIER efficiently evaded without damage a subsequent depth charge attack by escorting destroyers.....The sinking of the 15,000-ton tanker was confirmed by other sources."

Another endorsement read as follows: "The attack on the large tanker was vigorously and efficiently carried out. The commanding officer successfully evaded the severe depth charging that followed. The numerous sightings of aircraft and lack of enemy air attacks indicates an alertness and high state of training." There were 41 air attacks made on this patrol, which terminated on 18 September 1942 in Freemantle, Australia.

For her fourth war patrol, GRENADIER proceeded to the approaches to Haiphong, Indo-China. The main object of this patrol was to lay a minefield of 32 mines off Haiphong, but eight torpedoes were carried to conduct an offensive patrol against enemy shipping in the South China Sea between Latitude 12 and 18 degrees north.

The mine plant was successfully executed at night as GRENADIER dodged junks and islands in water which was, in parts, as shallow as 26 feet and laid one of the first submarine minefields of the war. The fifth mine exploded prematurely, 45 minutes after planting.

Shortly after midnight on the morning of 12 November, a surface approach was made on a freighter near Cape Varella. It was believed that the target course and speed had been well checked and the bridge personnel saw the torpedo tracks run under the freighter. The third and last torpedo caused a large commotion under the enemy's bridge as though its air flask had exploded. At this time the freighter doused a small light which had been showing and turned in toward the beach.

At 0657 the same morning, a corvette was sighted at close range in poor visibility. A dive was made, the approach started, and the first look revealed the enemy ship to be at a range of less than 1,000 yards and coming in at high speed. Depth charges were dropped close aboard forcing GRENADIER to the bottom with considerable force, carryin

- 4 - USS GRENADIER (SS 210)
Also (SS 525)

away both sound heads. Salt water was taken in the after battery compartment causing chlorine gas to be formed which caused much suffering
among the crew, but with no permanent casualties.

Upon surfacing in the evening of 16 November, the handicap of having no sound gear was illustrated. The visibility was poor and a corvette was sighted close aboard immediately after surfacing. During
the subsequent depth charge attack, everyone was wishing that the sound
gear was still intact so that the tables could have been turned.

Among the incidents of this patrol GRENADIER sighted a diplomatic
ship and a hospital ship near the Gulf of Tonkin. Then, at 0728 on
30 November the submarine had the heart-breaking experience of sighting an aircraft carrier of the RYUJO class at 8,000 yards and a heavy
cruiser and destroyer at 15,000 yards heading south in a heavy rain
squall in the Strait of Makassar. When sighted, the ships were at
high speed with an angle on the bow of at least 80° starboard. Since
it was impossible to close, GRENADIER surfaced to pass on the contact
report to Radio Darwin. This patrol ended in Fremantle on 10 December
1942.

During the refit period at Fremantle Lieutenant Commander Carr was
relieved by Lieutenant Commander J. A. Fitzgerald, USN, as the submarine's commanding officer.

The fifth war patrol of GRENADIER began on 1 January 1943 and was
conducted in the approaches to Soerabaja, Makassar, and Balikapapan,
the vicinity of Saleier Strait, Pulassi Island, and the northern entrance to Bali Strait.

At 0620 on the morning of 10 January in the northern approaches
to Soerabaja, GRENADIER battle-surfaced on a 60-ton, two-masted schooner flying the Jap merchant flag. The schooner was sunk by gunfire
from the 3-inch and automatic weapons.

In the afternoon of 12 January in the same area, a steamer of 750
tons was sighted towing a well loaded hulk barge of about 500 tons.
The seas and wind were sufficient to hold the speed down so that the
submarine was able, at 1705, to join the formation as third ship in
column waiting for darkness. After nightfall, she surfaced, started
mounting the machine guns, and closing distance.

It was necessary to lash 7x50 binoculars to the 3-inch gun to use
as sights since the regular sights had flooded and at 2042 fire was
opened on the steamer. Seventeen minutes later the cease fire order
was given with the ship afire and beginning to settle. A few minutes
later she opened fire on the barge, ceasing after three minutes to
watch both enemy vessels sink.

On 22 January 1943, after ascertaining with a lead line (the
fathometer was out of commission) that there was enough water in which

- 5 -   USS GRENADIER (SS 210)
Also (SS 525)

to dive, a convoy consisting of two 7,000-ton cargo vessels escorted by a destroyer and a patrol vessel was sighted hugging the coast just south of Balikpapan. The approach was made and three torpedoes were fired at the leading vessel and two at the second. One hit was made on the first ship and two on the latter. The counter-attack by the enemy escorts with depth charges in about ten fathoms of water prevented the skipper from observing the results of the hits. Several hours later, a quick look showed only the escort vessels, oil on the surface, and large column of heavy black smoke.

On the last day of January, off the entrance to Makassar City in the Celebes, GRENADIER made the unfortunate exchange, with a small enemy steamer, of three torpedoes for some depth charges -- neither having any effect.

The commander Task Force 51, endorsed the report of the fifth war patrol as follows: "The GRENADIER operated for a considerable part of this patrol in relatively shallow water in spite of the handicap resulting from the failure of the fathometer -- the patrol throughout was marked by a spirit of aggressiveness which, with additional experience, will produce maximum results on future patrols."

Commander, Submarine Squadron 6 said, "Assigned patrol areas were thoroughly covered by the GRENADIER; determined attempts were made with torpedoes and gunfire."

GRENADIER was credited with inflicting the following damage on the enemy during this patrol: Sunk -- 1 schooner, 60 tons; 1 tug, 750 tons; and 1 barge, 500 tons. Damaged -- 2 freighters totaling 14,000 tons.

GRENADIER's sixth war patrol began on 20 March 1943 from Fremantle, Australia. She headed for the Andaman Sea, from the Gulf of Martaban down through the Mergui Archipelago to Malacca Strait, to investigate and destroy enemy shipping. GRENADIER was the first American submarine to be in this area. Pictures were taken of the harbor at the Island of Sabang.

On the night of 6 June, a small freighter of about 2,000 tons was sighted off Puhket Island. A surface torpedo attack resulted in her damage and, to the officers and men on the bridge, what appeared to be an attempt to beach the vessel. Later information, received from several different Japanese sources, revealed that this ship had been sunk. After the explosion, the wounded ship fired on the submarine with two guns (estimated to be 5-inch) using tracer ammunition, most of the shells going over GRENADIER or landing in the sub's wake. This fire was returned until the freighter got too close in to the beach.

The next several weeks were uneventful, showing no evidence of shipping in this area, and a request was made by the impatient GRENADIER to change to a more fruitful area. At the same time that orders were received to shift to Sunda Straits, two freighters of about 3,000 tons were picked up. It being night, a surface attack was commenced in bright moonlight but unfortunately GRENADIER was sighted when she had closed to 2,500 yards. At this time the submarine commenced firing with her 3-inch and automatic weapons and the two enemy ships returned the fire with what appeared to be 5-inch guns. The commanding officer deemed it advisable to retire and attempt to gain a position ahead of the ships for a submerged approach in the morning. However, a slight miscalculation put the freighters, which were using a high speed and erratic zig-zag plan, out of range when the attack was resumed.

It again became necessary for the tenacious GRENADIER to surface with the intent of sweeping wide around the two ships in order to gain a position for a submerged attack. At about 0830 on 21 April 1943 a heavy naval bomber was sighted heading for the submarine. A quick dive was made and what was estimated as two 1,000-pound bombs exploded as GRENADIER was passing the 90-foot depth. The explosion was just above the forward part of the after torpedo room and lights immediately went out while the boat took a down-angle of about 20 degrees. Power to the screws was lost, so the Captain ordered to put her on the bottom, which was at about 45 fathoms.

Gauges were broken throughout the boat and the overhead of the after torpedo room was found to be stove in to a great extent. The soft patch and air induction in the maneuvering room were leaking on the maneuvering cubicle, and the cubicle had been sprung against the overhead, fusing wires and causing electrical fires in the maneuvering room. In the after torpedo room there was a tangled mass of torpedoes, bodies and bunks; but miraculously there were no major casualties among the men. The thick, strong back by the torpedo loading hatch was buckled. The hydraulic steering and stern plane gears were put out of commission, but by the excellent work of Pianka, Machinist's Mate first class, and Shaw, Machinist's Mate second class, a jury rig was improvised. The propeller shafts had been warped and there was considerable leakage around their bearings while the after torpedo tubes were so warped that it was impossible to operate the tube doors.

Squads were organized to fight the fire in the maneuvering room and it finally brought under control, but intermittent fires were continually breaking out which, along with the leakage, overcame any progress on repair of electrical equipment.

Remaining on the bottom all day using emergency lights, without power to run the air conditioning or air circulating units, and with the fires using up a great deal of the precious oxygen -- it became necessary to use carbon dioxide absorbent throughout the boat and to bleed oxygen into the air from the oxygen flasks.

GRENADIER surfaced that night and work was continued. As she came up and the pressure was released against the after torpedo room hatch, it sprang out to such an extent that it was possible to put a hand around a portion of the "knife edge."

By this time it was apparent that there was no hope of being able to repair the submarine sufficiently to get underway, or even be able to dive again. Therefore, all classified equipment and publications were destroyed and a fruitless attempt was made to transmit a radio message telling of GRENADIER's plight and the crew's intention to abandon ship to the nearby Pilgrim Island.

Shortly after dawn on the morning of 22 April 1943, several ships were sighted on the horizon, coming in. A Zero headed in on the submarine but 20-millimeter gunfire forced the plane to drop her bomb several hundred yards short. It could be seen that the plane had been hit, and subsequent intelligence obtained in Penang, Malay States, revealed that the pilot had been killed and the plane crashed.

At about 0830 the skipper ordered GRENADIER abandoned and all hatches were left open. The Chief-of-the-Boat, Chief Torpedoman's Mate Withrow, opened the vents and came topsides to have the decks submerge under him; as the whole crew watched their home, of which they had become so proud, plummet to the bottom -- and turned to face the oncoming Japanese vessels with hearts of lead.

After a little more than an hour in the water, the entire crew of GRENDIER was captured by a Japanese naval escort vessel, a converted merchant ship of about 2,000 tons, and taken into Penang. There the Japanese naval forces proved themselves to be nothing human by their starvation, continual beatings and other torture methods to gain information from their captives. Time after time the prisoners would be tortured until they lost consciousness rather than submit to their captors, who claimed that the crew was still their enemy and acted accordingly.

This state of being was to continue until the crew reached a registered camp, at which time they would become prisoners-of-war. It took some of the men nearly two years to reach this exalted status.

After a week in Penang, Commander Fitzgerald, Commander Whiting (executive officer), and Lieutenant Commander Harty (communications officer) were flown to a naval non-registered, interrogation camp in Ofuna, Japan, run by the Yokosuka Naval Base. Chief Radioman Knutson was flown to Soerabaja, Java, where he was questioned by German naval officers, and from them received extremely severe treatment. He was later flown to the camp in Ofuna.

The remaining members of the crew left Penang in a filthy hold of a steamer on the 5th of August 1943, and arrived in Singapore two days later to be interned in a blocked-off portion of an Indian prisoner-of-war camp in Selitar, just outside the captured English naval base

- 8 - USS GRENADIER (SS 210)
Also (SS 525)

in Singapore. There the men were fairly unmolested but still received very small rations, no medical care and were required to work in the naval base. However, by this time not many were able to stand, much less work.

These men left Singapore on 26 September 1943 in a hold of the ASAMA MARU. One man, Electrician's Mate second class L.L. Barker, was too ill to travel and was left behind, but fortunately joined some of his shipmates at a later date in Japan. The voyage on the ASAMA MARU was highlighted by severe mass beatings when the watch would change -- missing no one. At the end of the trip the prisoners were put into small launches and taken to a small village near Shimonoseki on 9 October 1943. Two days later, 29 of these men were taken to the interrogation camp in Ofuna and later the remaining 41 were interned in a prisoner-of-war camp in Fukuoka.

Over the course of the next 15 months, the members of GRENDIER's crew in Ofuna gradually spread out over the northern part of Honshu in various prisoners-of-war camps. Few who saw the submarine's crew after six months of captivity would have believed that many could have lived; but God was with them and only four died -- all in a camp in Fukuoka. These four, all fine men, were: Charles Doyle, MoMM1c, USN; Charles F. Linder, MoMM2c, USNR; George W. Snyder, Jr., MM3c; and Justiniano G. Guico, StM1c, USNR.

DAMAGE TO ENEMY BY USS GRENADIER

First Patrol	Damaged	1 Freighter, 5,000 tons
Second Patrol	Sunk	1 Freighter, 9,500 tons 1 Passenger ship, 14,900 tons
Third Patrol	Sunk	1 Tanker, 1,500 tons
Fifth Patrol	Sunk	1 Schooner, 60 tons 1 Tug, 750 tons 1 Barge, 500 tons 2 Freighters, 14,000 tons
Sixth Patrol	Sunk	1 Freighter, 2,000 tons 1 Plane
Total Sunk	42,710 tons plus 1 plane	
Total Damaged	19,000 tons	

- 9 - USS GRENADIER (SS 210)
Also (SS 525)

USS GRENADIER (SS 210) earned four Battle Stars on the Asiatic-Pacific Area Service Medal for participating in the following operations:

1 Star/Midway -- 3-6 June 1942

1 Star/Submarine War Patrol, Pacific -- 4 February to 23 March 1942

1 Star/Submarine War Patrol, Pacific -- 13 July to 18 September 1942

1 Star/Submarine War Patrol, Pacific -- 1 January to 20 February 1943

* * * * *

USS GRENADIER (SS 525)

A second Navy ship to be named GRENADIER was authorized by Act of Congress on 19 July 1940 and her keel was laid at the Boston Navy Yard, Boston, Massachusetts, on 8 February 1944. USS GRENADIER (SS 525) was, like the SS-210, named for a family of soft-finned, mostly deep-sea, fishes having a tapering body and also to perpetuate the name of the former submarine which was lost due to enemy action in Malayan waters on 21 April 1943.

SS-525 was christened and commissioned in dual ceremonies at the Boston Naval Shipyard, Charlestown, Massachusetts, on 10 February 1951. Mrs. John A. Fitzgerald, wife of the commanding officer of the first GRENADIER sponsored the new ship.

USS GRENADIER (SS 525), sister ship of USS GRAMPUS (SS 523), is one of a group of streamlined submarines constructed for the Navy under the "Greater Underwater Propulsive Power" (GUPPY) project. The perfection of the snorkel or breathing apparatus, such as that installed on GRENADIER, allows increased submerged endurance.

This modernized submarine is 306 feet in length, 27 feet abeam, has a speed of 20 knots, and displaces 1,570 tons.

USS GRENADIER (SS 525) is attached to the U. S. Atlantic Fleet with her home port at New London, Connecticut, and home yard at Boston, Massachusetts.

* * * * *

Compiled: October 1951

SS210/A12   U.S.S. GRENADIER

Serial (052)   C/o Fleet Post Office,
                                 Pearl Harbor, T.H.,
                                 March 23, 1942.

DECLASSIFIED

From: Commanding Officer.
To :   Commander Submarines, Pacific Fleet.

Subject: U.S.S. GRENADIER - Report of First War Patrol.
                   Period from February 4, 1942 to March 23, 1942.
                   Area Four.

     1.   Narrative:

February 4 - Departed Pearl.

February 8 - A Japanese submarine shelled Midway at dusk. This vessel was due to arrive Midway the next morning, but was not informed as to the above.

February 9 - Fueled at Midway, and resumed course to Area Four.

February 18 - Began submerged running during daylight, about 600 miles from Honshu. From departure until this date, a trim dive was made about every other day.

February 23, 1930 Z.T. (King). Lat 34-37.4 N Long 143-11.5 E. On surfacing sighted glare as from searchlight, bearing 198° True. C/C to 000 to charge batteries before investigating; 2030 - lost glare; 2100 C/C to 180, continued on this course until 2300 but failed to make any contact; resumed course to area.

February 24 - Arrived in area; raining all day, visibility poor, periscope observations on the hour. Heavy seas and rain at night, visibility very poor, no Nav. fix, dived 0330.

February 25 - Weather moderated and cleared during the day, periscope observations every half hour. Sea calm, bright moonlight on surfacing. Sighted Inubo Saki and Katsuura Wan Lights about 2200.

February 26 - About 0230, while closing coast south of Katsuura Wan, trimmed down too well and took considerable water down the Conning Tower hatch, flooding out the trim and drain pumps, low pressure blows, main hydraulic pump and one air compressor. About 0300 sighted light bearing 135 relative, appeared to be a signal light, probably from a sampan. Dived, working vents by hand, began restoring flooded machinery to operating condition. After surfacing at night, ran south toward Miyake Shima. About

                           - 1 -   ENCLOSURE (A)

<u>CONFIDENTIAL</u>

Subject: U.S.S. GRENADIER - Report of First War Patrol.
- -

2100 sighted light on port quarter, similar to one seen the preceding night. Dived. About 2200, while ready to surface, sighted another white (all around) light through periscope, probably on sampan. Opened out on this light about a mile and surfaced, nothing in sight.

February 27 - Dived about 20-30 miles N.E. of Miyake Shima, which had not been sighted. On course 000 during day. Surfaced 1900 in bright moonlight, about 30 miles east of Nojima Saki, having been set well to N.E. during the day. Headed for Miyake Shima.

February 28 - Dived about 0500, about 20 miles N.E. of Miyake Shima, which had not been picked up. Spent day about Long. 139-45 E., Lat. between 34-17 and 34-27, with Miyake Shima, Nu Shima and To Shima in sight. Visibility very good. Nothing sighted. Surfaced about 1900 on course 150°. Sighted small DD bearing 010 Relative, angle on bow 60 port. Dived to make periscope approach, as moon was behind DD, and speed of DD appeared small. Some trouble with ship porpoising, and when steadied down did not see DD, or pick up on sound. Surfaced about 2015, in bright moonlight.

March 1 - Patrolling north of Miyake Shima, to be between Miyake Shima and Nojima Saki in morning. About 0300 attacked by plane which dropped bomb or depth charge, and which exploded during diving, when the keel depth was about 35 feet. Noise in Conning Tower was about same as when 3" gun is fired. No damage. On northerly courses toward Nojima Saki. About 1130 sighted well deck freighter bearing 035 True, on course 270, distance 8000 yards. Unable to close for attack. Patrolling on westerly and easterly courses about 15 miles south of Nojima Saki. Surfaced S.E. of Nojima Saki at 2000. Raining, position doubtful due to current. Ran east, then south, then west during night.

March 2 - Fix at 0300. Dived 0515, Lat. 34-16 N, Long. 140-20 W, continued on course 270° until 1645, when course was reversed to 090. Raining during day, visibility very poor, seas increased in afternoon. Periscope observations every half hour until noon, then every hour. Depth control difficult at periscope depth in afternoon. Surfaced 2000 in heavy seas from 240°. Ran eastward until 0100, then reversed course to westward. Two sights obtained, indicating that usual set to N.E. had not obtained since last fix.

March 3 - Dived 0600, Lat. 34-16.5 N, Long. 139-58 W. Seas too heavy to make periscope observations at short intervals, maintained listening watch, periscope observations about every three hours. About 1810 picked up screws on sound, bearing 017 relative.

- 2 -   ENCLOSURE (A)

Subject: U.S.S. GRENADIER - Report of First War Patrol.

- -

Periscope observation showed to be large sampan. Went to 130 feet. Surfaced. Overcast occasional showers.

March 4 - About 0000 obtained moon and star fix showing set of 066°, 1.6 knots since 0300, 2 March. Fix Lat. 34-20 N; Long 141-47 E. Set course 290, to return to area. About 0300 sky cleared, moon full, sea calm, visibility excellent. Dove about 0415, on course 000, as moon will be up all next night and desired to get north of Tateyama, assumed to be the source of airplane patrols. By being north of Tateyama, only those planes patrolling to north of east would be able to silhouette us against the moon. Surfaced 1845. Moonrise 1900. Sky clear, visibility excellent. Steamed into and away from moon, maintaining position about 35-10 N, 141-45 E.

March 5 - At 0400 dived. Lat. 35-19 N, Long. 141-45 W. Course 000. Sky became overcast during day, and wind freshened. Surfaced 1830; seas rough; overcast, raining. Courses southwest during night; heavy seas, very poor visibility.

March 6 - Dived 0510. Lat. 34-46; Long. 140-30. Course 135° True. 1837 surfaced. Sights showed we had been set well to northward during day. Due to this, decided to try area just north of Inuboe Saki light.

March 7 - Dived 0510. Lat. 36-20 N, Long. 141-00 E. Sighted two freighters about 0800, but unable to close as tracks were too far to westward. C/C to westward for 2.5 miles, then resumed north and south courses. At 1436 sighted freighter to northward, on southerly course. At 1447 fired four torpedoes, heard one explosion, quite loud in Conning Tower. Target did not sink, and fired two more torpedoes. The Forward Room heard three thuds in addition to the explosion heard in the Conning Tower. Continued to hear screws while clearing area on easterly course. Screws drew to 180 relative, and it is possible the ship was being beached. 1817 surfaced. Raining, very heavy seas. Proceeding to southern part of area.

March 8 - At 0045 visibility zero due to rain and snow. Dived. At 1845 surfaced. Sights showed little progress to southward. Seas calm, sky overcast, proceeding to southern part of area.

March 9 - 0356 dived; lookout reported plane on port beam, having sighted bright white light. (Believed to be Venus). 1851 surfaced. 1948 dived due to bright illumination of sky, believed to be aircraft flare. 2053 surfaced. 2233 decided to return to Pearl, set course 090.

- 3 -   ENCLOSURE (A)

CONFIDENTIAL

Subject: U.S.S. GRENADIER - Report of First War Patrol.
- -

March 10-12 - Uneventful.

March 13 - Began surface running in daylight. 1345 sighted tops
of masts and stack of merchant vessel bearing 198° True. Dived
on 198° True, but lost contact. 1505 surfaced, nothing in sight.

March 14-23 - Uneventful.

From this patrol, there appeared to be little traffic in
the vicinity of Miyake Shima, indicating that southbound traffic
is using the route closer to the mainland. Also, traffic between Nojima Saki and the north was invariably sighted close to
the coast. Due to the considerable amount of rain and low visibility weather, and the currents, it is desirable to keep landmarks in sight whenever practicable. Then in low visibility,
position can at least some of the time be maintained with a
landmark in sight, and thus in a place where there is a possibility of getting a target.

In bright moonlight, due to the proximity of air bases, it
is considered difficult to maintain position close to the traffic
routes in this area, especially when a full moon lasts all night.
An extension of this area to the northward, which could be covered
under such conditions, is recommended.

2.   Weather. Enroute to station, moderately rough seas
from west to north obtained about half the time. On station,
eight days were clear or partly overcast, with rain usually
attended by fairly rough weather, for six days.

3.   Tidal Information. About same as given in the Coast
Pilot. A drift of 1.5 to 2.0 knots may be expected as normal.

4.   Navigational Aids. Not much data was obtained,
but Katsuura Wan and Nojima Saki lights were seen on one occasion,
and probably Shioya Zaki light on another. The lights are probably turned on for limited periods when requested. The vol-
canic light from O'Shima described in the Coast Pilot is out.

5.   Enemy vessels sighted:

Zone Time	Zone Des.	Position Lat.	Long.	Enemy Course	Enemy Speed	Type of Vessel
1900	-9	34-27N	139-15.8E	100°	?	Small DD
1055	-9	34-35N	139-30 E	270°	16 Kts	3 island 5000 ton freighter
0700	-9	36-19N	141-06 E	040°	10 kts	3 island 3000 ton freighter
0730	-9	36-19N	141-06 E	220°	15 kts	3 island 5000 ton freighter

- 4 -   ENCLOSURE (A)

CONFIDENTIAL

Subject: U.S.S. GRENADIER - Report of First War Patrol.
- -

Enemy vessel sighted: (continued)

Zone Time	Zone Des.	Position Lat.	Long.	Enemy Course	Enemy Speed	Type of Vessel
1410	-9	36-27 N	141-06 E	180°	12 kts	Gatsu San Maru 4516 tons
1345	-10	34-52 N	155-26 E	--	--	Merchantman

6.   Description of all aircraft sighted: None sighted, one heard.

7.   Particulars of attacks:

Contact Number	No. of Torp.Fired	Point of aim	Track Angle	Depth Setting	Est. Draft	Torp. Perf.	Est. Speed	Torpedo Run(Yd:
5	6	Funnel (Amidships)	108	15	20	Unknown	12	1500

Result of attack: A very loud explosion was heard in the Coning Tower, about a minute and a half after firing. Shortly thereafter, three distinct thuds were heard in the Forward Room. The target seemed lower in the water when last seen, but the screws continued to be heard, and faded out on 180 relative. As this ship was headed **East**, it would appear that the target was headed West, toward the nearest beach.

8.   Enemy A/S measures. From February 25 to March 6, the moon was full or nearly full, and in the sky all night. With a moderate amount of air patrolling, and follow up of submarine contacts by anti-submarine vessels, this area would be untenable for a submarine during periods of an all night, nearly full, moon. However, this vessel was fairly close in for four bright nights and only one airplane contact resulted. There was no follow up, by surface vessels and, during the time in the area, no evidence of any coordinated anti-submarine work by surface vessels. It is believed that this area could be better covered when the moon is not showing at night, as position could be maintained closer to the beach.

9.   Major defects experienced.

(a) Unable stop engine on dive. February 5, on dive following sighting of plane, No. 3 engine could not be immediately stopped, as neither the throttle nor emergency stop were effective. The engine speeded up, and the ventilating fan carried away breaking the generator casing. Engine was finally stopped by closing the fuel supply valve.

Recommendation: Since the throttle and emergency stop both

- 5 -   ENCLOSURE (A)

CONFIDENTIAL

Subject: U.S.S. GRENADIER - Report of First War Patrol.
- -

operate on the fuel rack, a derangement in the fuel rack can prevent stopping of the engine. It is recommended that provision be made to stop the engines from the operating platform by means that will quickly stop the fuel supply to an engine.

(b) Tube door inoperative. February 9. Upon leaving Midway, number 9 torpedo tube was ordered made ready. The outer door could not be opened. Unable to determine cause while at sea.

(c) Flooding of Torpedo No. 17311. This torpedo flooded each of the four times its tube was flooded, cause unknown. After the third flooding, the tube tail buffer gasket was renewed, but on flooding the tube the afterbody leaked about three gallons in one hour. This torpedo was pulled and put in the racks.

(d) Flooding of Pump Room. February 26. While trimming down, took considerable water down the Conning Tower hatch. This water ended up in the Pump Room with the following results:

    (1) No.3 Distribution Panel. Splashed by water from Control Room deck coming down around No.2 periscope housing, shorting out both high pressure air compressors, and the refrigerator circulating water and brine motors. About 18 inches of water finally accumulated in the bilges, shorting out the entire panel, causing loss of main hydraulic plant motor, trim and drain pump motors, both high pressure air compressors, QC-JK training motor generators, refrigerating and air conditioning motors, and both turbo-blower motors.

    (2) No. 1 periscope starting panel - flooded from bilges.

    (3) No.2 high pressure air compressor - water flooded in bottom of motor from the bilges, flooding the field windings.

    (4) 200# air compressor motor - flooded from bilges.

    (5) Starting resistances for Turbo Blowers, Drain Pump, Trim Pump, Hydraulic Plant Motor and both High Pressure Air Compressors. All these starting resistances were flooded by spray from water running down from the Control Room.

    (6) QC-JK training motor generator - fields flooded from bilges.

(e) QC projector holding down interlock. Did not operate properly allowing projector to raise with sea pressure during dive. This permits play in the coupling, burning of pins and sockets, etc.

                          - 6 -   ENCLOSURE (A)

CONFIDENTIAL.

Subject: U.S.S. GRENADIER - Report of First War Patrol.

- -

(f) Flexible coupling unit between reduction gear box and JK projector training shaft. This coupling (canvas) wore rapidly, and a coupling of more durable material is recommended.

10.   Radio Reception. NPM provided primary means of communication. NPM Submarine schedules were observed and copied without any interference except for occasional fading between the hours of 1745 and 1930 (Int) while in the area. Comtaskforce 7 4155 KCS series were copied satisfactorily on the way out and while 500 miles from the area. Three days before arrival in area began to experience interference on 4155 KCS series. Interference consisted of long dashes. On February 22 secured 4155 series and set watch on 4235 KCS as per Comtaskforce 7 191456 of February. Lost contact with Comtaskforce 7. Japanese broadcast station transmitting on 4240 and 3475 KCS interfered with 4235 series. On return trip experienced difficulty in clearing traffic through NPM on 4235 series. On two occasions NPO heard us calling NPM before contact was made with the latter.

Last serial received - No. 9
Last serial sent   - No. 4

11.   Sound conditions and density layers. Sound conditions while in the area were in general poor due to high water noises. This was particularly true in the vicinity of Inubo Saki. Noises were frequently heard just after sunset, which changed considerably in true bearing. After considerable experience with these noises (just before surfacing) and without being able to find a definite cause, the noise was charged to schools of fish.

No data was obtained on density layers.

12.   Health and habitability. Very good in general. A number of the officers and crew had colds, some of which were severe colds.

13.   Factors of endurance remaining (March 9, 1942):

Torpedoes	Fuel	Provisions (days)	Personnel(days)
18	18,798 Gals.	21	14

A. R. JOYCE.

Copy to: Commander Subron SIX
         Commander SubDiv SIXTY-TWO.

- 7 -   ENCLOSURE (A)

SUBMARINE DIVISION SIXTY - TWO

FB5-62/A16-3   eb

Serial : 024

                                                    Pearl Harbor, T.H.
                                                    24 March 1942

CONFIDENTIAL

From: The Commander Submarine Division SIXTY-TWO.
To :   The Commander Submarines, Pacific Fleet.

Subject: U.S.S. GRENADIER, War Patrol - Comments on.

    1.   The results of the GRENADIER's war effort for a
period of forty-seven (47) days resulted in a total failure.
It is possible, but not probable, that a small 5000 ton freighter was damaged at the expense of six (6) torpedoes. Such an
expenditure cannot be tolerated against a freighter target that
will sink if hit with one torpedo.

    2.   Navigational risks must be carefully considered
by commanding officers. It is believed that determined skill-
ful operation near enemy coasts is possible and will produce
sinkings. If a navigation light is sighted the probability of
shipping being present is good and it should be well worth
while to remain in vicinity of the light.

    3.   It is considered that the GRENADIER handled re-
pair of a serious main generator casualty in an excellent manner.
Since this derangement occurred on second day of departure, the
successful use of the generator after repair during remainder
of patrol indicates sound engineering judgement.

    4.   The untimely flooding of pumproom auxiliaries
soon after entering area was a distracting physical and mental
problem for crew and officers.

    5.   Factors of endurance remaining indicate that the
GRENADIER could have remained on patrol for a period of ten to
fourteen additional days. The commanding officer stated that he
returned because he was tired. Commanding Officers must have
confidence and place responsibility in the hands of their
juniors so that they will never be tired.

                                                    F.H. O'LEARY.

Copy to: Comsubron SIX.
            GRENADIER.

                              -8-   ENCLOSURE (B)

FC5-6/A16-3   SUBMARINE SQUADRON SIX   (6/Mc

Serial 092   Care of Postmaster,
                                           San Francisco, California,
                                           March 24, 1942.

CONFIDENTIAL

From: The Commander Submarine Squadron SIX.
To :   The Commander Submarines, Pacific Fleet.

Subject: U.S.S. GRENADIER (SS210) - Report of First War
          Patrol.

    1.   This, the first war patrol of the GRENADIER,
covered a period of 48 days, of which 34 were spent enroute
and 14 were spent on station. According to the report, the
least remaining endurance of the factors affecting the length
of the patrol was fourteen days. No explanation is offered
for the GRENADIER's early return to port.

    2.   The material performance of this patrol was
very good. The main difficulties encountered were a result
of taking water down the conning tower hatch which cannot be
attributed to defective material. Personnel endurance appeared to be very good, but the patrol was not long enough to be
a good criterion of this factor.

    3.   The number of contacts made on this patrol was
disappointing as it was thought that this area contained a
large volume of enemy shipping, located, as it is, across the entrance to important enemy ports. One attack was made with
doubtful results and the expenditure of six torpedoes. The
torpedo supply does not warrant such a prodigal use of torpedoes.
Torpedoes must be fired to hit and the results must not be
left in doubt. It is believed that this patrol would have
been more productive had the area been exploited more thoroughly.

                                        A. R. McCANN.

Copy to:
    Comsubdiv 62.
    CO U.S.S. GRENADIER.

                         -1-   ENCLOSURE (C)

FF12-10/A16-3(5)   SUBMARINES, PACIFIC FLEET

Serial 0321   Care of Postmaster,
                                     San Francisco, California,
                                     March 27, 1942.
COMSUBPAC PATROL REPORT No. 17
U.S.S. GRENADIER - FIRST WAR PATROL.

CONFIDENTIAL

From: The Commander Submarines, Pacific Fleet.
To   :   Submarines, Pacific Fleet.

Subject: U.S.S. GRENADIER (SS210) - First War Patrol -
             Report of.

Enclosure: (A) Copy of CO GRENADIER Conf ltr SS210/A12
                 Ser. 052 of Mar. 23, 1942.
             (B) Copy of CSD 62 Conf ltr FB5-62/A16-3 Ser.
                 024 of Mar. 24, 1942.
             (C) Copy of CSS 6 Conf ltr FC5-6/A16-3 Ser.
                 092 of Mar. 24, 1942.

    1.   The following are quotations from the Command-
ing Officer's report:

    (a) "0300 sighted light bearing 135 relative, appeared to
        be a signal light, probably from a sampan. Dived ..
        ......"

    (b) "About 2100 sighted light on port quarter, similar to
        one seen preceding night. Dived. About 2200, while
        ready to surface, sighted another white (all around)
        light through periscope, probably a sampan. Opened
        out on this light about a mile and surfaced, nothing
        in sight".

    (c) "Sighted small DD bearing 010 relative, angle on the
        bow - 60° port. Dived to make periscope approach,
        as moon was behind DD, and speed of DD appeared small.
        Some trouble with ship porpoising, and when steadied
        down, did not see DD, or pick up on sound."

    2.   These were the only night contacts reported.
Three of the lights sighted were not investigated at all; in
fact, one was deliberately avoided. The destroyer contact,
with destroyer silhouetted in the moon, was ideal for a surface attack. No attempt was made to develop this, but rather,
GRENADIER dived and lost contact.

    3.   On the return trip, four days from the area,
tops of mast and stack of a merchant vessel were sighted, where-

                        -1-

FF12-10/A16-3(5)   SUBMARINES, PACIFIC FLEET

                                                                an
Serial 0321   Care of Postmaster,
                               San Francisco, California,
                               March 27, 1942.
COMSUBPAC PATROL REPORT No. 17
U.S.S. GRENADIER - FIRST WAR PATROL.

<u>CONFIDENTIAL</u>

Subject: U.S.S. GRENADIER (SS210) - First War Patrol -
                Report of.
- -

upon the GRENADIER immediately dived and lost contact. With
the surface speed available, it is considered that GRENADIER
could have obtained a favorable position for a submerged attack or at least discovered what kind of a ship it was. The
possibility of tankers fueling submarines or other vessels
at this distance from Japan must be considered.

        4.   After firing four torpedoes at the only day-
light target (one of which hit) and seeing that it was not
sinking, two more torpedoes were fired, whereupon GRENADIER
proceeded to clear the area.

        5.   GRENADIER returned from patrol with approxi-
mately fourteen days endurance remaining.

        6.   GRENADIER is credited with the following dam-
age inflicted upon the enemy:

                One freighter of 5,000 tons - DAMAGED.

                                        T. WITHERS.

DISTRIBUTION:
Pacific List 7CM-41:
  List I, Case 2,
    P1(5), SSF.
Atlantic List 11CM-41:
    SO(2).
Special:
    EN3(5), EN10(1); EN28(5),
    ND14(2); NY1(1), NY9(1),
    NY10(2), Subschool NL(8),
    ComsubSWPac(2), Cominch(5),
    Supships Groton Conn (2).
    MP1(2).

E. R. Swinburne
E. R. SWINBURNE,
Flag Secretary.

1ST COPY

SS210/A12

Serial 39

U.S.S. GRENADIER

U.S.S. GRENADIER - REPORT OF SECOND WAR PATROL

PERIOD FROM APRIL 12, TO JUNE 10, 1942.

TIME ZONES -9(I) AND + 12(Y)

1. Narrative.

April 12 - Underway from Submarine Base, Pearl Harbor in accordance with Commander Task Force Seven, Operation Order 35-42, escorted by U.S.S. LITCHFIELD. At 2030 (V) LITCHFIELD headed back for Pearl.

April 14 - At 1040 (X) sighted masts of merchant ship bearing 310°T and heading toward Pearl. Dived and closed ship which was identified as probably the U.S.S. THOMAS JEFFERSON.

April 16 - At 0605 (X) sighted Midway Island and established identification with the signal tower at 0615 (X). At 0615 (Y) passed U.S.S. CACHALOT outside the reef and heading for Pearl. Moored starboard side to dock at 0642 (Y) and proceeded to fill up with fuel and water and to effect minor repairs. Underway at 1740 (Y) to clear channel before dark. Air coverage was supplied both on arrival and departure.

April 17-24- No occurences of special interest. On April 21 began running on one engine part of each day to conserve fuel as fuel consumption on two engines was too high.

April 25 - At 1256 (K) in Lat. 30-09 N, Long. 143-08 E, radar picked up an airplane distance 5-6 miles. Almost immediately thereafter a monoplane bearing 165° and headed for the ship was sighted, estimated range 4 miles, altitude 1500 feet. Made a quick dive to 145 feet and while passing 90 feet heard explosions of two bombs. At 1336 heard explosion of a third bomb some distance away. Surfaced after dark and continued on way. Skies were clear and the sea glassy smooth all day.

April 26 - Ran submerged during daylight hours due to close proximity to Tori Shima in the Southern Island Group.

- 1 -   ENCLOSURE (A)

41240

DECLASSIFIED

Subject: U.S.S. GRENADIER - Second War Patrol - Report of.

- -

April 29 -   At 0445 (I) radar indicated nearest island 11
                miles. Dived to await daylight and fix position.
                At 0600 made landfall and fixed position about
                8 miles east of Nokano Shima. Proceeded sub-
                merged into area via Nokano Shima Suido. Con-
                siderable difficulty was experienced with cur-
                ents in this passage. Considering today as the
                first day in the area the time spent enroute was
                16 days. Surfaced at 2005 and set course for
                Kusakaki Shima. At 2152 made first sampan contact
                in the area. Due to the excellent visibility
                with a full moon dived and closed to investigate.
                Believed it to have been a patrol vessel. Lost
                contact at 2245 and surfaced. Rounded Kusakaki
                Light and set course for Danjo Gunto.

Day 1 -   While patrolling submerged off Danjo Gunto made
                contact with six sampans during the day, all
Contact #1   believed fishing. Upon surfacing at 2040 sight-
                ed light of two sampans on the port quarter and
                a ship bearing 160°T, distance about 4 miles.
                Because of the bright moon, dived and conducted
                a submerged approach on the ship, a large three
Attack #1   island freighter, estimated 5,000 tons. Attack-
                ed and sank this ship. Continued patrol to
                the northward.

Day 2 -   At 0355 sighted luminous exhaust ring of low
                flying plane and dived.

Day 3 -   At 0825 picked up a small trawler which passed
                close aboard. Did not attack due to small size,
Contact #2   about 50 tons. At 0822 sighted masts of a small
                single stack freighter, estimated 1,500 tons,
Contact #3   bearing 262°T, zigzagging on a base of about
                060°, range 12,000 yards. Made an approach but
                failed to reach favorable firing position.
                This vessel may have been the "X" ship reported
                by GUDGEON. At 1150 sighted a warship tentatively
                identified as a FG of the Uji Class. Was unable
                to close for an attack due to large angle on
Contact 4   bow and range.

Day 4 -   At 2330 broke off patrol of northern part of area
                and set course to the Southward in hopes of
                intercepting enemy ships reported by ComTaskForce
                7 to be concentrating in Kagoshima Bay.

                        - 2 -   ENCLOSURE (A)

DECLASSIFIED

Subject: U.S.S. GRENADIER - Second War Patrol - Report of.

- -

Day 5 -   At 1026 sighted smoke on the horizon, drawing
                 rapidly to the left. Could not close for an
Contact #5   attack. May have been a ship or a sampan. At
                 1243 made an approach on a target which at
                 close range was identified as a powered sampan.
                 Did not attack.

Day 6 -   At 0030 received despatch cancelling intelligence
                 of men-of-war in Kagoshima Bay, took up patrol
                 in vicinity of Kusakaki Light. Due to thick
                 weather which developed during the day set
                 course at 2020, to patrol in the vicinity of the
                 intersection of the Shanghai - Yokahama and
                 Nagasaki - Formosa shipping lanes. Made one
                 sampan contact during the evening.

Day 7 -   Uneventful except for two sampan contacts.

Day 8 -   At 1852 in Lat. 30-40 N, Long. 127-54 E, inter-
                 cepted a south bound convoy of at least 6
Contact #6   medium freighters and the Taijo Maru. Conducted
                 attack and made at least two hits on the Taijo
                 Maru. Encountered strong AS measures by planes
Attack #2   and surface escorts and was heavily depth
                 charged, suffered no important material damage.

Day 9 -   AS search and depth charging of the area contin-
                 ued throughout most of the day.

Day 10 -   Patrolling in eastern part of the area in the
                 direction of Nagasaki Ho. Sighted four sampans
                 during the day.

Day 11 -   Patrolling to westward toward the Moji Formosa
                 shipping lanes. Only contacts were with six
                 sampans during the day.

Day 12 -   At 0952 sighted a small steamer, a three island
                 vessel of about 500 tons, bearing 350°T on
                 course about 250°T range about 5 miles. Range
                 and angle on bow, about 80° port, prevented
                 closing to attack. Sighted only one sampan
                 today.

Day 13 -   At 2030 began clearing the area in accordance
                 with ComTaskForce 7 despatch instructing GREN-
                 ADIER shift to area. Made three sampan con-
                 tacts today.

                        - 3 -   ENCLOSURE (A)

DECLASSIFIED

Subject: U.S.S. GRENADIER - Second War Patrol Report of.

- -

May 14 -   Clearing area - enroute area -. Sighted four
sampans prior to nightfall. At 2305 sighted
two sampans, one lighted and one darkened,
evidently patrolling between Kusakaki and Yoka
Shima, changed course to avoid detection.

May 15 -   Cleared area - via Tokara Kaikyo and set course
for Bungo Suido cutting through area -. Contacted four sampans today, three in Tokara Kaikyo.

May 16 -   At 2200 ran into a heavy fog bank setting down
from the Bungo Suido. Ran to southward to clear
the fog and took up patrol on course 070° and
reverse in hope of intercepting "Wounded Bear"
during the night.

May 17 -   Conducted patrol south of Bungo Suido until
2015. At this time set course for Pearl.
Unable to continue longer in area due to
shortage of fuel.

May 19 -   Ran submerged during daylight due to proximity
to Tori Shima.

May 20 - 24 - Uneventful. Running on surface on one engine to
conserve fuel. On May 24, #3 main engine put
out of commission with a cracked liner in
#2 cylinder.

May 25-30 -   At 0500 (L), May 25 increased speed to 80-90
combination on two engines in anticipation of
orders to proceed to Midway. At 1200 (L)
altered course to proceed to Midway for fuel
and provisions via altered route prescribed by
ComTaskForce 7. At 0300 (M), in Lat. 31-05 N,
Long. 171-25 E, sighted beam of light in sky
which looked like a searchlight beam though it
could have been moonlight through a rift in the
clouds. Closed for one hour, and saw nothing
further and resumed course. A report of this
incident was made to ComTaskForce 7. At 0925 (M),
May 28, increased speed to arrive at Midway before
sunset the next day. At 1624 (Y), May 28 moored
to the dock at Midway alongside U.S SIC.RD.
Other ships present were USS GUDEN, KITTYHAWK
and CRYSTAL. GUDEN, KITTYHAWK, and SICARD departed Midway at 0500 (Y), May 29. At 1600 (Y),
May 29, underway in accordance with despatch
orders from ComTaskForce 7, proceeding via
assigned route to patrol station on the 200 mile
circle bearing 310-330T from Midway, in addition
to taking on fuel, water and provisions at Midway,

- 4 -   INCLOSURE (A)

DECLASSIFIED

Subject: U.S.S. GRENADIER - Second War Patrol - Report of.

- -

May 25-30 Con- made repairs to #1 electric still and renewed
t'd   one cylinder liner in #3 engine.

May 31 -   At 0400 (Y), arrived on station and took up
                patrol, running submerged during daylight.

June 1 -   Patrolling on station. At 0930 (Y) sighted
                PBY plane patrolling on north westerly course
                from Midway. Completed repairs to #3 engine
                and put it back in commission.

June 2 -   At 0045 (Y) set course 225°T, shifting station
                in accordance with despatch instructions to
                patrol sector bearing 290°-310°T from Midway
                and to remain within 20 miles of center of
                sector chord. Arrived on new station and
                took up submerged patrol at 0420 (Y). Sighted
                PBY plane on patrol at 0651 and 1440 (Y).

June 3 -   Patrolling on station. At 0645 (Y) sighted a
                PBY plane patrolling on northwesterly course,
                well clear.

June 4 -   Patrolling station. About 0615 (Y) intercepted
                plane contact report on enemy. 2CB's and 1TB,
                bearing 320° distance 170 miles from Midway,
                course 135°T, speed 25 knots. Since this
                force was already beyond us, continued submerged
                patrol looking for other enemy units. At 0744
                sighted unidentified aircraft bearing 043T on
                southwesterly course. When plane turned and
                headed toward GRENADIER went to deep submergence.
                At 0837 surfaced and proceeded toward Midway
                but was chased down by unidentified plane flying
                toward ship at 0855 (Y). When area was clear of
                aircraft, surfaced and continued on course toward
                Midway, hoping to intercept retiring enemy
                units. At 1420 (Y) changed course to 090T passed
                about 60 miles north of the island after inter-
                cepting a despatch from U.S. PORTLAND that she
                had been attacked 150 miles north of Midway.
                This was the first indication received as to
                where the action was taking place. At 1535 (Y)
                was forced down by large seaplane, probably a
                PBY, flying toward the ship. Continued surface
                running when area was clear. At 2030, in accord-
                ance with instructions from ComTaskForce 7, set
                course for new patrol station on the 100 mile
                circle from Midway, the sector bearing 290-300T.
                Arrived on station at 2355 (Y).

                        - 5 -   ENCLOSURE (A)

Subject: U.S.S. GRENADIER - Second War Patrol - Report of.

- -

June 5 -   Patrolling on station. At 0502 (Y), while submerged at
            periscope depth, felt a strong explosion which seemed
            fairly close but nothing was sighted. At 0848 (Y) sur-
            faced and began retiring along median of section toward
            Midway in accordance with instructions. Commenced pa-
            trolling on the 12 mile circle from Midway at 1450 (Y).
            Several PBY planes were sighted while enroute but all
            kept well clear.

June 6 -   Patrolling on station. At 0220 (Y), started shifting to
            new patrol station on sector bearing 250-260T from Mid-
            way. Dived during morning twilight and resumed in and
            out patrol on surface at 0545 (Y). At 1154 (Y), set
            course 132T, heading for Pearl, in accordance with des-
            patch instructions from ComTaskForce 7.

June 7-   Enroute Pearl via routing points 25 and 26. Rendezvous
10 -   with LITCHFIELD and GATO set for daylight 10 June in
            Lat. 21-15-11, Long 159-00 W. Sighted GATO to north
            of GRENADIER track at 1810 (A), June 8. Contacted PBY
            plane at 1300 (X) and another about 1345 (X) June 8.
            Sighted PBY plane on southwesterly course at 0615 (X)
            June 9. Made scheduled rendezvous with GATO and LITCH-
            FIELD and proceeded to Submarine Base, Pearl.

2. WEATHER

        Weather enroute to and from station and in the
vicinity of Midway was exceptionally favorable and mild
with light winds and smooth seas. In area ___ patrol
conditions were only fair. For the first week on station the bright full moon and smooth seas made surprise
surface encounters at night entirely impossible. During the remainder of time in this area the sky was generally overcast with a light surface haze forming about
sunset. Variable shifting winds and heavy rain squalls
were frequently encountered. It being difficult to
maintain periscope depth at times due to heavy seas
which were noticeable to depths of one hundred feet.
Visibility in the northern portion of the area was con-
sistently poor and limited the extent of the patrol in
this sector as it was impossible to fix position with
any certainty for two or three days at a time.
        On the other hand the weather in area ___ was
clear and warm with glassy smooth seas making a successful of periscope attack out of the question. On
the night of May 16th, just prior to the expected
arrival of the "Wounded Bear", a heavy fog set out of
Bungo Suido making it necessary to withdraw to the south.

                    - 6 -   ENCLOSURE (A)

DECLASSIFIED

Subject: U.S.S. GRENADIER - Second War Patrol - Report Of.

- -

3. TIDAL INFORMATION

No definite information on this subject was obtained, the strong currents which exist in most parts of area ___ are considerably affected by the state of the tide, however.

4. NAVIGATIONAL AIDS.

The lights on Kusakaki Shima, Gaja Shima and Yaku Shima were noted to be burning with their published characteristics. The latter two were not burning when the Commanding Officer was previously in this area.
No other aids were noted.

5. DESCRIPTION OF ENEMY SHIPS ENCOUNTERED

Contact	Location	Course	Speed	Time	Description
#1	31-47N 127-35E	295°	10	2040 (I) May 1.	Large three island freighter. Details were difficult to make out in the dark but it appeared to be of the "Africa Maru" Class. Tonnage, 9,500 gross. First Attack.
#2	33-09N 127-19E		8	0626 (I) May 3	Small trawler. Looked like an old schooner fitted with box-like deck house amidships to house engine. Estimated about 75 feet. Deck house may have been hiding a gun.
#3	33-16N 127-20E	060°	10	0822 (I) May 3.	Three island freighter resembling "Kyofu Maru" Ship was very light in water and rolling considerably in moderate seas. Crows nest forward and built up structure aft. Believed to be a patrol vessel. Could not get into attack position. May be the "Q" ship encountered by GUDGEON.

- 7 -   ENCLOSURE (A)

Subject: U.S.S. GRENADIER - Second War Patrol - Report of.
- -

Contact	Location	Course	Speed	Time	Description
#4	33-23N 127-15E	120° Approx. zigzagging	15	1158 May 8	Single stack PG of Uji Class or a light minelayer. Unable to close for an attack, initial angle on bow about 80°, range 15,000 yards.
#5	31-50N 128-04E			1026 (I) May 5	Sighted smoke of fast ship or sampan which drew rapidly out of sight. Did not see vessel.
#6	30-47 N 127-39E	190° zigzagging	10	1852 (I) May 8	Convoy consisting of at least six single stack, three island freighters and passenger liner identified as the "Taiyo Maru" 14,900 tons. ░░ not observe escort vessels or planes. Did not observe freighters closely, concentrating on attack on the passenger ship or auxiliary cruiser.
#7	32-21N 127-38E	250° Possibly zigzagging	10-12	0952 (I) May 12	Small steamer, estimated 500-1000 tons, three island, single stack type. Ship was stubby with high forecastle and a relatively tall stack, old coal burner. After Is-

land was built up abnormally high and masts appeared to be heavily shrouded. Initial angle on bow of 80° and long range prevented closing to close range. Did not attack. Possibly a patrol vessel.

The only other contacts made were with sampans. A total of 31 sampans were sighted. Some were fisherman while others were undoubtedly patrol craft. The fishing craft were invariably showing a large white light at night. Some sampans were observed to be showing a bright red light at night. Sometimes this light was observed to be steady while at other times it was flashed on and off at intervals. It is believed that these are some sort of patrol craft.

Subject: U.S.S. GRENADIER - Second War Patrol - Report of.

- -

6. ENEMY AIRCRAFT SIGHTED.

One enemy air plane was sighted during daylight. This plane attacked GRENADIER with three bombs in Lat. 30°-09°N., Long. 143-08E., on April 25, at 1256 (K). It was a single wing landplane, possibly a light bomber (Type Showa Sho 98).

At 0355 (I), May 2, sighted luminous exhaust ring of low flying plane and dived. Plane was not observed but was probably sent out to locate GRENADIER following attack on freighter, the previous evening.

On May 8, was attacked by bombs from planes immediately following attack on Taiyo Maru. Planes were providing air coverage for the convoy and were not observed.

No other contacts with enemy aircraft were made.

- 9 -   ENCLOSURE (A)

DECLASSIFIED

Subject: U.S.S. GRENADIER – Second War Patrol – Report of.

7. Particulars of Attacks.

Attack	No. Torpedoes Fired	Firing Interval	Track Angle	Range	Depth Set	Est. Drift	Enemy Speed	Point of aim	Offset Angle
#1	4	40 sec.	104S	1430	24	18-20	10	Stack	0
		8 min.	110S	1380	24		10	"	0
		2 min.	114S	Approx 1800	24	feet	0	"	0
				1800					
		2 min.	1238	Approx 1800			0	"	0
#2	4		1085	1460	24	18-24	10	Fwd.	2 L
		23	1143	1430	28	feet	10	Stack	0
		15	1175	1420	28		10	"	0
		15	1223	1410	24		10	"	2 R

Torpedo Performance : Results : Evidence of sinking

Attack #1: First torpedo ran normally. Performance of others unknown as all should have hit : First torpedo was a definite hit. Second was not heard but should have hit fwd. of first. Last two were misses : Smoke seen aft, fire issuing from stack and ship settling. Screws stopped when hit. Not in sight upon surfacing one hour after attack.

Attack #2: Torpedoes 1&4 functioned normally. If torpedoes 2 & 3 were not hits was due to failure of magnetic exploders to function : From strong explosions heard :torpedoes 1&4 were definite hits. Torps. 2&3 should have been hits : No evidence other than the number of hits and the prolonged depth charging which followed the attack. An old ship of this type probably could not survive two or more torpedoes.

– 10 –

ENCLOSURE (A)

DECLASSIFIED

Subject: U.S.S. GRENADIER - Second War Patrol - Report of.

- -

7. PARTICULARS OF ATTACKS (CONTINUED)

Attack
#1
At 2040 sighted lights of two sampans on port quarter and smoke and outline of a ship bearing 160°T distance about 4 miles. Dived and closed ship which was identified as a large three island, single stack, freighter on estimated course 295, speed 10 knots, made submerged approach.

2121
Fired torpedo from #3 tube at estimated range of 1500 yards and 105° starboard track angle. Sound man had not reported torpedo running normally so at 21-21-40 fired torpedo from #4 tube. At 21-21-05 first torpedo hit under after well deck with a loud explosion and a cloud of smoke was seen to issue from after part of the ship. Her propellers stopped immediately and were not heard again. No explosion was heard from the second torpedo although it ran normally and should have hit forward of the first torpedo. However about a minute after the first torpedo hit smoke and fire was seen shooting high out of the freighters stack for several minutes. It also appeared that part of the stern was blown away by the first torpedo.

2130
Target had not sunk though it had settled considerably by the stern so fired one torpedo from #7 tube using target speed zero. Since this torpedo apparently missed fired another torpedo from #8 tube. This also apparently missed. All torpedoes were fired using a depth of 24 feet to get benefits of the magnetic exploder.

2133
Decided against further torpedo expenditure and began to clear area submerged.

2145
Observed target through periscope. Ship was dead in the water with stern awash and bow high, evidently in sinking condition.

2233
Surfaced and could see no sign of target, assumed it had sunk since last observation. Proceeded away from area and commenced charging. It was a brilliant moonlight night with calm seas and a full moon. Battery was badly in need of a charge as we had been submerged since 0445.

- 11 -   ENCLOSURE (A)

DECLASSIFIED

Subject: U.S.S. GRENADIER - Second War Patrol - Report of.

- -

7. PARTICULARS OF ATTACKS (CONTINUED)

Attack
#2

At 1852 picked up smoke bearing 048°T. At 1854 observed masts and stacks of large vessel with other masts and smoke beyond. As the range was closed it became evident that we had encountered a south bound convoy consisting of at least six freighters with a large liner in van. At 1900 came to normal approach course to intercept the liner which was identified as the Taiyo Maru. No escort vessels were sighted but assumed their presence as well as probable air coverage until dark. Decided to accept counter measures and attack before dark, assuming that sinking of the large transport would have the most damaging effect on the convoy. By trailing after dark it might be possible to get one or two freighters but we probably could not get in and attack on the Taiyo Maru.

Sea conditions were good for a periscope attack and by sparing use of the periscope and running deep between exposures a good attack position was attained for an estimated 105° starboard track and 1500 yards range.
Four torpedoes were fired as follows:

Torpedo	Time	Depth Setting	Gyro Offset	Tube No.	Time of explosion.
#1	19-31-58	24'	2°L	4	19-33-08
#2	19-32-21	28'	0	1	Not heard
#3	19-32-36	28'	0°R	2	Not heard
#4	19-32-51	24'	2°R	3	19-33-54

Two loud explosions, definitely torpedo hits, were heard and from the times noted it is evident that torpedoes 1 & 4 were hits. Either the magnetic exploders on torpedoes 2 & 3 failed to function or they were not heard due to exploding under the ship. With the spread used, if #1 & #4 were hits, #2 & #3 torpedoes also should have been hits. The sound operator reported that all torpedoes appeared to be running normally.

Torpedoes 2, 3 & 4 were fired on generated bearing.

- 12 -   ENCLOSURE (A)

DECLASSIFIED

Subject: U.S.S. GRENADIER - Second War Patrol - Report of.

- -

7. PARTICULARS OF ATTACKS (CONTINUED)

At 1933 started changing course to the right and
within a minute heard the explosions of a stick of
bombs close overhead. Started for deep submergence
and while passing 90 feet heard several more bombs. At
1938 heard and felt a series of three powerful explosions. These could have been explosions from the sinking ship or depth charges though they were not close
aboard and did not sound like depth charges and no water
turbulence was noted. About this time fast screw noises
on three bearings were noted closing in on us and evasion tactics at slow speed were started. At 1941 two
depth charges exploded fairly close aboard and from then
until 2300 a total of 36 charges were felt. Some of
these were too close for comfort while later on some
appeared to be several thousand yards away. During the
depth charge attacks all hands conducted themselves in
a most creditable manner. The effect of the torpedoes
on the Taiyo Maru could not be observed due to the
prompt AS measures encountered. However, it is felt
that with at least two and possibly more, torpedo hits
in her the old ship definitely sank. That the enemy
was chagrined at our getting in undetected on the convoy was evidenced by their depth charging the area all
the next day.

8. ENEMY AS MEASURES.

The attack on the Taiyo Maru was promptly followed
by AS activity by planes and escort vessels. Two
sticks of bombs were dropped by planes within a minute
of firing, probably in the vicinity of the torpedo im-
pulse bubbles. Shortly after firing the screws of
three vessels were heard closing the GRENADIER and at
1941 the first two definite depth charges were felt
close aboard. A total of 36 charges were felt between
then and 2300.

The procedure used by the attacking vessels seemed
to be for one to close in and launch charges while the
other two ran at slow speed listening. No supersonic
signals were heard. It is also believed that depth
charge projectors were employed.

- 13 -   ENCLOSURE (A)

DECLASSIFIED

- -

At depths greater than 150 feet our starboard shaft emits a loud squealing noise and the trailing vessels appeared to have no difficulty trailing us until we stopped using that shaft. The attacking vessels appeared to expect us to retire to the westward and gradually worked off in that direction. Accordingly GRENADIER retired at slow speed to eastward. No depth charges were heard after 2300, although screw noises were picked up for a short time after that.

Several charges went off close enough to severely jar the ship, stirring up dust, breaking two lights in the control room, affecting depth control somewhat and causing a rushing of water and jarring of gear in the superstructure. During most the attack GRENADIER was running at 250 feet. It is believed that the depth charges were set for a shallower depth.

At 0145 GRENADIER surfaced and put in a quick charge, diving again at 0408 when possible screw noises were heard but nothing could be seen. After diving suspicious noises were heard. These sounds were heard during most of the forenoon.

At 0450 depth charging of the area was again started and continued until 1100. A total of 22 charges were heard, the nearest one estimated to be about 1,000 yards distance. GRENADIER ran silent at deep submergence to avoid detection by planes as seas had become smooth. Began running at periscope depth at 1730 when sun was fairly low. Between 1900 and 1945 heard a series of 6 more depth charges in the distance but nothing could be seen. No further AS activity was noted.

9. MAJOR DEFECTS EXPERIENCED.

(A) Fathometer:
Prior to reaching Midway outbound, the NM Fathometer was reported out of commission due to grounds in the wiring to the projector. This equipment was out of commission the entire trip.

(B) Electric Stills:
The water distilled by the electric stills was of poor quality the entire patrol. The evaporator coils

- 14 -   ENCLOSURE (A)

DECLASSIFIED

DECLASSIFIED

Subject: U.S.S. GRENADIER - Second War Patrol - Report of.

received extremely rough treatment during cleaning by
the repair crew at the base and the stills were not
properly assembled. Some leaks were repaired while at
Midway on the outbound trip but due to minor leaks the
water made was excessively salty. Several coils should
be renewed. A thorough test of this equipment should
be made prior to the next patrol.

On the return trip to Midway #1 still was disas-
sembled and on arrival the coils were sent to the shop
and repaired, and tested. The still was assembled on
station and performed satisfactorily.

(C) Tail Shafting:
Both shafts squeal badly in starting and stopping
due to improper clearance of rubber strips in stern
bearings. This condition has been the subject of correspondence with the Bureau but corrective action has
not been taken. In addition, the starboard shaft
emits a loud squealing noise when operated at low
speeds at depth greater than 150 feet. This is a distinct military deficiency which prevents running silent.
This vessel should be docked to correct this condition
prior to another patrol.

(D) Cracked Liners:
On May 24, while running at 150 RPM on #3 Main
Engine a cracked liner developed in #2 cylinder putting
this engine out of commission. This liner was replaced
while at Midway on the return passage and reassembling
was completed on patrol station on June 1.

On June 6, a cracked liner developed on #4 engine
shortly after starting it up. Repairs were not effected as no spare liner was on board. Both of the liners
which developed cracks are in cylinders which became
overheated on the passage of this vessel from Portsmouth to Honolulu.

(E) On the return passage a severe banging noise developed in the superstructure or in #1 Main Ballast
Tank. It has not been traced down but may be that
the residual drain piping in #1 Main Ballast Tank has
been carried away incident to depth charging.

- 15 -   ENCLOSURE (A)

DECLASSIFIED

Subject: U.S.S. GRENADIER - Second War Patrol - Report of.
- -

(F) Sound Training Generator.
A short circuit occured between two commutator bars in the armature on the motor end of the training motor generator upon departure from Pearl. Repairs were effected by ship's force prior to arrival at Midway.

10.   Communications -
Radio Reception: NPM submarine schedules were observed without difficulty. While on station, considerable static interferred with low frequency schedules during early morning hours. On three occassions strong Jap signals on 4115 blocked out NPM high frequency broadcasts. Radar causes some interference with high frequency reception. In accordance with Comtaskfor 7 despatch 250111 of May, set continuous watch on 4265 KCS series while patrolling off Midway. No difficulty was experienced in clearing traffic through NPM, NM, NAS, NPS. By checking with the list of arbitrary words assigned, it was noted that three messages to the GRENADIER were not received.

Last message sent   ___IGLO___

Last message received __DECOY__

Radar: Based on ranges obtained on various types of aircraft and known landmarks it appears that the Radar beam is projected at an angle of about one degree to the horizontal. From this it may be assumed that the expected radar range (in miles) on any object will be equal, roughly to the height of the object (in hundreds of feet) above sea level. For example a 5,000 foot peak will be indicated at distances up to 50 miles whereas a plane flying at 500 feet will pass out of range at 5 miles and one at 1,000 feet at 10 miles.

Yoku Shima (Island)   6351'   at 65 miles.
Saishu to (Island)   6388'   at 65-70 miles.
Aircraft (over Midway) above 2,000' at 21 miles.

General: On june 6, at 0030 XRay, Lat. 23-14-00 E,Long. 167-02-00N, attempted to exchange recognition signals with a navy patrol plane and was informed our signals were incorrect. Ten minutes later exchanged the same signals with a second navy patrol plane with no difficulty.

11.   Sound Conditions and Density Layers.
In general sound conditions were only fair, with the usual water noises being encountered off the Japanese Coast. At no time was a target picked up by sound, before it was sighted. During the depth charge attack, one projector lower interlock roller, was forced off its track. On the other projector, the roller was flattened out by sea pressure, at deep submergence.

12.   Habitability was very good. The air conditioning system was run almost continuously and kept the ship cool and the

- 16 -   ENCLOSURE (A)

DECLASSIFIED

Subject: U.S.S. GRENADIER - Second War Patrol - Report of.

- -

humidity sufficiently low. ...

The health of the crew, in general, was excellent. Onl one man was admitted to the sick list for a foot injury. The same man suffered an attack of acute appendicitis while at Midway on the return trip. He was transferred to the station and operated on. There were numerous cases of headaches during the patrol caused by the long daily dives. Three cases of minor injuries were treated by the pharmacist mate. Only two men were treated for constipation.

The food was of high standard, of good variety and well prepared. No attempt was made to turn night into day for meals.

13. Limiting factors of endurance.

Factors of Endurance remaining upon arrival at Midway were:

TORPEDOES	FUEL	PROVISIONS (DAYS)	PERSONNEL DAYS)
16	18,000 gallons	30	21

Factors of endurance remaining upon arrival at Pearl were:

TORPEDOES	FUEL	PROVISIONS	PERSONNEL
16	26000	30	10

Fuel and provisions were taken on at Midway, May 28, 19

14. The factor of endurance which caused ending this patrol was fuel. Fuel on hand on clearing the area was approximately 47,000 gallons.

15. General.
The scarcity of contacts with worthwhile targets is considered due to the use of convoys in the patrol area by the enemy. It is regretted that GRENADIER was not more fortunate in making contacts.

The health and morale of the personnel was of a high order the entire period. At the time of leaving area practically all hands were showing some effects of strain and tension. Recuperation while enroute to Midway was marked.

Fuel used in shifting station from Area to Area caused terminating the patrol somewhat earlier than would have been necessary had station been maintained in Area .

-17-   ENCLOSURE (A)

FB5-62/A16-3   SUBMARINE DIVISION SIXTY-TWO   eb
                                Care of Postmaster,
Serial 04A   San Francisco, California,
                                June 11, 1942.

~~DECLASSIFIED~~

From: The Commander Submarine Division SIXTY-TWO.
To :   The Commander Submarines, Pacific Fleet.

Subject: U.S.S. GRENADIER - Second War Patrol - Comments on.

        1.   The GRENADIER has returned from a very successful patrol in enemy controlled waters and remained at sea for fifty-nine days. In spite of strong enemy anti-submarine measures, including three long depth charge attacks, the commanding officer returned his ship without damage to material or personnel.

        2.   It is noted that the radar gave very good results and warned of the approach of aircraft. The commanding officer covered his areas very thoroughly but due to weather and not operating in the shipping lanes only three contacts with enemy shipping were developed. Operations in the vicinity of important lighthouses as O Shima, Me Shima, Jusakaki Shima and Marato might produce more enemy contacts. In patrolling in the open sea it is believed that the courses of patrol should be along the estimated shipping routes such as Straits of Formosa-Shimonoseki, Nagasaki-Straits of Formosa and Yokohama-Straits of Formosa rather than normal to those tracks.

        3.   It is reported that two torpedoes fired at the Taijo Maru failed to detonate when they went under the target. Four commanding officers of this division have reported apparent failures of the Mark 6 exploder. Disarming of the counter-mining device either may or may not eliminate failures. In the future, it is strongly recommended that torpedoes be set so as to run between the keel and two feet less than the estimated draft of the vessel attacked. This procedure should cause the torpedo to be just as effective as directly under the target and might eliminate the reported failures.

        4.   The GRENADIER is credited with the following damage:

Sunk	Vessel	Tonnage
1	Freighter (Africa Maru Class)	9,500
1	Taijo Maru	14,900
	Total	24,400

The Japanese acknowledged the loss of the Taijo Maru.

        5.   The GRENADIER returned to port with the officers and men in the highest state of morale and health. The Division Commander congratulates the commanding officer, officers and men of the GRENADIER for their excellent performance.

Copy to:
   Comsubron 6, GRENADIER   - 1 -   F. M. O'LEARY.

                                      ENCLOSURE (B)

SUBMARINES, PACIFIC FLEET

FF12-10/A16-3(5)   ay

Serial 0688   Care of Fleet Post Office,
                                               San Francisco, California,
COMSUBPAC PATROL REPORT NO. 35   June 18, 1942.
U.S.S. GRENADIER - SECOND WAR PATROL

~~DECLASSIFIED~~ I A L

From: The Commander Submarines, Pacific Fleet.
To :   Submarines , Pacific Fleet.

Subject: U.S.S. GRENADIER (SS210) - Report of Second War
            Patrol.

Enclosure: (A) Copy of subject report.
            (B) Copy of Comsubdiv 62 Conf. ltr. FB5-62/A16-3,
                Serial 04A of June 11, 1942.

    1.   The results obtained on this patrol are highly
gratifying.

    2.   It is impossible to accurately prove or disprove
the statement made in paragraph 3 by Commander Submarine Division
Sixty-Two regarding failures of the Mark 6 exploder. The Commanding Officers referred to are as follows:

    (a) GUDGEON - Commanding Officer stated one torpedo surely
passed under target without exploding. The submarine in
first case was at a range of at least 1200 yards from target. Commanding Officer stated that the wake of torpedo
was seen to pass under the ship aft of the stack. By the
Commander Submarines, Pacific Fleet - This was a miss
ahead. The submarine in second case was at a range of
2000 yards from target at periscope depth. Commanding
Officer stated that the second torpedo fired was seen to
pass under the target. By the Commander Submarines,
Pacific Fleet - It is believed to be almost impossible to
determine from periscope depth at a range of 2000 yards
from target that a torpedo passed under the target.

    (b) TROUT - Commanding Officer makes no mention in patrol
report of torpedoes being seen to run under targets and
failing to explode.

    (c) TRITON - Commanding Officer states that one torpedo
set to run at 30 feet passed under the target (which was
dead in the water) and did not explode. By the Commander
Submarines, Pacific Fleet - With torpedo running at such
a depth and knowing definitely that torpedo passed under
target, it is highly probable that the anti-countermining
device locked and did not unlock thus preventing the
exploder from functioning.

                        - 1 -

FF12-10/A16-3(5)   SUBMARINES, PACIFIC FLEET   Jk

Serial 0688   Care of Fleet Post Office,
                                     San Francisco, California,
                                     June 18, 1942.

COMSUBPAC PATROL REPORT NO. 35
U.S.S. GRENADIER - SECOND WAR PATROL

~~DECLASSIFIED~~ I A L

Subject: U.S.S. GRENADIER (SS210) - Report of Second
                War Patrol.

- -

(d) GRENADIER - Commanding Officer fired 4 torpedoes the
first of which is believed to have exploded under the
after part of the ship. A ship's officer was taking the
time between explosions and stated that a second explosion
occurred one minute after the first one. By the Commander
Submarines, Pacific Fleet - The first torpedo was aimed
to hit the middle of the target. It is believed that the
first torpedo hit aft which slowed the target sufficiently
to cause the next three torpedoes to miss ahead. What
the second explosion was it would be guess work to state;
it may have been an explosion within the target -- such as
a boiler explosion. The point of aim is the Middle of
Target. If a spread of four torpedoes is fired at a target,
the spread should be so calculated that the first torpedo
will hit 50 yards forward of MOT, the second to hit at
the MOT, the third to hit 50 yards aft of MOT and the
fourth to hit 100 yards aft of MOT.

3.   Submarine torpedo misses may be attributed to
the following:

    (a) Errors in range estimates.
    (b) Errors in speed estimates.
    (c) Errors in course estimates.
    (d) Natural dispersion of torpedoes which is large.
    (e) Inexperience of Torpedo Data Computer Operator.
    (f) Guess and snap decisions by approach officer.
    (g) Targets maneuvering to avoid.
    (h) Physical condition of the approach officer.

4.   Commanding Officers will continue to set torpedoes at a depth not less than five feet greater than the
maximum draft of the target.

5.   It is not understood why the last two torpedoes
fired on attack number one, in an attempt to finish off the
freighter quickly after the freighter was stopped, were fired
from such a long range. After a ship has been hit and stopped,
the submarine should approach close enough to insure almost
certain hits.

- 2 -

SUBMARINES, PACIFIC FLEET

FF12-10/A16-3(5)

Serial 0688

Care of Fleet Post Office,
San Francisco, California,
June 18, 1942.

COMSUBPAC PATROL REPORT NO. 35
U.S.S. GRENADIER – SECOND WAR PATROL

~~DECLASSIFIED~~ I A L

Subject: U.S.S. GRENADIER (SS210) – Report of Second War
Patrol.

- -

6. The GRENADIER is credited with inflicting the
following damage on the enemy:

<u>SUNK</u>

1 Freighter   -   9,500 tons
1 Passenger Ship -   <u>14,900</u> tons

Total 24,400 tons

R. H. ENGLISH.

DISTRIBUTION:
  (21CM-42)
List I, Case 2:
  P1(5), SSx
Special:
  EN3(5) EN10(1); EN28(5);
  Comsublant (2); Subschool, NL(8);
  ComsubSWPac (2); Cominch (5);
  Combat Intel (1).

E. R. SWINBURNE,
Flag Secretary.

1ST COPY

U.S.S. GRENADIER

SS210/A16-3

001
S **DECLASSIFIED**

September 18, 1942.

From: Commanding Officer.
To :   Commander-in-Chief, United States Fleet.
Via :   Official Channels.

Subject: War Diary of Third War Patrol Report.

Enclosure: (A) War Diary, Period July 13, 1942 to September 18,
            1942.

    1.   Enclosure (A) is forwarded herewith.

B. L. CARR

DECLASSIFIED-ART. 0445, OPNAVINST 5510.1C

BY _OP-0989C_ DATE _5/26/72_

DECLASSIFIED

43544

U.S.S. GRENADIER

U.S.S. GRENADIER - Report of 3rd War Patrol

Period from 13 July 1942 to 18 September 1942.

Area 15.   Operation Order 61-42.

1. NARRATIVE

July 13   Underway in company with USS BREZE and SILVERSIDES. Made
           Trim Dive and submerged to 310 feet to check tightness.
           Accompanying ships returned to Pearl after dark.

July 15   Sighted PBY Patrol Plane
1200 (X)   (Air Contact #1)

July 17   Crossed 180th Meridian.
1320(Y)

July 18   Held battle surface and fired 5 rounds from 3" gun for
           training.

July 20   Submerged during daylight to avoid detection while entering
           the Marshalls.
2124 (M)   Passed between Wotje and Maloleop Atolls.

July 21   Because of apparent lack of air patrol decided to remain
           on surface in area between Radik and Ralik Chains.
0953(M)   Made sight and radar contact with unidentified plane. Made
           quick dive to 150 feet. Ten minutes later returned to
           periscope depth and set continuous periscope watch. (Air
           Contact #2).
1200 (L)   Surfaced for latitude sight - submerged again - total time
           90 seconds.
2222   Passed Lib Island 6 miles to port.

July 22   Lat. 08-03N, Long. 165-31E. Sighted Army Scout Bomber
0707(L)   bearing 205°T, distance 7 miles. (Air Contact #3) - Made
           quick dive.
0845(L)   Surfaced.

- 1 -

U.S.S. GRENADIER

<u>S E C R E T</u>

U.S.S. GRENADIER - Third War Patrol - Report of.

- -

July 23- Remained on surface - nothing sighted.

July 24- Submerged due to unfavorable cloud conditions and proximity
1021 (L) to Nomoi Island.
1625 (K) Surfaced.

July 25-
1015 (K) Entered assigned sector of Area.
1500 (K) Dived for training and to avoid detection. Tol Island
bearing 045°T, distance 100 miles.

July 26-
0320 (K) Sighted Tol Island bearing 052°T, distance 35 miles.
0500 (K) Commenced patrol at periscope depth.
0736 (K) Sighted seaplane, Nakajima Type 97 (Air Contact #4)
1030 (K) Sighted patrol plane Reconnaissance Type 9 K-1 Hiro which
appeared to be landing between Fefan, Moen and Dublon
Islands. (Air Contact #5)
1525 (K) Sighted large sampan (Ship contact #1)

July 27- Uneventful.

July 28-
1011 (K) Sighted catcher boat of Tama Maru Class lying off Aulap
Pass. (Ship contact #2).
1152 (K) Sighted twin engine flying boat landing inside reef
opposite Ollan Island (Air contact #6)
1200 (K) About 2.5 miles south of reef took pictures of Tol and
Ollan Islands.
1215 (K) Sighted Mitsubishi Type 96 Heavy Bomber (Air Contact #7)
1322 (K) Sighted smoke inside reef. Sighted unidentified plane
landing on either Fefan or Dublon Islands (Air Contact #8).
1400 (K) Sighted what appeared to be a submarine inside reef.
(Ship contact #3).

- 2 -

U.S.S. GRENADIER

<u>S E C R E T</u>

Subject: U.S.S. GRENADIER - Third War Patrol - Report of.

- -

1. <u>NARRATIVE</u>

July 28 - (cont.)

2000 (K) Sighted patrol vessel, put it on stern and opened
range. (Ship Contact #4). After losing sight we
slowed down, changed course and it passed astern,
apparently on same course. It had probably sighted
us because we allowed it to get within about 3000-
4000 yards before speeding up. The moon was very
bright.

July 29 -
0947(K) Sighted large flying boat (Air Contact #9).
1025(K) Sighted catcher type patrol vessel patrolling off
Aualap Pass (Ship Contact #5).
1200(K) Took pictures of Tol Island.
1320(K) Sighted Plane similar to PBY. (Air Contact #10).
1418(K) Sighted smoke on or alongside Fefan Island.
1425(K) Sighted Mitsubishi Type 96, Heavy Bomber (Air Contact
#11)
1950(K) On the surface. Sighted patrol vessel and opened out
until it disappeared.

July 30 -
0015(K) Sighted smoke bearing 176°T, Lat. 06-46N, Long. 151-01E,
headed for it - very bright moonlight. We thought
we saw the outline of a large ship, bow on, and
dived for an attack. It turned out to be smoke. At
about 0130 the catcher type patrol vessel was sighted
and passed about 1000 yards abeam. (Ship Contact #6).
0212(K) Surfaced.
1435(K) Sighted Nakajima Nake 93, Floatplane Fighter.
(Air Contact #12)
1545(K) Sighted Kawanisi Type 97, Flying Boat (Air Contact #13)
1650(K) Lat. 07-11.5N, Long. 151-22E. Sighted and torpedoed
large tanker, escorted by destroyer of Tomozuru Class.
Ship was sighted bearing 080°T, distance 18,000 yards,
course 285°T, zigzagging. The tanker could not be
positively identified from photographs. For description
see contact sheet. We were depth charged by the destroyer
(Ship Contacts #7 & 8)

- 3 -

U.S.S. GRENADIER

S E C R E T

Subject: U.S.S. GRENADIER - Third War Patrol - Report of.
- -

1. NARRATIVE

July 30 - (cont.)

2000(K)   Surfaced in bright moonlight.

July 31 -
0245(K)   Sighted the catcher type patrol vessel maneuvered to keep
          clear. (Ship Contact #9).
          Remainder of day uneventful.

August 1 -
0040   Sighted smoke. Closed to investigate - turned out to be
          catcher type patrol vessel accompanied by a smaller vessel
          that was fairly long and of low freeboard, probably a
          patrol sampan. (Ship Contact #10 & 11).
0135   Sighted low sampan type vessel running toward us (bright
          moonlight). Put it astern and ran on two engines, however
          could not shake him, so went to full and finally lost him
          astern (this was probably the one seen with the other
          patrol vessel) (Ship Contact #12).
          He was about 2 miles away when first sighted. Should have
          changed course after shaking him, but could not have reach-
          ed favorable position for submerged patrol if we had.
0401   Lat. 7-00N, Long. 151-25E. Sighted ship bearing 110°T,
          distance 3 miles. It had the outlines of a destroyer, and
          seemed to be lying to. Watched it for a few minutes then
          dived. Had difficulty with the trim and did not get up to
          periscope depth until half an hour later. Heard screws and
          sighted the ship bow on the horizon. When it was fairly
          light, the ship passed close astern of us and was identified
          as the Q-Ship reported by the G.R. Shortly thereafter it
          speeded up and finally disappeared in the direction of
          Otta Pass. (Ship Contact #13).
          It is believed possible that it was warned of our approach
          by the patrol vessel previously sighted.
0828(K)   Sighted a buoy or raft with a red flag on it. Lat. 07-01N,
          Long. 151-24E.
1328(K)   Sighted ship bearing 002°T, closed it and identified it as
          the Q-Ship sighted earlier this morning. (Ship Contact
          #14).

- 4 -

U.S.S. GRENADIER

<u>S E C R E T</u>

Subject: U.S.S. GRENADIER - Third War Patrol - Report of.

- -

1. <u>NARRATIVE</u>

August 2- Patrolling at periscope depth closing Aualap Pass,
       glassy sea.
0900(K) Sighted large unidentified plane (Air Contact #14).
       Sighted smoke, closed and identified the catcher type
       patrol vessel (Ship contact #15). Noted that it was
       carrying a small plane on deck.
1103(K) Sighted long black sampan (Ship Contact #16). It is
       believed that this is the patrol boat that we sighted
       on two occassions at night.

August 3- Glassy seas again.
0813(K) Heard first of 7 depth charges, apparently coming from
       the eastward - nothing sighted.

August 4- Lat. 07-04N, Long. 151-30E. Sighted masts of two destroyers
0630(K) destroyers bearing 197°T, distance 10 miles course 025°T.
       They were steering zig-zag courses at a speed of about 18
       knots. The closest they came was about 4 miles, and were
       last on bearing of about 100°T, apparently passing to the
       south of Kuop Islands. The sea was glassy smooth, and the
       bubbles from our periscope, and air leaks, were plainly
       visible fifty yards astern. (Ship Contact 17 & 18).
1522(K) Sighted Nakajima Naka 93 - Type 97 - Floatplane Fighter.
       (Air Contact #15).
1706(K) Sighted Type 95 Reconnaissance Floatplane. (Air Contact
       #16).

August 5 -
1315(K) Sighted the catcher type patrol vessel. The sea was
       glassy smooth and as he would pass close, went to 140 feet,
       periscope exposure at close range being impracticable. He
       passed about 2000 yards astern. (Ship Contact #19).

August 6 -
1428(K) Sighted Nakajima Naka 93 - Type 97 - Floatplane Fighter
       (Air Contact #17)

August 7 -
0727(K) Sighted Aiche Tokei A.I. 92. Reconnaissance Floatplane.
       (Air Contact #18)

- 5 -

U.S.S. GRENADIER

S E C R E T

Subject: U.S.S. GRENADIER - Third War Patrol - Report of.
- -

1. NARRATIVE

August 7 - (Cont.)
0958(K)   Heard first of 10 depth charges from the eastward last
           one at 1043, nothing in sight.
1238(K)   Sighted buoy or raft with square red flag on it.
           Lat. 07-04N, Long. 151-18E. This is similar to the
           one sighted August 1. They are probably of no signifi-
           cance, but the fact that they could contain some detector
           or mine, constitutes a mental hazard in approaching and
           retiring during darkness.

August 8 -
1248(K)   Sighted Mitsubishi Type 97, Heavy Bomber. (Air Contact
           #19).
1455(K)   Sighted Nakajima Naka 93, Type 97, Floatplane Fighter.
           (Air Contact #20).
1655(K)   Sighted Mitsubishi Type 97, Heavy Bomber. (Air Contact
           #21).
1735(K)   Sighted Nakajima Naka 93 - Type 97 - Floatplane Fighter,
           apparently one sighted at 1455. (Air Contact #22).
1739(K)   Sighted the catcher type patrol vessel. The plane sighted
           at 1735 was circling over it. (Ship Contact #20).

August 9 -
1605(K)   Sighted Nakajima Naka 93 - Type 97, Floatplane Fighter
           (Air Contact #23).

August 10 -
0738(K)   Sighted Nakajima Naka 93 - Type 97, Floatplane Fighter.
           It turned and headed for us. As the sea was glassy, with
           a deep swell, making periscope detection ideal, we went
           deep. This is the first time that we were forced down -
           by planes. Came back to periscope depth at 0800.
           (Air contact #24).
0819(K)   Sighted above plane again. He again headed for us.
           At the same time we made out the masts and upper works
           of the Q-Ship sighted on 1 August. It was coming straight
           for us. We went deep and rigged for depth charging.
           The Q-Ship approached at high speed, stopped, then
           commenced circling around us. The very rapid change of
           bearing and the fact that his screws were plainly audible
           through the hull, indicated that he was close aboard.
           He finally came directly over us and stopped. We were
           running silent, attempting to get to 250 feet, however
           we struck a layer at 165 feet that we could not penetrate

- 6 -

U.S.S. GRENADIER

S E C R E T

Subject: U.S.S. GRENADIER - Third War Patrol - Report of.

- -

1. NARRATIVE

August 10 (cont.)

    without speeding up or flooding; both operations would probably have created sufficient noise to insure our detection. We waited to hear the first depth charge before taking steps to increase our depth; however none came. The ship finally kicked ahead, circled a couple of times and was lost by sound on about 272°T. This was a very reassuring test of our ability to run silent relative to the sensitivity of the Japanese listening gear. The listening conditions were ideal; glassy sea and other conditions so good that we were able to follow the approach of the Q-ship from about 10,000 yards. We can't figure out why he didn't drop at least one charge, unless perhaps the plane had misled him in the past. (Ship Contact #21).

1320(K)   Sighted Type 95 Reconnaissance Floatplane. (Air Contact #25).

1440(K)   Sighted above plane again (Air Contact #26).

2000(K)   Due to the fact that our presence was probably known and the glassy seas that were of advantage to the planes, decided to patrol out to the western limit of our area and reply to ComTaskFor 7 dispatch requesting details of attack on the tanker.
We patrolled at slow speed to maintain listening watch; for the weather was hazy and visibility bad.

August 11 Had received ComTaskFor 7 message relating to arrival of tender on the 12th, so postponed sending the dispatch and headed back for the islands.

1120(K)   Sighted Shawa Sho 98 Fighter Bomber. (Air Contact #27).

1703(K)   Sighted Type 97 - Osaka Light Bomber - Reconnaissance. (Air Contact #28).

August 12 -

0640(K)   Sighted Nakajima Naka 93 - Type 97 - Floatplane Fighter (Air Contact #29).

0839(K)   Sighted unidentified plane over Tol Island. (Air Contact #30).

2000(K)   Having seen no sign of the tender decided to again try to send the message referred to on the 10th.

- 7 -

U.S.S. GRENADIER

S E C R E T

Subject: U.S.S. GRENADIER - Third War Patrol - Report of.
- -

1. NARRATIVE

August 13 -
0030(K)   Received ComTaskFor 7 dispatch stating that the tender
           would not arrive until 13th,
           By this time we were so far out that we could not get
           back into position.
2130(K)   Received ComTaskFor 7 dispatch changing areas, but
           not transmit on supposition that one of the northern
           boats might be running down the western edge of our area
           and the disclosure of the presence of a submarine there
           might bring out patrols that would prevent him from running
           on the surface the next day. We decided to remain in this
           area and get rid of the dispatch next day.

August 14 -
2000(K)   Finally transmitted the dispatch via NPG. We wasted the
           better part of three days jockying around to send a dispatch
           that was not vital, however we were in a position to inter-
           cept traffic heading for Truk from the west.

August 15 -
           Uneventful - working back into position.

August 16 -
           Decided to get into position first south of Nuop Islands,
           as it was felt that traffic to or from Otto or Aualap
           Passes would come close to this reef,
0930(K)   Sighted Nakajima Naka 93 - Type 97, Floatplane Fighter.
           (Air Contact #31).
0952(K)   Lat. 06-48N, Long. 151-56E. Sighted smoke bearing 334°T,
           and drawing to the westward.
1023(K)   Sighted convoy of four ships, with a plane circling overhead
           At the time of sighting they presented a 90° angle on the
           bow; so we paralleled them at 2/3 speed. The most we ever
           saw was their masts and the top of the stack of one emitting
           smoke. Their closest range was about 8 miles; however we
           seemed to be losing bearing slowly and decided to follow and
           make a night attack. The largest ship was smoking continu-
           ously and enable us to keep their bearing.
1600(K)   Visibility reduced and lost sight of smoke. (Ship Contact
           #22).
1914(K)   Surfaced. Perhaps we should have surfaced sooner, but due
           to the presence of the plane, felt that if we were spotted
           interception would be impossible. Went to 17 knots and
           commenced search.

- 8 -

U.S.S. GRENADIER

<u>S E C R E T</u>

Subject: U.S.S. GRENADIER - Third War Patrol - Report of.

- -

1. <u>NARRATIVE</u>

August 17 -
0230(K)   No luck reduced speed to 14 knots.
0500(K)   Submerged on course 270°, maintaining continuous periscope
          watch. Figured that we were ahead of the convoy and if
          they were enroute New Hanover we should see them.
1600(K)   By this time it was quite evident that we had missed the
          convoy; so attempted to transmit contact report - could
          get no answer - so broadcast it.
2000(K)   Lat. 04-24.5N, Long. 151-12E.
          Tried to send the contact again; raised Washington & Nor-
          folk but they could not copy it - broadcast again.
August 18 Decided to patrol back to Truk along the Truk - New Hanover
          route in the hope of intercepting the AK reported due
          at New Hanover on the 21st.

August 19 As we were due to clear the area on the 20th decided to
          work to western limit on chance of intercepting the ship-
          ;ing reported due from the East Indies.

August 20 -
          Received ComTaskFor 7 dispatch directing us to remain on
          station to limit of endurance - headed back for Truk.

August 21 -
0540   Sighted Tol Island bearing 358 distance 36 miles.
1042   Sighted smoke - closed it - turned out to be the catcher
          type patrol vessel. (Ship Contact #23).
1450   Sighted masts of ship moving at high speed on course
          350°T, distance 11 miles, bearing 261°T. It is believed
          to have been a destroyer, however we never got close
          enough to see more than the masts (Ship Contact #24).
1950   While patrolling on surface at slow speed sighted two
          ships. A few minutes later a larger ship was sighted,
          heading in our direction. The other two signaled with
          blinker lights and it turned away. These ships came out
          a rain squall to the eastward. The only good horizon was
          ahead of us. (The moon was very bright - bearing 180,
          altitude about 60°). It is possible that the larger ship
          spotted us and thought we were the escort and so headed
          for us. We headed for the ships on four engines but lost
          them in the rain squall at 2020 (K). They must have
          been high speed ships because we searched for 6 hours in
          bright moonlight but never saw them again. (Ship Contact
          #25)

- 9 -

U.S.S. GRENADIER

S E C R E T

Subject: U.S.S. GRENADIER - Third War Patrol - Report of.
- -

1. NARRATIVE

August 22 -
0100(K)   Sent contact report via Darwin radio.
           Headed back to take up patrol off Piaanu Pass in
           accordance with station shift directed by ComTaskFor 7.
2325(K)   Sighted Tol Island bearing 020°T, distance 36 miles.

August 23 -
           Commenced patrol off Piaanu Pass.
0625(K)   Sighted airplane too far away to identify. (Air Contact
           #32).

August 24 -
           Took pictures of Tol and adjacent islands.

August 25 -:26
           Uneventful.

August 27 -
1230(K)   Sighted large fishing sampan. (Ship Contact #26)
1525(K)   Sighted large unidentified plane of flying boat type in
           distance. (Air Contact #33).

August 28 -
1940(K)   While on the surface sighted searchlight and floodlights
           on Tol. They were on very briefly.

August 29 -
1350(K)   Sighted a Nakajima Naka 93 - Type 97, Floatplane Fighter.
           (Air Contact #34).

August 30 -
1105(K)   Sighted unidentified airplane in the distance behind Tol
           Island. (Air Contact #35).
1425(K)   Sighted large sampan engaged in fishing. (Ship Contact
           #27).
1651(K)   Sighted the catcher type patrol vessel. (Ship Contact #28

August 31 Having sighted nothing off Piaanu Pass decided to patrol
           on the 270° line from the pass. This might give us a
           chance of contacting ships that may be slipping in or out
           under cover of darkness.

September 1 -
           Uneventful.

- 10 -

U.S.S. GRENADIER

S E C R E T

Subject: U.S.S. GRENADIER - Third War Patrol - Report of.
- -

1. NARRATIVE

September 2 -
0600(K)   Cleared Area 15, enroute for Perth in accordance with
          instructions of ComTaskFor 7.
0640(K)   Sighted seven or eight large logs or uprooted trees.
          Running on surface maintaining radar watch.

September 3 - 6 -
          Uneventful - Running on surface. Sighted many uprooted
          trees.

September 7 -
0000(I)   Passed through Djailolo Passage.
0600(I)   Submerged for the day.
1407(I)   Surfaced. Weather was hazy and as there was a possibility
          of not getting sights at night, we were desirious of pickin
          up Pisang Island. On surfacing Wildi Isles, were sighted
          bearing 270T, distance 17 miles.
1522(I)   Sighted Pisang Island bearing 177°T, distance 35 miles.
1645(I)   We were getting close to Pisang, so submerged again.

September 8 -
          Passed through Manipa Strait. We were submerged and had
          to buck a current of about 1.6 knots throughout the day.

September 9 -
          Running Submerged.
1200(I)   Surfaced for latitude sight and submerged again.
1555(I)   Surfaced in order to pick up Gunung Api.
1819(I)   Sighted Gunung Api bearing 212T, distance 17 miles.

September 10 -
          Passed between Wetar and Romang Islands. Submerged at day-
          light and passed between Kisar and Lette Islands, and
          between Lette and Timor.
0810(I)   When abeam of Kisar Island sighted a large bomber. It
          seemed to have taken off from the island. There is a
          possibility that there is a base or landing field there.
          The plane was either a Fiat B.R.-20, or a Lockheed Hudson,
          camouflauged with light and dark grey paint. (Air Contact
          #36).

September 11 - 12 -
          Uneventful. Running submerged during the day.

- 11 -

U.S.S. GRENADIER

<u>S E C R E T</u>

Subject: U.S.S. GRENADIER - Third War Patrol - Report of.
- -

1. <u>NARRATIVE</u>

September 13 -
          Running on the surface.
0630(H)   Sighted Mitsubishi Type 96 Heavy Bomber. Dived.
          (Air Contact #37).
0720(H)   Surfaced.
0812(H)   Radar contact with plane distance 28 miles. Followed it o
          radar and lost contact at 22 miles. Nothing sighted. Did
          not dive. (Air Contact #38).

September 16 -
0750(H)   Sighted PBY Plane (Air Contact #39)
1430(H)   Sighted PBY Plane (Air Contact #40)
          Conducted battery discharge.

September 17 -
0800(H)   Sighted PBY Plane (Air Contact #41)

September 18 - Made rendezvous and proceeded to Fremantle.

- 12 -

U.S.S. GRENADIER

S E C R E T

Subject: U.S.S. GRENADIER - Third War Patrol - Report of.

- -

2. WEATHER

Weather in general was favorable during this patrol.
Several periods of glassy calm seas occured during the patrol
which would have made an undetected periscope approach almost impossible, and which reduced night visibility by eliminating the
horizon. These periods were as follows:
1.   2 August   to   7 August
2. 10 August   to   15 August
3. 17 August   to   19 August
4. 22 August   to   26 August

Although Tol Island was frequently obscured by rain, we experienced very little of it. Clouds were not nearly as prevalent as
we were led to think from the ONI Report.

3. TIDAL INFORMATION

(a) During the first part of the patrol, south of Truk, an
easterly and southeasterly set consistent with the pilot chart was
experienced. During the last ten days off Piaanu Pass strong (1 to
1.5 knots), variable currents, probably of a tidal nature, were experienced.
(b) Density layers were found in the Truk Area on two occasions;
one on July 25, and three on July 30.
July 25: The layer was found between 195 and 250 feet. It was
accompanied by a change of temperature of from 85 to 84 between
210 and 225 feet.

July 30: The first layer occured at 170 feet; the second and by
far the best layer found was between 235 and 245 feet and the
last at 290 feet. Due to enemy A/S measures no temperatures
were taken.

(c) On the trip between Truk and Djailolo Pass a strong easterly
set of from 3/4 to 1 knot was observed. This was in contradiction
to the pilot chart which indicated variable westerly currents.

4. NAVIGATIONAL AIDS

No navigational aids were observed during the patrol. The
radar proved to be of invaluable assistance when ranges on peaks
could be properly analyzed.

- 13 -

U.S.S. GRENADIER

S E C R E T

Subject: U.S.S. GRENADIER - Third War Patrol - Report of.
- -

5. Surface Craft Contact Sheet

Contact	Time	Our Position	Bear °T.	Dist.	Course	Speed	Description & Remarks
1	1525(K) 7-26	07-08N 151-35E	290	3 mi.	340°	4	Large fishing sampan - painted black.
2	1011(K) 7-28	07-12N 151-30E	071	6 mi.	190°	0	Catcher type patrol vessel of Tama Maru Class (See Plate 94 Japanese Merchantman). He carries a gun forward - also small plane. Has handling booms on either side of deck house. Patrols at about 6 knots - high speed screw. Emits dense clouds of black smoke and is a thorough nuisance He has pulled us out of position numerous time, trying to investigate smoke sighted. (Plane is Nakajima Naka 93 - Type 97 Floatplane Fighter).
3	1400(K) 7-28	07-13N 151-35E	060	5 mi.	?	?	Appeared to be a submarine.
4	2000(K) 7-28	07-01N 151-26E	040	4 mi.	270	?	Same as #2.
5	1025(K) 7-29	07-07N 151-43E	060	5 mi.	220	?	Same as #2.
6	1015(K) 7-30	06-46N 151-01E	170	-	-	-	Smoke that later turned out to be same ship as #2 on course 000°, speed 6 knots.
7	1650(K) 7-30	07-11.5N 151-22 E	080	9 mi.	285	12	Large Tanker - From comparison of size of DD it appeared that it was 500-550' long and was showing about 25' freeboard. The water line did not show and it had the appearance of a loaded ship. The stack and deck house were aft, pilot

- 14 -

U.S.S. GRENADIER

Subject: U.S.S. GRENADIER - Third War Patrol - Report of.
- -

5.   SURFACE CRAFT CONTACT SHEET

Contact	Time	Our Position	Bear °T	Dist.	Course	Speed	Description & Remarks
7 cont.	1650(K) 7-50	07-11.5N 151-22E	080	9 mi.	285	12	house forward, there were three masts the forward mast was regular stick type, middle mast and after masts were goal posts. They were both Dutch Type Goal Posts. On the port side of the poop deck was a heavy derrick, either triangular or quadralateral in cross section and tapering up. The stack was fairly low and round. There was little or no sheer. The bow was of the straight type; unfortunately the type of stern did not register. The ship was painted black with white upper works. The paint looked new. Red lead could be seen in spots where the black had flaked off. There is no ship in the recognition booklets that fits the description and it may have been a new one. The impression of size was given by the dimunitive appearance of the destroyer in comparison.
8	1650(K) 7-30	07-11.5N 151-22E	080	9 mi.	285	12	Destroyer of the Tomozuru Class, escorting contact #7. He was patrolling ahead and on either bow. He was using echo-ranging continuously throughout the approach and the attack.
9	0245(K) 7-31	07-04N 150-43E	185	5 mi.	225	?	Same as #2.
10	0040(K) 8-1	06-34N 150-32E	106	6 mi.	270	?	Same as #2.
11	0040(K) 8-1	06-34N 150-32E	106	6 mi.	270	?	Low sampan type vessel - appeared to be about 100' long (Silhouette)
12	0135(K) 8-1	06-32N 150-35E	301	2-3 mi.	045	12	Same as above (11).

- 15 -

U.S.S. GRENADIER

S E C R E T

Subject: U.S.S. GRENADIER - Third War Patrol - Report of. - - - - -
- -

5.   SURFACE CRAFT CONTACT SHEET

Contact	Time	Our Position	Bear On	Dist.	Course	Speed	Description & Remarks
13	0401(K)	7-00N 8-1 151-25E	110	3 mi.	320	?	This appears to be the Q-Ship reported by the GAR. It has a nice sheer, is around 250' long, deck gun mounted in a shield forward, large deck house, two goal post masts with a high stick mast and crows nest in the middle of the forward one. The legs of the masts are staggered and give the impression of tripods when seen from the beam. The ship has high speed twin screws, and when it is hull down looks like a freighter. The ship in our navy that closely resembles its general lines is the new type sea going tug. It is doubtful if its tonnage is more than 800-1000.
14	1328(K)	07-00N 8-1 151-31E	002	15 mi.	085	?	Same as #13.
15	1040(K)	07-00N 8-1 151-31E	007	8 mi.	270	6	Same as #2 (passed within 1000 yds).
16	1103(K)	07-06N 8-2 151-41E	-	1½ mi.	-	-	This is the low black sampan reported under Contact #11. It is quite low and appears to be about 100' long. There is a deck house amidships & another shelter just aft of it. The screw is of the high speed type.
17 & 18	0630(K)	07-04N 8-4 151-30E	197	10 mi.	025	18	Momo Class Destroyers.
19	1315(K)	07-08N 8-5 151-13E	056	10 mi.	225	6	Same as #2 (came within 4000 yds)
20	1739(K)	07-02N 8-8 151-26E					Same as #2.

- 16 -

U.S.S. GRENADIER

<u>S E C R E T</u>

Subject: U.S.S. GRENADIER - Third War Patrol - Report of.

- -

5.   <u>SURFACE CRAFT CONTACT SHEET</u>

Contact	Time	Our Position	Bear °T	Dist.	Course	Speed	Description & Remarks
21	0819(K) 8-10	07-02N 151-27E	041	6 mi.	220	?	Same as #13.
22	1023(K) 8-16	06-50N 151-54E	305	12 mi.	215	9	Convoy of four ships. Possibly light cruiser, transport and two patrol ships
23	1042(K) 8-21	06-56N 151-42E	074	8 mi.	225	4-8	Same as #2.
24	1450(K) 8-21	07-00N 151-45E	261	11 mi.	350	15	Unidentified destroyer.
25	1950(K) 8-21	06-45N 151-48E	000	6 mi.	150	12	Three unidentified ships one large one and two smaller ones.
26	1230(K) 8-27	07-23N 151-11E	023	6 mi.	200	6	Large fishing sampan.
27	1425(K) 8-30	07-22N 151-20E	110	5 mi.	225	6	Same as #2.
28	1651(K) 8-30	07-20N 151-21E	163	15 mi.	270	6	Same as above.

- 17 -

U.S.S. GRENADIER

S-E-C-R-E-T

Subject: U.S.S. GRENADIER - Third War Patrol - Report of.
- -

6. AIRCRAFT CONTACT SHEET

Contact #	Time & Date	Our Position	True Bear	Dist.	Course	Alt.	Description & Remarks
1	1200(K) 7-15-42	17-43N 168-13W	106	7 mi.	220	1200	PBY U.S.N.
2	0953(M) 7-21-42	08-28N 168-44E	062	TO DISTANT			
3	0707(L) 7-22	08-04N 165-33E	205	7 mi.	?	?	Army Scout Bomber (enemy)
4	0736(K) 7-26	07-01N 151-22E	180	5 mi.	220	1000	Nakajima Type 97
5	1030(K) 7-26	07-02N 151-29E					Patrol Plane Reconnaissance Type 9K1 Hiro.
6	1152(K) 7-28	07-14N 151-32E					Large twin engine flying boat
7	1215(K) 7-28	07-15N 151-33E	065	4 mi.	135	1200	Mitsubishi Type 96 Heavy bomber
8	1400(K) 7-28	07-14N 151-35E					Little torpedo plane (?)
9	0947(K) 7-29	07-08N 151-42E	040	10 mi.	?	2000	Twin engine flying boat
10	1320(K) 7-29	07-10N 151-40E	029	10 mi.	?	?	Similar to PBY
11	1425(K) 7-29	07-08N 151-39E	133	4 mi.	025	1500	Mitsubishi Type 96 heavy bomber
12	1435(K) 7-30	07-12N 151-19E	180	6 mi.	060	1000	Nakajima Naka 93 Fleatplane, fighter
13	1545(K) 7-30	07-13N 151-19E	337	4 mi.	040	2000	Kawanisi Type 97 flying boat.

- 18 -

U.S.S. GRENADIER

S-E-C-R-E-T

Subject: U.S.S. GRENADIER - Third War Patrol - Report of.

- -

6. AIRCRAFT CONTACT SHEET

Contact #	Time & Date	Our Position	True Bear	Dist.	Course	Alt.	Description & Remarks.
14	0900(K) 8-2	07-05N 151-25E	020	19 mi.	-	-	Large plane - unidentified.
15	1322(K) 8-4	07-18N 151-23E	310	7 mi.	270	-	Nakajima Naka 92 type 97 Floatplane fighter
16	1706(K) 8-4	06-57 N 151-22E	025	10 mi.	330	1500	Type 95 Reconnaisance Float Plane
17	1428(K) 8-6	07-08N 151-18E	019	5 mi.	240	1000	Same as 15
18	0727(K) 8-7	06-57N 151-26E	090	4 mi.	310	-	Aiohi Tokei A.I. 92 Reconn. Float Plane
19	1248(K) 8-8	07-04N 151-36 E.	125	15 mi.	000	2000	Mitsubishi Type 97 heavy bomber
20	1455(K) 8-8	07-02N 151-33	003	6 mi.	250	1000	Same as #15
21	1605(K) 8-8	07-00N 151-34E	007	10 mi.	270	-	Same type as #19
22	1735(K) 8-8	07-00N 151-31E	150	6 mi.	315	-	Same as #15
23	1605(K) 8-9	07-06N 151-26E	190	7 mi.	214	-	Same as #15
24	0738(K) 8-10	07-02N 151-25E	065	5 mi.	E	1000	Same as #15. This plane spotted us.
25	1320(K) 8-10	06-54N 151-18E	060	4 mi.	N	-	Type 95 Reconn. Floatplane
26	1440(K) 8-10	06-52N 151-18E	270	2 mi.	N	-	Same as #25

- 19 -

U.S.S. GRENADIER

S-E-C-R-E-T

Subject: U.S.S. GRENADIER - Third War Patrol - Report of.
- -

Contact	Time & Date	Our Position	True Bear	Dist.	Course	Alt.	Description & Remarks
27	1120(K) 8-11	06-56N 150-52E	030	6 mi.	SW	1500	Shawa Sho 98 - Fighter Bomber.
28	1703(K) 8-11	06-46N 150-57E	160	4 mi.	050	-	Type 97 Osaka Light bomber reconnaisance
29	0640(K) 8-12	07-03N 151-15E	130	2 mi.	SW	1000	Nakajima Naka 93 - Type 97 Floatplane Fighter
30	0839(K) 8-12	06-58N 151-17E	040	15 mi.	E	-	Unidentified
31	0930(K) 8-16	06-48N 151-49E	350	8 mi.	?	-	Same as #29
32	0625(K) 8-23	07-19N 151-10E	090	20 mi.	N	-	Unidentified plane
33	1525(K) 8-27	07-20N 151-08E	082	20 mi.	S	-	Unidentified plane
34	1350(K) 8-29	07-26N 151-18E	219	5 mi.	270	1000	Same as #29
35	1105(K) 8-30	07-23N 151-19E	100	8 mi.	-	-	Unidentified plane briefly sighted thru clouds.
36	0810(I) 9-10	07-57S 127-23E	200	2 mi.	-	800	Fiat B.R. -20 or Lockheed Hudson
37	0630(H) 9-13	13-48S 120-29 E	062	10 mi.	W	-	Mitsubishi Type 96 Heavy bomber
38	0812 9-13	13-59S 120-27E	-	30 mi.	-	-	Radar contact - did not sight.
39	0750(H) 9-16	25-33S 112-12E	171	6 mi.	280	1000	PBY
40	1430(H) 9-16	27-00S 112-30E	321	12 mi.	095	1000	PBY
41	0800(H) 9-17	29-47S 113-23E	175	15 mi.	225	1000	PBY

- 20 -

U.S.S. GRENADIER

S-E-C-R-E-T

Subject: U.S.S. GRENADIER - Third War Patrol - Report of.

- -

7. SUMMARY OF SUBMARINE ATTACKS

ATTACK #1	TORPEDO	Time of Firing: 1713(K).
DATE	30 July 1942	A large bubble was noted when the torpedoes were fired.
LOCATION	Lat. 7° 11.5'N Long. 151° 22'E.	To clear our firing position it was necessary to run with periscope down before ob-
TORPEDOES FIRED ON EACH ATTACK	3 (Mk. 15)	servation of sinking could be made the DD forced us down. We came to periscope
HITS	2	depth after dark, to keep from being spotted by planes.
NUMBER SUNK (TONNAGE)	1 10,000 tons or more	Sunset was one hour after the attack and the moon did not rise until just before we surfaced.
TYPE OF TARGET	TANKER	
RANGE MORE THAN		REMARKS:
		EVIDENCE OF SINKING:
1500 YARDS	1900	1. Two torpedo hits with heavy explosion between the two hits.
PERISCOPE DEPTH	YES	2. Sounds of small boat screws as if abandoning ship.
DEEP SUBMERGENCE	AFTER ATTACK	3. Heavy increase in noise level in direction of target.
ESTIMATED DRAFT TARGET	20 Feet.	4. Oil persisting in area for several days.
TORPEDO DEPTH SETTING (Actual)	20 Feet.	
BOW OR STERN SHOT	STERN	
TRACK ANGLE	98°P., 103°P, and 109°P	
GYRO ANGLE	1½°L, 3°L, 5°L	
ESTIMATED SPEED TARGET	12 knots	
FIRING INTERVAL	19 sec, 20 sec.	
SPREAD - AMOUNT AND KIND	3° (3L-0-3R) Divergent	

- 21 -

U.S.S. GRENADIER

S-E-C-R-E-T

Subject: U.S.S. GRENADIER - Third War Patrol - Report of.
- -

8.   ENEMY A/S MEASURES.

   The patrol vessels and planes listed in paragraph one were in evidence to keep us on the alert for them. The smoke of the catcher type vessel frequently drew us out of position in an effort to identify it. We believe that we were only spotted once from the air. Bombs or depth charges were not noticed in any of the planes.

   The destroyer escorting the tanker used echo-ranging continuously and ineffectively. He dropped two charges shortly after the torpedoes hit, and then after an interval three or four close together and very close to us. We were at 300 feet and it is believed that at least two were directly overhead. Light bulbs were broken, and locker doors jarred open. The packing in #2 starboard shaft sprung a leak that shot a stream of water up to the overhead of the motor room; however it was quickly stopped by tightening the packing.

   The destroyer was using its echo-ranging while trying to locate us, but it is believed that they relied mainly on sound. After the above mentioned charges were dropped, the DD searched for some time but apparently could not locate us. We were running silent at slowest speed. The new wooden bearings in the stern tubes are very quiet.

9.   MAJOR DEFECTS EXPERIENCED.

   BOW PLANES: The starboard plane has developed a series of loud knocks when during normal operation, they are put on rise by either hand or power.
   FLOOD VALVE: The After Group flood valve or operating gear in M.B.T. #2B has gone adrift and hammers loudly when on the surface at speeds over 5 knots.
   FATHOMETER: Junction box has flooded rendering the equipment inoperative.

   HOLDING DOWN ROLLERS FOR SOUND HEADS: These are made of plastic and become flattened when the ship goes to any depth over 150 feet. The flattening causes a knock, that is quite audible, when the heads are rotated. We took a couple of rollers off a torpedo handling cradle, cut them down, and find they are very satisfactory.
   AIR LEAKS: These have been very bad. We ground in the manifolds a couple of times on station. It was found that three of the bottles in tank 2-C were leaking and they were bled down and cut out of the system. These air leaks, especially during the periods of glassy seas, were very much in evidence from the periscope.

- 23 -

U.S.S. GRENADIER

S-E-C-R-E-T

Subject: U.S.S. GRENADIER - Third War Patrol - Report of.
- -

10.   COMMUNICATIONS

Radio Reception: NPM and VHM submarine schedules were observed without difficulty except on two occassions the VHM schedule faded out completely. Traffic was cleared thru NPG and VHM. One message as sent broadcast was apparently not received. No traffic was sent or received on 450 KCS.

Last Message sent to CTF 7 ...... Ermine
Last Message Received from CTF 7 .... Igloo

Last Message sent to CSSWP ..... 141200 of September
Last Message received from CSSWP .... ef

Radar was used extensively in navigation and on two occassions gave warning of enemy aircraft..

11.   SOUND CONDITIONS:

Sound conditions were fair with the usual water noises encountered. During the depth charge attack both projector lower inter-lock rollers were forced off their tracks and flattened out.

12.   HEALTH AND HABITABILITY:

Except for one officer who suffered a heart attack the health of the crew has been very good, in fact better than on the previous patrols.
The boat has been comfortable throughout the patrol.

13.   MILES STEAMED ENROUTE TO AND FROM STATION:

Enroute to   Enroute from

14.   FUEL AND OIL EXPENDED:

Fuel   Oil

15.   FACTORS OF ENDURANCE REMAINING:

TORPEDOES	FUEL	PROVISIONS	FRESH WATER	PERSONNEL
21		4(1)	2200	0(2)

1. This is a balanced ration. Our supply of fresh meat, flour, sugar and canned fruit is low. We could go three weeks longer on canned meat, rice, beans, and canned vegetables.

- 23 -

U.S.S. GRENADIER

S-E-C-R-E-T

Subject: U.S.S. GRENADIER - Third War Patrol - Report of. - - - - -
- -

2. Zero days are not meant to carry the impression that the crew is in a state of mental or physical collapse, or that their morale is low. It does mean that they are no longer on their toes and that they have been at sea long enough.

16. The Patrol was ended due to expiration of time alloted by ComTaskFor 7.

17. REMARKS

TORPEDOES - The torpedoes expended were Mark XV. Remaining torpedoes are in excellent condition. The only outer doors opened during the patrol were in the tubes containing the torpedoes that were fired, and they were not opened until it was certain that they would be the tubes used.

SURFACE PATROL - At night we patrolled on one engine at 4 knots. This gave good listening conditions, and permitted floating the battery. It was also economical of oil. This slow speed was no great handicap on diving, diving times averaged about 50 seconds.

TIME ON STATION:
Approximately 40 days were spent in assigned sectors, and most of this within 30 miles of Tol Island. It is felt that three weeks in an area so small is ample; a longer period takes the zest out of the patrol. A shift of area after the above period would be welcome.

PERSONNEL:
The morale of the officers and crew has been commendable. The total lack of any derangement to machinery or auxiliaries, that could be attributed to carelessness or lack of foresight, is a credit to the Engineer and First Lieutenant and the personnel under their supervision.
The unsung heroes of these patrols are the cooks, theirs is a difficult task, and one that is always well done.
The numerous sightings of aircraft on this patrol speaks well of the alertness of the officers at the periscope.

B. L. CARR.

- 24 -

70

SUBMARINE DIVISION SIXTY-TWO

FB5-62/A16-3

Serial   OO-1

S-E-C-R-E-T

Care of Fleet Post Office,
San Francisco, California,
21 September 1942.

FIRST ENDORSEMENT to
CO U.S.S. GRENADIER War
Diary period from 7-13-42
to 9-18-42.

From: The Commander Submarine Division SIXTY-TWO.
To :   The Commander in Chief, U.S. Fleet.
Via :   (1) The Commander Submarines, SOUTHWEST PACIFIC.
          (2) The Commander U.S. Naval Forces, WESTERN AUSTRALIA.
          (3) The Commander Submarine Squadron SIX.

Subject: War Diary - U.S.S. GRENADIER - Period from 7-13-42 to
          9-18-42 - Comments on.

    1.   This patrol covered a period of sixty-seven days of which
forty were spent in the vicinity of the Truk area. It was the first patrol
of the present commanding officer.

    2.   Of the twenty-eight surface contacts, seven were with sampans
and eleven with catcher type patrol craft. The commanding officer did not
attempt to sink the latter because he believed his torpedoes could not be set
to run above twenty feet. When possible enemy craft of all kinds must be
vigorously attacked with any means available. The deck gun must be kept in a
condition of readiness.

    3.   The one attack on the large tanker was vigorously and
efficiently carried out. The commanding officer successfully evaded the
severe depth charging that followed. The numerous sightings of aircraft and
the lack of enemy air attack indicates an alertness and high state of training.

    4.   The GRENADIER returned in an excellent material condition.
The ship was clean. The morale, health and appearance of the officers and
crew, with one exception, was excellent. The patrol was terminated by the
operation order.

    5.   The Division Commander congratulates the commanding officer,
officers and crew of the GRENADIER on another job well done. It is recommended that the GRENADIER be credited with the following damage on the enemy:

        SUNK - Either one 10,000 ton or larger tanker, by two hits
               from a three (3) torpedo spread.

                                    F. M. O'LEARY.

FC5-6/A16-3
Serial 00-12

SUBMARINE SQUADRON SIX   (6)/OL

Care of Fleet Post Office,
San Francisco, California,
September 30, 1942.

S-E-C-R-E-T

SECOND ENDORSEMENT to
CO USS GRENADIER War
Diary period from
7/13/42 to 9/18/42.

From: The Commander Submarine Squadron SIX.
To :   The Commander-in-Chief, U.S. Fleet.
Via :   (1) The Commander Submarines, Southwest Pacific.
               (Commander Task Group 51.1).
           (2) The Commander U.S. Naval Forces,
               Western Australia.
               (Commander Task Force 51).

Subject: U.S.S. GRENADIER - War Diary of Third War Patrol.

   1.   Forwarded, concurring in the comments of the Division
Commander. This patrol was made incident to the transfer of the GRENADIER
from Submarines, Pacific Fleet, to Submarines, Southwest Pacific.

   2.   Material performance during this patrol is considered
to have been excellent. The few defects specifically mentioned by the Commanding Officer are susceptible to easy correction by the tender and relief
crews and the GRENADIER will be in all respects ready for another patrol
after a short tender refit.

   3.   A large number of contacts were made with aircraft
and various types of patrol vessels. At least one "catcher" type patrol
vessel was observed to carry a small plane; several sampans, presumably
patrol vessels, were painted black.

   4.   This is the first patrol conducted by the present
Commanding Officer who has recently fleeted up from Executive Officer of
the same ship. The Squadron Commander desires to add his congratulations
to those of the Division Commander for a well conducted patrol by the now
Commanding Officer, officers and crew of the GRENADIER.

   5.   After submission of the War Diary the Commanding
Officer stated that he believed that he had originally under estimated
the size of the tanker sunk and that she was of at least 15000 tons dis-
placement. It is therefore believed that the GRENADIER inflicted the
following damage on the enemy:

      1   15000 ton tanker - Sunk.

                                A. R. McCANN.

SSWP/A16-3/
Serial S-0065

SUBMARINES, SOUTHWEST PACIFIC
U.S.S. SARGO (SS188), FLAGSHIP

~~CONFIDENTIAL~~

October 6, 1942.

THIRD ENDORSEMENT to
CO USS GRENADIER Secret
War Diary SS210/A16-3
Serial 001 of 9-18-42.

Reg. No Com Sub Ron-6. #645 (A-3-G/4166)
R.3. No.............. 11 094

From: The Commander Submarines, SOUTHWEST PACIFIC.
To :   The Commander-in-Chief, U.S. FLEET.
Via :   (1) The Commander U.S. Naval Forces, WESTERN
                AUSTRALIA.
            (2) The Commander U.S. Naval Forces, SOUTHWEST
                PACIFIC AREA.

Subject: U.S.S. GRENADIER - War Diary of Third War Patrol.

1.   The GRENADIER arrived in FREMANTLE from PEARL
after a patrol lasting sixty-seven (67) days. With the exception
of one officer who has been physically disqualified for submarines, the other officers and crew were in excellent physical
condition and high state of morale. The ship was in very good
material condition.

2.   Numerous contacts were made with anti-submarine
vessels during the forty day patrol off SOUTH ENTRANCE to TRUK.
It is considered that some of those vessels, in particular DD,
Q-Ship, catcher type patrol and sampans, should have been
hunted and sunk. By surfacing earlier, the four ship convoy
on 16 August might not have been lost and a big bag might have
resulted. The enemy must be doggedly pursued without regard to
area restrictions until he is sunk.

3.   The attack on the tanker was well executed and
the GRENADIER efficiently evaded without damage a subsequent
depth charge attack by the escorting destroyer.

4.   During the patrol the GRENADIER expended only
three (3) torpedoes and inflicted the following damage on the
enemy which was confirmed by other sources:-

            One 15,000 ton AO - Sunk.

                                    C. A. LOCKWOOD, Jr.

DISTRIBUTION:
COMINCH   (2)   COMSUBSLANT   (2)
VICE OPNAV   (1)   COMTASKFOR-51   (1)
CINCLANTFLT   (1)   COMSUBRON-2   (1)
CINCPACFLT   (1)   COMSUBRON-6   (1)
COMSOUWESPACFOR (1)   COMSUBRON-5   (1)
COMSOUPACFLT   (1)   DIVCOMS,RON-2   (1)
COMSUBSPAC   (5)   DIVCOMS,RON-6   (1)
                       EACH S/M, W.A. (1)

CLASSIFICATION THIS CORRESPONDENCE
CHANGED TO .. Confidential
AUTHORITY ..... FGS.
DATE.......... 11/2/42....

FILMED

SS210/A16-3   U.S.S. GRENADIER

Serial #004

~~DECLASSIFIED~~

℅ Fleet Post Office,
San Francisco, California,
December   , 1942.

From: The Commanding Officer.
To :   The Commander-in-Chief, United States Pacific
              Fleet.
Via :   Official Channels.

Subject: War Diary (Fourth War Patrol Report).

Enclosure: (A) War Diary, Period 13 October 1942 to
                 December 19 2.

1.   Enclosure (A) is forwarded herewith.

                              B.L. CARR.

DECLASSIFIED-ART. 0445, OPNAVINST 5510.1C
BY OP-0909C DATE 5/26/72   DECLASSIFIED

U.S.S. GRENADIER, War Diary, 4th War Patrol, 13 October 1942 to
December 1942.

The U.S.S. GRENADIER arrived on 20 October 1942, in Albany, West Australia,
after her third war patrol. From that date until 11 Sept 1942, the
GRENADIER was undergoing tender overhaul alongside the U.S.S. ELIAS. On
11 October 1942, she proceeded to Fremantle, W.A., arriving 13 October 1942.
There she topped off with fuel and stores and received her patrol orders
and departed on patrol that same night.

GRENADIER'S patrol orders required her to proceed to the approaches to
Haiphong, Indo China and lay a minefield of thirty-two mines and then to
conduct an offensive patrol against enemy shipping in the South China Sea,
between latitudes 12 degrees north and 18 degrees north until 20 November
1942, when she was to return to Fremantle, W.A.

NARRATIVE

October 13, 1942: 1755 (I) Underway in accordance with CSSWP Operation
Order No. 60-42.

2155 (I) Exchanged calls with U.S.S. SALMON.

POSITION

	0800	1200	2000
Lat:	-	-	31-50 S
Long:	-	-	115-27 E

Miles steamed: 72.3   Fuel expended: 660.

October 14, 1942: Underway on surface.
0837 (I) Sighted P.B.Y. Dived.
0905 (I) Surfaced.

POSITION

	0800	1200	2000
Lat:	29-51-15 S	29-14-15 S	27-39-49 S
Long:	113-36-15 E	113-09-45 E	112-50-05 E

Miles steamed surface: 313.9   Submerged: 1.2
Fuel expended: 2705.

October 15, 1942: Underway on surface.
1500 (I) Made trim dive.
1620 (I) Surfaced.

POSITION

	0800	1200	2000
Lat:	25-13-45 S	24-27-00 S	22-57-00 S
Long:	112-16-15 E	112-26-00 E	112-41-30 E

Miles steamed surface: 310.3   Submerged: 4.3
Fuel expended: 2680.

Page 1

SECRET

October 16, 1942: Underway on surface.
                0755 (I) Sighted P.B.Y.
                0759 (I) Sighted P.B.Y.
                1204 (I) Moored to fuel barge at Exmouth Gulf.
                1352 (I) Underway.
                1630 (I) Sighted P.B.Y.
                1712 (I) Sighted P.B.Y.

POSITION

	0800	1200	2000
Lat:	21-36-45 S	22-13-15 S	21-32-15 S
Long:	114-12-30 E	114-10-30 E	113-36-30 E

Miles steamed surface: 272.1. Fuel expended: 2400.
Received: 7530.

October 17, 1942: Underway on surface.
                1107 (I) Made training dive.
                1121 (I) Surfaced.
                1608 (I) Made training dive.
                1626 (I) Surfaced.

POSITION

	0800	1200	2000
Lat:	19-26-30 S	18-39-30 S	16-52-00 S
Long:	113-30-30 E	113-40-00 E	113-47-00 E

Miles steamed surface: 338.1 Submerged: 2.4.
Fuel expended: 266.5

October 18, 1942: Underway on surface.
                1323 (I) Training dive.
                1345 (I) Surfaced.
                1917 (I) Sighted unidentified plane - dived.
                1928 (I) Surfaced.

POSITION

	0800	1200	2000
Lat:	14-13-45 S	13-22-30 S	11-40-00 S
Long:	114-32-40 E	114-46-00 E	115-17-15 E

Miles steamed surface: 350.3 Submerged: 1.8
Fuel expended: 2840.

October 19, 1942: Dived on approaching Lombok Strait, at 0605 (I).
                0634 (I) Sighted Nusar Besar Isle, bearing 354 T.
                        Distance 15 miles.
                2003 (I) Surfaced. Commenced passage through strait.
                2220 (I) Completed passage through strait.

Page 2

SECRET

October 19, 1942 (Cont'd)

POSITION

	0800	1200	2000
Lat:	09-01-00 S	08-53-30 S	08-49-00 S
Long:	115-40-00 E	15-41-00 E	115-44-00 E

Miles steamed surface: 152.0 Submerged: 37.1
Fuel expended: 1595.

October 20, 1942: Underway on surface.

POSITION

	0800	1200	2000
Lat:	06-30-00 S	05-38-00 S	04-05-00 S
Long:	116-43-30 E	117-00-45 E	118-03-30 E

Miles steamed surface: 341.5 Submerged: ___.
Fuel expended: 2720

October 21, 1942: Underway on surface.
    0620.(I) Made quick dive to avoid detection by two
                small sailing vessels.
    0752 (I) Surfaced.
    1842 (I) Dived to avoid detection by sailing sampan.
    1943 (I) Surfaced.

POSITION

	0800	1200	2000
Lat:	01-48-00 S	00-56-00 S	00-33-30 N
Long:	118-28-00 E	118-38-00 E	119-10-30 E

Miles steamed surface: 302.3 Submerged: 7.2
Fuel expended: 2235.

October 22, 1942: Underway on surface.
    1717 (I) Dived to await darkness for transiting Sibutu
                Pass.
    1940 (I) Surfaced.
    2347 (I) Completed passage through pass.

POSITION

	0800	1200	2000
Lat:	02-41-30 N	03-35-30 N	04-33-15 N
Long:	119-56-00 E	119-52-45 E	119-47-45 E

Miles steamed surface: 290.9 Submerged: 6.8
Fuel expended: 2110.

Page 3

SECRET

October 23, 1942: Underway on surface.

POSITION

	0800	1200	2000
Lat:	06-56-15 N	07-33-30 N	08-53-45 N
Long:	119-34-00 E	119-48-00 E	120-19-00 E

Miles steamed surface: 295.5 Submerged: ---
Fuel expended: 2025.

October 24, 1942: Underway on surface.
      1813 (I) Dived on very positive radar airplane contact.
             The weather was rainy and misty.
      1955 (I) Surfaced.

POSITION

	0800	1200	2000
Lat:	10-46-00 N	11-25-00 N	12-23-00 N
Long:	121-25-00 E	121-18-30 E	120-24-00 E

Miles steamed surface: 310.4 Submerged: 3.6
Fuel expended: 1890.

October 25, 1942: Underway on surface.
      2320 (I) Sighted steamer bearing 007 degrees T, distant,
2000 yds. Weather bad - raining - seas very
heavy. Approached on the surface on 110 degree
track. Suddenly noticed that angle on bow was
decreasing and that we were crossing his track
and were in to almost 500 yards. We had thought
the ship was about 5000 tons and could now see
that it was less than 1000 tons. We sheered
clear. It was apparent that his draft was less
than 10' and it would have been impossible to
fire a torpedo at so shallow a setting in that
sea. It was also impossible to man the deck gun.
Heading into the sea our maximum speed on two
engines was 8 knots, and they were coming green
over the bridge.

POSITION

	0800	1200	2000
Lat:	13-26-15 N	13-36-00 N	13-50-45 N
Long:	118-16-30 N	117-34-45 E	116-18-30 E

Miles steamed surface: 205.4 Submerged: ---
Fuel expended: 2015.

Page 4

SECRET

October 26, 1942: Underway on surface, weather still stormy.

POSITION

	0800	1200	2000
Lat:	14-18-45 N	14-28-30 N	14-47-15 N
Long	114-45-45 E	114-08-30 E	112-51-15 E

Miles steamed surface: 221.0 Submerged: ---
Fuel expended: 1420.

October 27, 1942: Underway on surface:

POSITION

	0800	1200	2000
Lat:	15-33-30 N	15-40-00 N	16-25-30 N
Long:	111-12-30 E	110-32-30 E	109-35-00 E

Miles steamed surface: 224.0 Submerged: ---
Fuel expended: 1450.

October 28, 1942: 0718 (I) Submerged.
                   2000 (I) Surfaced.

POSITION

	0800	1200	2000
Lat:	17-27-00 N	17-35-00 N	17-51-30 N
Long:	108-11-30 E	108-03-00 E	107-45-30 E

Miles steamed surface: 116.5 Submerged: 37.7.
Fuel expended: 1055.

October 29, 1942: 0711 (I) Submerged.
                   2015 (I) Surfaced.
                   2142 (I) Commenced mine plant. We had a number of
                             sampans in sight during the plant but do not
                             think that they saw us. The fifth mine planted
                             took off after 45 minutes.
                   2322 (I) Completed mine plant and commenced retirement.

POSITION

	0800	1200	2000
Lat:	20-10-00 N	20-18-45 N	20-24-00 N
Long:	107-36-30 E	107-27-15 E	107-14-00 E

Miles steamed surface: 122.0 Submerged: 38.7
Fuel expended: 995.

page 5

SECRET

October 30, 1942: 0714 (I) Submerged.
                    2008 (I) Surfaced.

POSITION

	0800	1200	2000
Lat:	19-02-15 N	18-51-00 N	18-31-00 N
Long:	107-40-30 E	107-40-30 E	107-40-00 E

Miles steamed surface: 126.9 Submerged: 34.1
Fuel expended: 1170

October 31, 1942: 0714 (I) Submerged. Patrolling off Cape Mui Duong.
                    2014 (I) Surfaced.

POSITION

	0800	1200	2000
Lat:	18-04-30 N	18-00-00 N	17-45-00 N
Long:	106-41-00 E	106-40-00 E	106-40-30 E

Miles steamed surface: 58.7 Submerged: 35.0
Fuel expended: 400.

November 1, 1942: 0722 (I) Submerged, patrolling off Hon Dio.
                   2010 (I) Surfaced.

POSITION

	0800	1200	2000
Lat:	17-47-00 N	17-38-30 N	17-18-00 N
Long:	106-47-30 E	106-43-00 E	107-01-00 E

Miles steamed surface: 39.7 Submerged: 34.6
Fuel expended: 415.

November 2, 1942: 0716 (I) Submerged, patrolling off Tiger Island.
                   2013 (I) Surfaced.

POSITION

	0800	1200	2000
Lat:	17-20-00 N	17-10-00 N	17-04-00 N
Long:	107-10-00 E	107-12-00 E	107-23-00 E

Miles steamed surface: 47.1 Submerged: 38.1
Fuel expended: 460.

November 3, 1942: 0709 (I) Submerged. Patrolling near Tiger Island.

page 6

SECRET

November 3, 1942 (Cont'd) Bad visibility due to heavy rain.

POSITION

	0800	1200	2000
Lat:	17-25-00 N	17-25-00 N	17-25-00 N
Long:	107-26-30 E	107-15-00 E	107-17-00 E

Miles steamed surface: 46.2   Submerged: 34.6
Fuel expended: 385.

November 4, 1942: 0709 (I) Submerged. Patrolling near Tiger island.
        1050 (I) Sighted steamer bearing 338 degrees T.
Distant 7 miles. Made approach. Allowed
vessel to pass by at 1200 yards. She was a
yacht type steamer about 400 tons, flying
French colors. Too close to shore to surface
and engage with deck gun and too small to use
torpedoes on.
        2020 (I) Surfaced.
        2037 (I) Sighted lights of steamer bearing 002 degrees
T. Distant 8 miles. Made approach on surface,
examined at 1500 yards. Appeared to be same
small ship sighted this morning. Let her go
by. We believe that attacking these small
ships will only disclose our presence and warn
other worth while targets away

POSITION

	0800	1200	2000
Lat:	17-14-00 N	17-14-00 N	17-06-00 N
Long:	107-27-00 E	107-20-00 E	107-22-00 E

Miles steamed surface: 53.8   Submerged: 33.7
Fuel expended: 435.

November 5, 1942: 0705 (I) Submerged, patrolling near Tiger Island.
        2015 (I) Surfaced. Steered to patrol across traffic
lanes between Hainan, Cape Varella and
Touraine.
        2242 (I) Sighted lights of steamer bearing 131 degrees
True. Distant 10 miles. Made surface appr-
oach and examined from about 1000 yards. She
carried the white crosses of a diplomatic ship
so we let her go by.

POSITION

	0800	1200	2000
Lat:	17-15-00 N	17-12-00 N	17-09-45 N
Long:	107-12-00 E	107-08-00 E	107-10-30 E

Miles steamed surface: 65.5   Submerged: 35.1
Fuel expended: 525.

page 7

SECRET

November 6, 1942: 0707 (I) Submerged.
                   2010 (I) Surfaced.

POSITION

	0800	1200	2000
Lat:	16-56-00 N	16-53-00 N	16-47-15 N
Long:	109-11-30 E	109-23-00 E	109-46-00-E

Miles steamed surface: 99.0   Submerged: 36.9
Fuel expended: 740.

November 7, 1942.: 0707 (I) Submerged.
                    1025 (I) Sighted submarine bearing 319 degrees True.
                              Distant 6 miles. (Our position: Lat: 16-17-
                              00 N; Long: 110-15-00 E). Made submerged
                              approach. Identified vessel as U.S.S. T??BO
                              She passed 800 yards distant.
                    1954 (I) Surfaced, decided to patrol off Cape Batangan

POSITION

	0800	1200	2000
Lat:	16-21-00 N	16-15-30 N	15-55-00 N
Long:	110-17-00 E	110-13-00 E	109-50-00 E

Miles steamed surface: 55.7   Submerged: 35.2
Fuel expended: 340.

November 8, 1942: 0654 (I) Submerged.
                   1900 (I) Surfaced.

POSITION

	0800	1200	2000
Lat:	15-21-00 N	15-16-00 N	15-15-30 N
Long:	109-14-30 E	109-07-30 E	109-09-00 E

Miles steamed surface: 46.7   Submerged: 34.6
Fuel expended: 330

November 9, 1942: 0705 (I) Submerged, patrolling off Cape Batangan.
                   2009 (I) Surfaced.

POSITION

	0800	1200	2000
Lat:	15-12-00 N	15-02-00 N	14-37-00 N
Long:	109-14-30 E	109-08-00 E	109-12-00 E

Miles steamed surface: 49.4   Submerged: 33.9
Fuel expended: 375.

page 8

82

SECRET

November 10, 1942: 0701 (I) Submerged.
                     2000 (I) Surfaced.

POSITION.

	0800	1200	2000
Lat:	14-08-30 N	13-57-30 N	13-21-00 N
Long:	109-29-00 E	109-26-00 E	109-26-30 E

Miles steamed surface: 45.7 Submerged: 33.5
Fuel expended: 345

November 11, 1942: 0705 (I) Submerged:
               1301 (I) Passed Cape Varella abeam to starboard 4 miles.
               1655 (I) Sighted freighter on course 190 degrees T., bearing 317 degrees T., distant 8 miles - Could not close so paralleled to keep in sight for night attack.
               1940 (I) Surfaced - Commenced chase on 3 engines.
               2030 (I) Sighted light bearing 211 degrees T., distant 12 miles. Approached it and it turned out to be the freighter.

POSITION

	0800	1200	2000
Lat:	13-18-00 N	12-57-30 N	12-14-00 N
Long:	109-32-00 E	109-32-30 E	109-28-00 E

Miles steamed surface: 83.0 Submerged: 34.0
Fuel expended: 750.

November 12, 1942: (Continuing approach on Freighter).
               0015 (I) Fired two bow tubes - no hits - apparently no action on freighter. Commenced another approach.
               0035 (I) Fired another bow shot. Believe that it was a dud hit because it was set to run at 10', and lights were seen being flashed over the side and the freighter turned in toward the beach and turned off its lights. Another ship had been sighted in toward the beach and heading in our direction during this approach. The two ships exchanged signals in blinker lights, and at this time a heavy rain blotted everything out. As we were about 4000 yards off the beach at this time, and having lost sight of the target, decided to clear to eastward. It is thought that the misses were torpedo failures, we had the speed well figured in the long approach, and the ranges were checked by Q-C, just prior to firing, and no counter measures could be noted that were taken by the target.

SECRET

November 12, 1942 (Cont'd)

0655 (I) Sighted ship bearing 288 degrees T., distant about 6000 yards.

0657 (I) Dived to make approach and avoid detection as it was getting light. After leveling off raised periscope and saw that ship was a corvette distant less than 1000 yards and turning toward us at high speed. Started down and as we passed 70 feet, heard 5 charges, close and to port. In the next 4 minutes we heard 5 more, none as close as the first. Stern tubes were not ready so there was no chance to fire before going deep.

0810 (I) Hit the bottom, and carried away our sound heads.

1015 (I) Cleared from the bottom and commenced working up to periscope depth.

1130 (I) Raised periscope - All clear.

1310 (I) Sighted plane bearing 325 degrees T., distant 3 miles - Went to 150'.

1500 (I) Sighted plane bearing 040 degrees T., distant 5 miles.

2010 (I) Surfaced. Noted that all hands were suffering from symptoms indicating Chlorine gas aching joints, pain in throat and lungs, rasping cough and some cases of vomiting. Located chlorine gas in after battery well, and flushed it out. Believe that salt water had leaked into battery sump from heads that overflowed due to faulty sea valves. We were still south of our area and not having seen much traffic close to the coast decided to work to the northeast and patrol traffic lanes, off the coast.

POSITION

	0800	1200	2000
Lat:	11-43-30 N	11-32-00 N	11-16-00 N
Long:	109-22-00 E	109-24-00 E	109-43-00 E

Miles steamed surface: 72.1 Submerged: 21.6
Fuel expended: 1070.

page 10

SECRET

November 13, 1942: 0652 (I) Submerged.
1950 (I) Surfaced.

POSITION

	0800	1200	2000
Lat:	11-43-00 N	11-50-30 N	12-06-00 N
Long:	110-59-30 E	111-05-30 E	111-15-00 E

Miles steamed surface: 79-7 Submerged: 35.5
Fuel expended: 790.

November 14, 1942: 0650 (I) Submerged.
1856 (I) Surfaced. The effects of the chlorine are
beginning to wear off, however we now have
numerous cases of sore and swollen gums.

POSITION

	0800	1200	2000
Lat:	12-21-00 N	12-21-00 N	12-21-00 N
Long:	111-37-00 E	111-27-00 E	111-09-30 E

Miles steamed surface: 69.3 Submerged: 33.4
Fuel expended: 640.

November 15, 1942: Decided to patrol on surface at 6 knots. Made three
training dives.

POSITION

	0800	1200	2000
Lat:	12-44-00 N	12-44-00 N	12-28-00 N
Long:	112-14-00 E	112-28-00 E	113-11-00 E

Miles steamed surface: 130.1 Submerged: 4.1
Fuel expended: 775.

November 16, 1942: Patrolling on surface.
1218 (I) Sighted steamer bearing 045 degrees T., dista
about 12-15 miles. Course 180 degrees T.,
He presented a 45 degree angle on the bow so
decided to close his track on the surface.
Put our stern toward him and went to 4 engi
There was a great amount of smoke released in
starting the engines, and he was coming in
fast so it is probable that he spotted us
because he reversed course. We dived until
she passed from sight, then surfaced and
gave chase. We figured that she would eventually change course to starboard and probably
let us get in an attack. When sighted again
she had almost 90 degrees starboard angle

page 11

SECRET

November 16, 1942 (Cont'd)

on the bow. She would seem to move in and then out of sight again and bearing change was slight. She had as much speed as we, and it began to be questionable as to who was trailing who.

1613 (I) Heard transmission, close, on 500 K.C., in international code.

1645 (I) Sighted smoke bearing 225 degrees T., that appeared to be drawing rapidly to port. Thought it might be an A/S vessel summoned by the freighter and changed course toward it. Stopped and raised #2 periscope and saw convoy of 6 ships, some presenting zero and some small port angle on the bow.

1705 (I) Dived and commenced approach on convoy, could see smoke only now; however continued to draw to the left until 1730 (I) when it started changing to right; went to normal approach course and when convoy came in sight it was about 8 miles distant and presented about 90 degrees starboard angle on the bow. Saw we couldn't close; so decided to trail and attack at night. From course change, believe convoy either saw us or received our position from single vessel.

1951 (I) Surfaced.

2001 (I) Sighted ship bearing 285 degrees T., distant 5 miles (bright moonlight). The visibility was excellent except up where the convoy should be and there was a rain squall in that direction.

2007 (I) Sighted ship bearing 325 degrees T., distant 4000 yards, coming out of the squall, and closing; submerged to periscope depth but could not see anything so changed course to 190 degrees T., and surfaced at 2048.

2049 (I) Sighted corvette or destroyer about 2000 yards distant bearing 330 degrees T., turning towards us at high speed. Dived. Stern tubes were not ready so went deep.

2052 (I) Heard 2 depth charges not too close. Commenced evading tactics. Not having sound gear put us at a disadvantage. We could probably have detected the ship before we surfaced the second time and would have avoided being spotted.

POSITION

	0800	1200	2000
Lat:	12-35-00 N	12-49-00 N	12-30-30 N
Long:	114-32-45 E	114-19-20-E	114-16-30 E

Miles steamed surface: 121.9   Submerged: 24.6
Fuel expended: 945.

page 12

SECRET

November 17, 1942: 0020 (I) Surfaced – Nothing in sight. Ran into heavy
rain. The convoy had a 4 hour or more start
on us and the lilkehood of overtaking it was
slight; so decided to stand toward the
Paracel Islands in case they came up that way

0650 (I) Submerged. Decided that patrolling on the
surface made us too visible, and with Radar
mast up, and 5 feet of periscope shears above
heads of lookouts we were liable to be sighted
first. Figure we can patrol at 50 feet with
17 feet of periscope out and cover about same
area as on surface.

1900 (I) Surfaced.

POSITION

	0800	1200	2000
Lat:	12-50-00 N	13-04-00 N	13-28-00 N
Long:	113-07-00 E	113-00-00 E	112-59-00 E

Miles steamed surface: 123.2 Submerged: 33.3
Fuel expended: 1320.

November 18, 1942: 0653 (I) Submerged.
1845 (I) Surfaced.

POSITION

	0800	1200	2000
Lat:	14-41-00 N	14-51-00 N	15-10-00 N
Long:	112-50-00 E	112-49-00 E	113-01-00 E

Miles steamed surface: 102.1 Submerged: 34.4
Fuel expended: 750.

November 19, 1942: 0645 (I) Submerged.
1904 (I) Surfaced.

POSITION

	0800	1200	2000
Lat:	14-30-00 N	14-26-00 N	14-16-00 N
Long:	114-18-00 E	114-27-30 E	114-50-00 E

Miles steamed surface: 82.5 Submerged: 33.2
Fuel expended: 515.

November 20, 1942: 0648 (I) Submerged.
1845 (I) Surfaced.

POSITION

	0800	1200	2000
Lat:	14-36-00 N	14-34-00 N	14-25-30 N
Long:	115-43-00 E	115-34-00 E	115-15-00 E

Miles steamed surface: 93.1 Submerged: 33.2
Fuel expended: 580.

page 13

SECRET

November 21, 1942: 0645 (I) Submerged.
                    1854 (I) Surfaced.

POSITION

	0800	1200	2000
Lat:	13-32-00 N	13-28-30 N	13-30-00 N
Long:	114-20-45 E	114-29-30 E	114-50-00 E

Miles steamed surface: 118.1 Submerged: 31.4
Fuel expended: 845.

November 22, 1942: 0647 (I) Submerged.
                    1857 (I) Surfaced. Decided to clear area via Palawan
                              Passage and patrol that area enroute Balabac
                              Strait.
                    2110 (I) Received instructions to intercept two cruiser
                              divisions enroute Manila from the south.
                              Assumed that ships coming from the southeast
                              would scarcely be stopping at Manila, since
                              such ports as Davao, Palau, or Truk would be
                              more available; so figured they were coming
                              from the southwest and decided to position
                              ourselves so that we could intercept ships rou
                              ing Lubang Island or going through Calavite
                              Pass. As the ships were due to arrive at
                              Manila at nightfall, this also insured us of
                              being in a position where we should sight them
                              during daylight.

POSITION

	0800	1200	2000
Lat:	12-40-00 N	12-33-30 N	12-18-00 N
Long:	116-16-00 E	116-24-30 E	116-47-30 E

Miles steamed surface: 111.3 Submerged: 32.6
Fuel expended: 810.

November 23, 1942: 0625 (I) Submerged.
                    1856 (I) Surfaced.

POSITION

	0800	1200	2000
Lat:	12-49-30 N	12-53-30 N	13-01-00 N
Long:	117-59-30 E	118-09-30 E	118-23-00 E

Miles steamed surface: 104.1 Submerged: 33.7.
Fuel expended: 800.

page 14

SECRET

November 24, 1942: 0625 (I) Submerged. Patrolling off Calavite. Pass.
                    1929 (I) Surfaced. Moonlight is very bright. Were able
                              to pick up mountains during night as distant
                              as 65 miles.

POSITION

	0800	1200	2000
Lat:	13-19-00 N	13-23-00 N	13-30-00 N
Long:	119-33-30 E	119-44-00 E	119-50-00 E

Miles steamed surface: 79.9 Submerged: 35.3
Fuel expended: 460.

November 25, 1942: 0605 (I) Submerged. Patrolling south of Lubang Island.
                    1929 (I) Surfaced.

POSITION

	0800	1200	2000
Lat:	13-30-00 N	13-38-30 N	13-31-00 N
Long:	120-03-00 E	120-06-30 E	119-59-30 E

Miles steamed surface: 78.2 Submerged: 36.9
Fuel expended: 485.

November 26, 1942: 0611 (I) Submerged.
                    1930 (I) Surfaced. Set course 180 degrees to return
                              to Fremantle.

POSITION

	0800	1200	2000
Lat:	13-27-00 N	13-29-00 N	13-12-00 N
Long:	119-50-00 E	120-00-00 E	119-59-30 E

Miles steamed surface: 108.9 Submerged: 35.1
Fuel expended: 860.

November 27, 1942: 0610 (I) Submerged.
                    1916 (I) Surfaced.

POSITION

	0800	1200	2000
Lat:	11-27-00 N	11-16-00 N	10-55-00 N
Long:	121-16-30 E	121-19-30 E	121-24-00 E

Miles steamed surface: 149.7 Submerged: 36.5
Fuel expended: 1305.

Page 15

SECRET

November 28, 1942: Underway on surface.

POSITION

	0800	1200	2000
Lat:	08-32-00 N	07-44-00 N	06-08-00 N
Long:	120-21-00 E	119-56-30 E	119-05-30 E

Miles steamed surface: 333.8   Submerged: —
Fuel expended: 2740.

November 29, 1942: 0215 (I) Completed passage through Sibutu Pass.
                    0703 (I) Submerged.
                    1900 (I) Surfaced.

POSITION

	0800	1200	2000
Lat:	03-36-00 N	03-37-30 N	03-08-00 N
Long:	120-05-00 E	120-05-00 E	120-00-30 E

Miles steamed surface: 174.2   Submerged: 36.4
Fuel expended: 1720.

November 30, 1942: 0607 (I) Submerged. Passing through Strait of
                              Makassar.
                    0728 (I) Sighted carrier, heavy cruiser, and one des-
                              troyer coming through a rain squall. The car-
                              rier bore 081 degrees T., distant 7-8000 yar
                              with a sixty to eighty degree angle on the
                              starboard bow. They were zigging and while
                              the angle on the bow gradually worked aft of
                              the beam, the range did not change greatly for
                              some time. The base course was assumed to be
                              210 degrees T., speed 15 knots.
                              The carrier appeared to be of the Ryujo class
                              except that the flight deck extended all the
                              way forward and the forward supports were
                              similar to those shown in pictures of the
                              Kaga. There was no superstructure above the
                              flight deck. In addition to the four masts
                              shown in the pictures of the Ryujo, there was
                              an additional mast aft with the colors flying.
                              Only the masts, stacks, and forward control
                              station of the cruiser was visible; however
                              their construction and size were such as make
                              its identification as a heavy cruiser fairly
                              certain.
                              Only the tip of the foremast of the destroyer
                              could be seen. The screening vessels were wel
                              ahead of the carrier. The closest range we

page 16

90

SECRET

November 30, 1942 (Cont'd)   could get on the cruiser was about 15,000
                                    yards.
                                    If the visibility in the direction from whi
                                    the ships came had been good, we could have
                                    easily picked them up at 15-20,000 yards and
                                    should have been able to get in an attack.
                                    Sound gear also may have permitted locating
                                    the target. However, rather than bemoaning
                                    our not getting in an attack, it might be
                                    well to recognize the tremendous odds that
                                    were in our favor, permitting us to see and
                                    report this force. There was no air coverage.
                                    We were in sight of land all day long and
                                    it was not considered advisable to surface
                                    and trail.
           0800 (I)   Carrier group out of sight.
           1928 (I)   Surfaced.
           2035 (I)   Sent contact report. Did not send immediate
                      after contact because was not certain that
                      we could reach Darwin on periscope antenna
                      during daytime. Also it would have informed
                      the carrier group that they had been sighted.
                      We sent the message routine and at the usual
                      times a surfacing sub might open up for
                      routine transmissions.

                        POSITION

           0800   1200   2000
Lat: 00-43-00 N   00-26-00 N   00-07-00 N
Long: 119-27-00 E   119-22-00 E   119-06-00 E

       Miles steamed surface: 144.5   Submerged: 39.1
       Fuel expended: 1300.

December 1, 1942:   0515 (I) Submerged.
                    1945 (I) Surfaced.

                        POSITION

           0800   1200   2000
Lat: 01-33-30 S   01-45-00 S   02-08-30 S
Long: 118-49-00 E   118-47-00 E   118-38-30 E

       Miles steamed surface: 127.3   Submerged: 43.2
       Fuel expended: 1215.

                        Page 17

SECRET

December 2, 1942: 0603 (I) Submerged.
                   1945 (I) Surfaced.

POSITION

	0800	1200	2000
Lat:	04-11-00 S	04-21-00 S	04-41-00 S
Long:	117-58-30 E	117-53-00 E	117-37-00 E

Miles steamed surface: 141.8   Submerged: 40.2
Fuel expended: 1500.

December 3, 1942: 0601 (I) Submerged.
                   2013 (I) Surfaced.

POSITION

	0800	1200	2000
Lat:	06-16-00 S	06-29-00 S	06-46-00 S
Long:	116-54-00 E	116-54-00 E	116-43-00 E

Miles steamed surface: 131.3   Submerged: 40.7
Fuel expended: 1230.

December 4, 1942: 0544 (I) Submerged - Commenced passage through Lombok
                                         Strait.
                   1551 (I) Cleared Strait.
                   2020 (I) Surfaced.

POSITION.

	0800	1200	2000
Lat:	08-23-45 S	08-32-45 S	09-00-30 S
Long:	115-50-30 E	115-44-00 E	115-36-45 E.

Miles steamed surface: 123.4   Submerged: 41.5
Fuel expended: 1320.

December 5, 1942: Underway on the surface.

POSITION

	0800	1200	2000
Lat:	11-36-15 S	12-31-15 S	14-23-00 S
Long:	114-50-00 E	114-34-45 E	114-00-15 E

Miles steamed surface: 353.7   Submerged: --
Fuel expended: 4065.

page 18

SECRET

December 6, 1942: Underway on surface. Made trim dive.

POSITION

	0800	1200	2000
Lat:	16-58-45 S	17-52-00 S	19-27-00 S
Long:	113-40-00 E	113-26-45 E	113-00-00 E

Miles steamed surface: 330.6 Submerged: 1.3
Fuel expended: 4010.

December 7, 1942: Underway on surface.
        0600 (I) Sighted Vlaming Head Light bearing 145 T, distan
                16 miles. Sighted USS TRINITY, HMAS GAWLER and
                USS WHIPPOORWILL.
        0805 (I) Sighted P.B.Y.
        0910 (I) Sighted P.B.Y.
        0935 (I) Closed TRINITY in the Gulf and she advised us
                that she was fueling barge to capacity and sug-
                gested that we keep our fuel. Commenced cleari.
                Gulf for Fremantle.
        1105 (I) Sighted P.B.Y.

POSITION

	0800	1200	2000
Lat:	21-37-00 S	21-40-00 S	22-14-30 S
Long:	114-21-00 E	114-11-00 E	112-39-30 E

Miles steamed surface: 323.9 Submerged: --
Fuel expended: 2855.

December 8, 1942: Underway on surface.
        1205 (I) Sighted P.B.Y.

POSITION

	0800	1200	2000
Lat:	21-41-30 S	25-28-00 S	27-05-30 S
Long:	112-31-45 E	112-22-45 E	112-29-00 E.

Miles steamed surface: 330.9 Submerged: --
Fuel expended: 2895.

December 9, 1942: Underway on surface:
        1030(I) Made trim dive.
        1050(I) Surfaced.

POSITION

	0800	1200	2000
Lat:	29-00-30 S	29-36-00 S	30-45-30 S
Long:	112-48-00 E	113-12-45 E	114-15-00 E

Miles steamed surface: 239.8 Submerged: 1.2
Fuel expended: 1485.

December 10, 1942: Underway on surface.
        0130 (I) Sighted the loom of Rottnest Island Light bearing
                138 T, distant 48 miles.
        0452 (I) Rendezvoused with U.S.S. ISABEL.
        1153 (I) Moored in Fremantle W.A. alongside,

18 (a)

SECRET

WEATHER

Northeast monsoon had set in, in China sea before GRENADIER'S arrival.

In initial passage from Phillipines to Tonkin Gulf encountered storm which was apparently caused by a typhoon to the north. Only one engine speed was possible and DR navigation was necessary.

Along coast of Indo China weather was changeable. Two or three days would pass with relatively calm sea and light monsoon breeze. Station close inshore could be maintained although visibility at best was ten to fifteen miles due to a surface haze and mountains along the coast were never visible even from four or five miles off the coast. A day or two of bad weather would then follow with strong northeast winds, rain squalls and overcast sky. Position fixing was impossible, and it was necessary to run off the coast.

In the Phillipines fine weather prevailed. The northeast monsoon was well established. Visibility was exceptional. Time after time islands and peaks were sighted as soon as they came within the theoretical visibility range

TIDAL INFORMATION

Off shore in the China sea west of Long: 112°, a south westerly current of about 1 knot was experienced. Along the northern Indo China coast a current of from 1 to 2.5 knots was experienced setting parallel to the coast line, general direction southeast. From Cape Batangan south to cape Padaran set was almost due south and drift up to 3 knots was experienced.

Between Long: 113 degrees E and 116 degrees E., and between Lats: 12 degrees N and 15 degrees N., a set of about 1.0 knots toward 020 degrees was experienced. This bore out pilot.

Strong eddy currents are encountered close inshore. It was frequently necessary to speed up a screw to help the rudder maintain the course. The chances of getting a hit with a torpedo passing through these eddys are problematical.

In Makassar Strait on the return trip a northeasterly set of about .5 knots was experienced instead of the .75 knot southerly set mentioned in the sailing directions.

SECRET

NAVIGATIONAL AIDS

On the night of 23 October, Unsang Point light on the northeast coast of Borneo was burning as a steady white light and not with the characteristics shown in light list.

On the night of 28 November, Unsang Point light was again burning. Each time its position was checked against a fix obtained by other bearings and its location is as shown on the charts.

Until the fathometer grounded out on 17 November, it proved to be of great value for navigation especially when operating close inshore along the Indo China coast, during the overcast weather encountered on the way to station   and

SECRET

SHIPS SIGHTED

DATE	TIME	POSITION	BEARING	DISTANCE	COURSE	SPEED	DESCRIPTION
25 Oct	2320	14-03 N 115-40 E	007 T.	1 mile	060	6	Small steam vessel of 1000 tons with single high stack. Believe it to have been a trawler. Estimated masthead height 60 ft. Estimated length 200 ft. Closed for attack but did not attack. Doubted whether or not he was worth a torpedo and in any case heavy sea made torpedo performance doubtful. Too rough to use deck gun.
4 Nov	1050	17-14 N 107-22 E	338 T	7 miles	170	8	Small yacht type steam vessel of 300 to 400 tons flying French colors. Estimated length 150 feet. Reached firing position but decided he was too small for a torpedo. Masthead height 50 feet.
4 Nov	2037	17-06 N 107-24 E	002 T	8 miles	140	5	Small steam yacht of 300 to 400 tons. Lighted with normal navigational lights. Estimated length 150 ft. Closed and examined him and decided to let him go by because of small size. Believed same vessel seen during day.
5 Nov	2242	17-10 N 107-30 E	131 T	10 miles	345	12	Diplomatic ship of about 5000 tons, 2 masts, one stack. Estimated length 300 feet. Lighted. Closed to about 1000 yard.
11 Nov	1655	12-29 N 109-34 E	317 T	8 miles	190	7	Cargo vessel of about 3500 tons. Two masts, single high stack, no gool posts, high bridge structure. Estimated masthead height 60 ft. Estimated length 300 ft. Made two unsuccessful attacks. At night this vessel burned lights, not regular navigational lights.

SECRET

SHIPS SIGHTED

page 22

DATE	TIME	POSITION	BEARING	DISTANCE	COURSE	SPEED	DESCRIPTION
12 Nov	0655	11-43 N: 119-20 E:	288 T	3 miles	100	15	Jap Corvette of 600 tons, one mast, one stack clipper bow. Gun forward.
16 Nov	1218	12-52 N: 114-19 E:	045 T	12 to 15: miles.	180	14	Cargo vessel of about 7000 tons. Two sets of goal posts, high bow. Estimated length 400 ft.
16 Nov	1700	12-27 N: 114-16 E:	225 T	15 miles:	330 T	7	Cargo vessel, 4000 tons. Estimated length 350 feet.
16 Nov	1700	12-27 N: 114-16 E:	225 T	15 miles:	330 T	7	Cargo vessel, 3000 tons. Estimated length 300 feet.
16 Nov	1700	12-27 N: 114-16 E:	225 T	15 miles :	330 T	7	Cargo vessel, 5000 tons. Estimated length 400 feet.
16 Nov	1700	12-27 N: 114-16 E:	225 T	15 miles:	330 T	7	Cargo vessel, 4000 tons. Estimated length 350 feet.
16 Nov	1700	12-27 N: 114-16 E:	225 T	15 miles:	330 T	7	Cargo vessel, 5000 tons. Estimated length 400 feet.
16 Nov	1700	12-27 N: 114-16 E:	225 T	15 miles:	330 T	7	Tanker 5000 tons, two masts, one high stack, high bow and stern with bridge aft. Estimated length 600 feet.
16 Nov	2007	12-33 N: 114-10 E:	325 T	3 miles	145 T	15	Jap Corvette. 600 tons.
30 Nov	0728	00-47 N: 119-27 E:	081 T	7000 to :8000 yds	180 T	15	Jap aircraft carrier similar to Ryujo except that flight deck extended all the way to the bow. She had five masts and no superstructure above the flight deck. She was in a rain squall at this time and this was the reason for not sighting the carrier until she was almost past. Came to normal approach course but was unable to close for a shot
30 Nov	0728	00-47 N: 119-27 E:	095 T	15,000 yds.	180 T ::	15	Jap heavy cruiser acting as a starboard screen for carrier.

SECRET

SHIPS SIGHTED

DATE	TIME	POSITION	BEARING	DISTANCE	COURSE	SPEED	DESCRIPTION
30 Nov	0728	00-47 N	087 T	18000 yds	180	15	Jap destroyer acting as port screen for
		119-27 E					carrier

It was noted that both screens were well out ahead of the carrier.

No air screens were observed, probably because of the rain and general bad visibility.

Page 23

SECRET

AIRCRAFT SIGHTED

DATE	TIME	POSIT	BEARING	DISTANCE	COURSE	ALTITUDE	DESIGNATION
14 Oct	0837	29-44 S: 113-30 E	125	8 miles	310	400 ft	P.B.Y.
16 Oct	0755	24-40 S: 114-16 E	170	8 miles	320	500 ft	P.B.Y.
16 Oct	0759	21-40 S: 114-16 E	190	6 miles	320	500 ft	P.B.Y.
16 Oct	1630	21-45 S: 114-14 E	332	7 1/2 mil	190	500 ft	P.B.Y.
16 Oct	1712	21-35 S: 114-12 E	325	8 miles	150	1000 ft	P.B.Y.
18 Oct	1917	11-46-30 S 115-11 E	135	7 miles	000	2000 ft	Bomber Monoplane. Land plane
12 Nov	1314	13-08 N 109-37-30 E	325	3 miles	090	500 ft	Type "S" Seversky.
12 Nov	1500	13-10 N: 109-40 E	040	5 miles	180	500 ft	Type 97 Nakajima.
7 Dec	0805	21-38 S: 114-21 E	180	15 miles	000	500 ft	P.B.Y.
7 Dec	0910	21-52 S: 114-18 E	205	11 miles	340	500 ft	P.B.Y.
7 Dec	1105	21-45 S: 114-20 E	200	12 miles	000	500 ft	P.B.Y.
7 Dec	1205	25-29 S: 112-22 E	300	15 miles	135	500 ft	P.B.Y.

Page 24

SECRET

ATTACKS

DATE	POSITION	TIME	TARGET	TORPEDOES FIRED	FIRING INTERVAL	FIRING RANGE	POINT OF AIM	GYRO ANG	TRACK ANGL	ENEMY SPEED	DPTH SET	SURF OR SUB
11-12 Nov:	11-18 N : 109-02.5 E:	0015	3500 tn: cargo vessel	2	17 sec	1000 yards: 850 yards:	VOT	345; 34.3	89P; 94P	6.5	5 ft:	both: Surface.
2. 12 Nov:	11-18 N : 109-02.5 E:	0035	same vessel	1	--	950 yards:	VOT: 000	91:	6.5	0 ft:	Surface.

METHOD SOLUTION:	TORPEDOES HEARD TO RUN	TORPEDOES SEEN TO RUN	SPREAD USED	SPREAD APPLIED	HITS	TUBES USED
1. TDC & TBT	Yes	Yes	4° divergent	TDC	.0	Bow
2. TDC & TBT	Yes	Yes	--	--	0	Bow

REMARKS: Target course and speed had been checked over an 8 hour period. Both torpedoes were seen to run. The wakes were followed by several bridge personnel and both tracks seemed to pass under the target. The first wake seemed to pass 40 feet forward of the bridge. The second wake seemed to pass under the bridge. Torpedo run seemed normal. No reason other than bad torpedo performance can be given for failure to sink the target unless both of the torpedoes passed under the target before steadying down at running depth.

2. Torpedo was seen to run. Again the wake was followed by bridge personnel and track appeared to pass about 50 feet abaft the bridge. Again no reason other than torpedo performance can be given for the miss. A dud hit is believed probable.

SECRET

ENEMY A/S MEASURES

Enemy air patrols were very weak. One plane was sighted 100 miles south of the Malay Barrier. Radar contact was made with an enemy plane 25 miles southwest of Mindoro P.I. Two enemy planes were sighted off Davaich Head, Indo China, but our presence was known on the day we contacted the Corvette and they were obviously making a special search.

With these exceptions no enemy air activity was noted. When going on patrol, passage from the Malay Barrier to the entrance to Tonkin Gulf was made on the surface except for trim dives, and it is therefore believed that more planes would have been sighted, if patrol activity had been great.

Surface patrols were also limited. The only surface patrols encountered were a corvette off Davaich Head, Indo China and a Corvette escorting a six ship convoy in the South China Sea. In the first case he was obviously searching for us after our unsuccessful attack on a merchantman in the early morning. On sighting us he headed directly for us at high speed and dropped pattern of 5 charges at our supposed position followed shortly after by 2 charges. Three single charges were dropped later. He used both pinging and listening in his hunt.

In the second case the Corvette apparently knew of our presence from the afternoon contact with the single ship. He trailed the convoy to protect it from astern. When he first sighted us he headed for us but after we dived made no attack. Since our sound heads were gone it is not known whether or not he used pinging. In any case he was waiting for us when we surfaced 40 minutes later, and this time he attacked with depth charges.

In both cases the GRENADIER used silent running and deep submergence to evade. The enemy was kept as near dead astern as possible.

On 30 November at the contact with the Carrier it was noted that the screening Cruiser and Destroyer were well ahead of the Carrier

SECRET

MAJOR DEFECTS

#4 Main Engine was out of commission for four days as a result of a fresh water leak due to a crack at the junction of the inboard exhaust manifold and the   steel flange at the forward end of the manifold. Inboard section of manifold removed after spending two days tearing up floor plates, removing electrical leads, and attempting to pry loose the manifold from the engine. Crack soldered and manifold replaced. No further trouble experienced during the rest of the patrol.

Both sound heads were ruined when the ship bottomed on 12 November off the Indo China Coast.

The Fathometer is grounded.

The advisability of carrying an ample supply of acetylene gas was well shown. Casualties requiring brazing and welding, which, though minor in nature, had to be remedied for efficient operation of the Engineering plant were quickly and permanently made.

Page 27

SECRET   REMARKS

Radio reception: was good throughout the patrol.

Sound conditions: were poor along the Indo China coast. Water was very noisy due to shallowness. In other areas no information could be gained due to loss of sound heads on 12 November.

Density layers: In the South China Sea in Lat: 12-33 N, Long: 114-10 E, while going deep to avoid depth charge attack it was necessary to flood in 10,000 lbs to remain at 240 feet and not come up, and standard speed had to be used until the additional water had been taken aboard. This water had to be pumped out for periscope depth trim. Near and off the Indo China coast the observations made by other boats were confirmed. Boat was light near the coast and heavy when diving well off shore.

Chlorine: The experience with Chlorine gas on 12 November was an unpleasant one. The efficiency of the whole ship's company was adversely affected for several days. The following symptoms were noted:

SYMPTOM	% AFFECTED
Pain in chest with each breath:	100
Dry hacking cough:	100
Nausea and vomiting:	70
Headaches for 12 hours:	60
Soreness of gums and throat:	70
Tiredness for several days:	50

Traffic routes: It is believed that only southbound traffic uses the route close inshore along the Indo China coast at this season of the year. The strong southerly set helps this traffic and would greatly increase the time and fuel required for the northbound traffic. A stay of ten days inshore along the coast showed coastal traffic north of Padaran to be negligible. It is also believed that the northbound traffic at this time of the year uses the eastern route mentioned in HO 125 (Sailing Directions for the Western Shores of the China Sea). The convoy sighted on 16 November used this eastern route.

Lighted ships: These were encountered along the coast and all seem to be of small tonnage. The system of lights used is rather deceptive. In addition to regular side and mast head lights (dimmed), they carry a brilliant light on each side almost directly below the sidelights and at a distance of almost half the freeboard from the waterline. Another brilliant all around light is carried on a high staff at the stern. Viewed from anywhere except close to the stern or bow, these give the appearance of range lights just appearing and the course of the target is hard to judge and you are almost on top of the ship before the ruse can be recognized. The brilliance of the lights makes it almost impossible to make out the outlines of the ship.

Page 28

SECRET

REMARKS (Cont'd)

Personnel: In spite of the ill health resulting from the chlorine, and the disappointment incident to our poor luck on attacks, the morale of the officers and crew has been excellent.

The smoothness with which the mine plant progressed was due to the excellent planning and supervision of the Gunnery Officer.

The continued operation and efficiency of all machinery is a credit to the heads of departments and the personnel under them.

Habitability was good.

```
Potable water endurance remaining...................Unlimited.
Battery water endurance remaining...................Unlimited.
Balanced ration food endurance remaining...........10 days.
Fuel endurance remaining...........................10 days. (21,000 gals)
Torpedoes remaining................................. 5
Personnel endurance................................. 5 days.

Total miles underway................................ 10,863.8.
Total fuel expended................................. 80,500 gals.
```

SUBMARINE SQUADRON SIX   (6)/OL

FC5-6/A16-3   U.S.S. TAUTOG, Flagship,
Serial #00-45   December 13, 1942.

FIRST ENDORSEMENT to
C.O.Grenadier 4th War
Patrol #004 of 12/10/42

S E C R E T

From: The Commander Submarine Squadron SIX.
To :   The Commander Task Force 51.

Subject: U.S.S. GRENADIER - Fourth War Patrol - Comment on.

1.   Forwarded. The fourth war patrol of the GRENADIER was a
combination mining and torpedo patrol; it covered a period of fifty-nine days
of which forty-six were spent north of the Malay Barrier. The passage from
Lombok Strait to the Tonkin Gulf was made almost entirely on the surface without sighting any aircraft and with only three contacts with surface craft, two
of which were small sailing vessels.

2.   Material performance during the patrol was excellent with
no mechanical derangements of any magnitude having been experienced. Sound
heads will be replaced if all material becomes available during current refit
which is being undertaken by Pelias. General cleanliness of machinery and
structure upon return from patrol was exemplary.

3.   Chlorine gas caused by salt water which leaked into the
after battery well affected the entire personnel of the ship for several days.
No serious sickness resulted and, except for this, health and habitability were
excellent.

4.   The mining mission was successfully carried out; one premature explosion resulted. Seventeen contacts were reported but only one was developed into an attack, which was unsuccessful; the Commanding Officer reports
that the three torpedoes fired at the one ship attacked appeared to run under
the target without exploding. Several small vessels which might have been
attacked were permitted to go unmolested because of their size. The Commanding
Officer stated that he considered that attacking these small ships would disclose
his presence and warn off more worth while targets. Except under the most unusual circumstances, all enemy vessels encountered must be destroyed, and it is
considered a mistake to with hold attacking a small target in hopes of finding
a larger one. Instructions to attack enemy cruisers scheduled to arrive off
Manila were not properly carried out. The GRENADIER stopped off Lubang Island
when she should have gone to a position off the entrance to Manila Bay. It is
unfortunate that the convoy sighted on November 16 and the carrier group sighted
on November 30 could not be closed sufficiently for an attack. More determined
efforts on this patrol might have been productive of better results. No damage
was inflicted on the enemy by this patrol.

                                        A.R.McCANN.
                                        A. R. McCANN.

A16-3
Serial 00158

COMMANDER ALLIED NAVAL FORCES

Ly

December 17, 1942.

S-E-C-R-E-T

SECOND ENDORSEMENT to
CO GRENADIER Secret
ltr. SS210/A16-3 Serial
004 of 12-10-42 (Fourth
War Patrol Report)

From: The Commander TASK FORCE FIFTY ONE.
To : The Commander in Chief, U.S. FLEET.
Via : The Commander Southwest Pacific Force.

Subject: U.S.S. GRENADIER - Fourth War Patrol - Comment on.

1.   Forwarded, concurring in remarks of Commander Submarine Squadron SIX as set forth in first endorsement.

2.   Routine periodic flushing of battery sumps with fresh water and soda solution should be carried out in order to prevent accumulation of acid which will liberate chlorine gas on contact with salt water.

3.   The submarine was engaged primarily in mining operations and was carrying only 8 torpedoes. She returned with 5 torpedoes remaining on board. The ship was further handicapped by the loss of both sound receivers during the early stages of the patrol.

4.   Out of a total of 17 contacts only 2 attacks were made, both of which were on the same ship. In the second attack only one torpedo was fired. The misses are believed to be due to inaccurate firing data. As has been repeatedly emphasized a spread of at least two torpedoes should invariably be used to provide for erratic torpedo performance as well as to compensate for errors in estimated course and speed of the target. Numerous small ships were sighted which were not attacked. The Force Commander takes this occasion to again point out that the loss of ships, regardless of tonnage, may be severely felt by the enemy.

5.   More aggressive action in the pursuit of the convoy sighted on November 16th might have been productive of greater results.

6.   It is noted that the patrol on November 24, 25 and 26, in an effort to intercept enemy cruisers believed to be proceeding MANILA from the South, did not cover the exit from VERDE ISLAND PASSAGE. The line of reasoning used by the Commanding Officer in arriving at his decision to patrol off LUBANG ISLAND, some sixty miles from MANILA BAY, is considered faulty as specific orders directed an attack on enemy cruisers "OFF MANILA".

7.   No damage was inflicted on the enemy by the GRENADIER during this patrol.

/s/ C. A. LOCKWOOD, Jr.

DISTRIBUTION				
COMINCH	(2)(Via Comsouwespacfor)	COMSOUWESPACFOR	(1)	COMTASKFOR 42 (1)
VICE OPNAV	(1) (" ")	COMSOUPACFOR	(1)	COMSUBRON 6 (1)
CINCLANFLT	(1)	COMSUBSPAC	(5)	DIVCOMS, RON 6 (1)
CINCPACFLT	(1)	COMSUBSLANT	(2)	EACH S/M, W.A. (1)

A16-3 SOUTHWEST PACIFIC FORCE 0889

Serial 1082

CONFIDENTIAL March 12, 1943

From: The Commander Southwest Pacific Force.
To : The Commander Task Force FIFTY ONE.

Subject: U.S.S. GRENADIER Fourth War Patrol, report
of, request for additional copies of.

1. It is requested that the Commander Southwest
Pacific Force be furnished three (3) additional copies of
subject report to replace copies which were forwarded to
the Commander-in-Chief, United States Fleet and the Vice
Chief of Naval Operations on NATS Flight 62100 which has
been reported missing.

J. CARY JONES,
Chief of Staff.

- -

FIRST ENDORSEMENT U.S. NAVAL FORCES 05/Bz
FE24-71/A16-3(6) WESTERN AUSTRALIA

(0373) March 23, 1943.

CONFIDENTIAL

From: The Commander TASK FORCE SEVENTY-ONE.
To: The Commander SEVENTH FLEET.

Enclosure: (A) 3 copies of U.S.S. GRENADIER Fourth War Patrol.

1. Enclosure (A) is forwarded herewith.

S.S. MURRAY,
Chief of Staff.

CONFIDENTIAL

UNITED STATES FLEET
COMMANDER SEVENTH FLEET

A16-3

Serial 00278

CONFIDENTIAL

Reg. No 02115 (106.7.4)

R.S. No 4 0883

MAR 30 1943

SECOND ENDORSEMENT to
CSWPF serial 1082 of
March 12, 1943.

From: The Commander SEVENTH FLEET.
To: The Commander in Chief, United States Fleet.

Subject: U.S.S. GRENADIER - Fourth War Patrol - report of.

1.   Forwarded.

J. CARY JONES,
Chief of Staff.

Copy to:
    VCNO (1 enc)
         (2 herewith)

1943 APR 13 14 46

COMMANDER IN CHIEF
U.S. FLEET
RECEIVED

46149
FILMED

1ST COPY

SS210/A16-3,   U.S.S. GRENADIER

Serial #02

DECLASSIFIED

CONFIDENTIAL

℅ Fleet Post Office,
San Francisco, California,
February 20, 1943.

From: The Commanding Officer.
To :   The Commander-in-Chief, United States Fleet.
Via :   The Official channels.

Subject: War Patrol Report. (Fifth War Patrol)

Enclosure: (A) War Patrol, Period January 1, 1943 to
              February 20, 1943.

1.   Enclosure (A) is forwarded herewith.

J. A. FITZGERALD.

DECLASSIFIED

155879

EMPLOYMENT SINCE LAST PATROL: ...

Dec 11, 1942: Returned to Fremantle, W.A., from fourth war patrol.
Began two week tender and relief crew refit.
Dec 12, 1942: Officers and crew sent to rest camps.
Dec 24, 1942: Officers and crew returned from rest camps. Lieutenant
Commander, B.L. CARR, U.S.N. was relieved as commanding officer by
Lieutenant Commander, J.A. FITZGERALD, U.S.N. Began readiness for sea
period.
Dec 28, 1942: Conducted sound test of equipment; ran over degaussing
calibration range; calibrated radio direction finder.
Dec 31, 1942: Conducted sound training and approach exercises with
H.M.A.S. WALLAROO. Test fired 20MM gun. Conducted deep dive; 250'.

INSTRUCTIONS FOR CURRENT PATROL

Commander Task Force 51; Operation Order No. 74-42.
When directed about January 1, 1943, depart Fremantle, W.A., proceed
via the bombing restriction lane to Exmouth Gulf and there fuel to
capacity. Thence proceed to the vicinity of Cape Varella on the Indo
China Coast via Lombok Strait, Makassar Strait, Sibutu Passage, Mindoro
Strait and north of Dangerous Ground exploiting possible trade lanes
enroute.
Conduct offensive patrol against enemy combatant, supply and transport
shipping. Upon arrival Indo China Coast conduct offensive patrol close
to the coast keeping to the northward of latitude 11 degrees - 40'
north. If unfavorable weather precludes effective patrol along Indo
China coast or area is not productive at end of sixth day on station,
report and await further orders.
Start return to Fremantle at sunset February 6, 1943 via reverse of
outbound route.

Above operation order modified by C.T.F. 51 serial 24, directing
GRENADIER patrol approaches Surabaya, Makassar and Balikpapan, remaining on northern approaches to Surabaya for one week pending further
developments. If patrol ineffective due to enemy anti submarine
measures, proceed approaches to west and south west Makassar - reporting
when advisable.
C.T.F. 51 serial 37 modified above to patrol areas off Balikpapan,
Makassar and back to Surabaya departing latter place February 10, 1943.
C.T.F. 51 serial 76 modified above to conduct patrol off Makassar so
as to arrive vicinity Saleier Strait February 2, thence to vicinity
Pulassi Island thence to northern entrance Bali Strait, via 8-00-00 S.
latitude, departing latter place at dark February 12, 1943.

page 1

NARRATIVE

Jan 1, 1943: 1st day.
0907: Underway fifth war patrol, clearing Fremantle harbor
enroute Submarine exercise area to conduct sound training, daylight submerged attacks and night surface attacks with H.M.A.S. DUBBO.
2137: With Rottnest Island Light bearing 077 degrees T, distance 24
miles, took departure. Proceeding on surface to and in bombing restriction lane.
1200: Latitude: 31-42-00 S. Longitude: 115-30-00 E.
Miles steamed: 92.3   Fuel used: 1050.

Jan 2, 1943: Second day.
Underway on surface in bombing restriction lane. Made five training
dives and held gunnery drills during the day.
1200: Latitude: 29-31-15 S. Longitude: 113-25-00 E.
Miles steamed: 313.2 Fuel used: 3205.

Jan 3, 1943: Third day.
Underway on surface in bombing restriction lane. Made training dive,
and conducted gunnery drills during day.
1200: Latitude: 24-42-00 S. Longitude: 112-24-30E.
Miles steamed: 353.4 Fuel used: 3620.

Jan 4, 1943: Fourth day.
Underway on surface in bombing restriction lane.
0540: Sighted Vlaming Head light bearing 160 degrees T., distance 19
miles.
0641: Sighted 2 PBY planes, bearing 165 T., distance 7 miles and 175 T
11 mi.respectively. Latitude: 21-39-30 S. Longitude: 114-07-00 E.
0719: Entered Exmouth Gulf.
0950: Moored to fuel barge.
1205: Completed fueling to capacity having received 9500 gallons diesel
oil.
1214: Underway, clearing Exmouth Gulf. Conducted emergency drills,
gunnery drills and made trim dive.
1200: Latitude: 22-14-00 S. Longitude: 114-10-00 E.
Miles steamed: 280.6 Fuel used: 2375. Fuel received: 9500.

Jan 5, 1943: Fifth day.
Underway on surface. Made eight training dives. Held battle surface
drills. Fired 3"/50 cal and 20MM for training, both day and night.
During day drills fired both 30 cal. machine guns and tommy guns.
2051: Received C.T.F. 51 serial 24, changing area of operations for
GRENADIER.
1200: Latitude: 18-19-00 S. Longitude: 113-59-00 E.
Miles Steamed: 311.3 Fuel used: 3010.

Jan 6, 1943: Sixth day.
Underway on surface. Made trim dive. Conducted various drills.
1200: Latitude: 13-21-00 S. Longitude: 114-56-00 E.
Miles steamed: 336.4 Fuel used: 3495

page 2.

Jan 7, 1943: Seventh day.
Underway on surface.
0517: Sighted Nusar Besar Island, bearing 000 T, distance 20 miles.
0523: Submerged.
1255: Commenced passage through Lombok Strait, current quite favorable, averaging about three knots to northward.
1800: Completed passage Lombok Strait.
1918: Surfaced.
1200: Latitude: 08-52-00 S Longitude: 115-43-00 E.
Miles steamed: 188.6 Fuel used: 1520.

Jan 8, 1943: Eighth day.
Underway on surface.
0245: Discovered fathometer to be grounded, and beyond remedy away from tender. This unfortunate incident was, needless to say, quite disconcerting; particularly in view of the new areas assigned GRENADIER.
0541: Submerged, sky very much overcast and fix doubtful.
0612: Changed course to 270 T, along 6-06-30 latitude line enroute Surabaya area.
1903: Surfaced. Sky overcast and strong westerly wind. No fix obtainable.
1907: Course 290 T, heading toward Great Masalembo from D.R. position in hopes that if a fix is not to be obtained tomorrow morning would at least be in sight of these islands and near a possible traffic lane. A couple stars through a rift about 2130 gave an indication that GRENADIER was to north east of D.R. position so at 2230, changed course to 270 T.
1200: Latitude: 6-06-30 S. D.R. Longitude: 116-12-30 E. D.R.
Miles steamed: 167.7 Fuel used: 1340.

Jan 9, 1943: Ninth day
Underway on surface. Wind strong from west, making about 11 knots on two main generators.
0445: Stopped and took a sounding with the lead - bottom at thirty-four fathoms, 270 seemed to be a good course.
0536: Submerged, having obtained a few stars for a fix.
0555: Sighted Great Masalembo Island bearing 312 T, distance 13 miles.
0632: Changed course to 241 T, paralleling possible, shipping lane and also to avoid a 13 fathom spot.
1021: Course 270 T. Making little headway, current averaging about 2 knots on 090 T. Desired to get closer to the shipping lane.
1918: Surfaced.
1945: Course 246 on probably route Balikpapan - Surabaya.
1200: Latitude: 05-47-30 S Longitude: 114-27-30 E.
Miles steamed: 160.2 Fuel used: 1290.

Jan 10, 1943: Tenth day.
Underway on surface.. Patrolling northern approaches to Surabaya.
0149: Course 270 T.
0548: Submerged, no star fix but believed to be on route Surabaya to west of Bawean by D.R.
0620: Sighted two masted schooner bearing 300 T, distance about 5

miles. At first believed to be of about 150 tons, but later decided
it to be about half that size. Lat: 06-19-00 S. Long: 112-44-00 E.
0622: Commenced approach for possible battle surface.
0707: Surfaced. Range about 1000 yards and closing.
0708: Commenced firing with 3". Much activity on deck of schooner
including hoisting of Japanese flag. First shot, 3" fired with idea
of forcing schooner to heave to - it did not, so continued firing with
3", 20MM and 30 cal. maching guns.
0719: Ceased firing. Schooner on fire.
0732: Submerged, having inspected schooner at about 50 yards.
0750: Schooner sank. Survivors in the boat, and on masts. Had observed twelve of crew at one time while schooner was afloat. Saw several
objects of about three feet square and six to eight inches thick enclosed in grass matting.
0808: Course north to sight Bawean Island and establish position,
weather still overcast.
1202: Sighted Bawean Island in haze; sun trying to break through clouds.
1238: Flamed up for noon sight.
1241: Submerged.
1922: Sighted Corvette distance about 6800 yards, course 350 T, bearing
259 T, speed about 10-12. Commenced approach, hoping Corvette would
zig toward GRENADIER and get in a shot before darkness. No luck.
1934: Broke off attack as target was lost in darkness on bearing 320 T.
2025: Surfaced, and established patrol on Surabaya - Tg. Selatan line.
1200: Latitude: 06-07-30 S Longitude: 112-42-30 E.
Miles steamed: 142.6 Fuel used: 940.

Jan 11, 1943: Eleventh day.
Underway on surface, patrolling northern approaches to Surabaya.
0528: Sighted loom of searchlight over horizon bearing 170 T.
0538: Submerged on course 160 T, had obtained stars which resulted in
a fair fix.
1010: Sighted Madura Island to south.
1020: Course 022 T.
1143: Sighted Surabaya swept channel entrance buoy bearing 088 T,
distance about 3 miles.
1512: Sighted steamer bearing 065 T, distance about 13000 yards, angle
on bow 20 Port. GRENADIER position: Lat 6-26-00 S, Long 112-55-00 E.
Commenced approach.
16-16-41: Attempted to fire #2 tube - torpedo did not leave tube because
of sticky stop bolt, packing too tight.
16-16-52: Fired #4 tube.
16-17-01: Fired #3 tube. No explosions heard, tracks not seen, definately
heard one torpedo run normal. Maru, similar to Rokko Maru, sighted
torpedo (s) and turned away to angle on bow of 170 starboard.
1622: Maru fired one shot from stern gun looked like a 3". Target
then became inquisitive and headed east, course 085.
1630: Started new setup for another attack, range now 1500 yards.
1636: Data seemed to be checking, still had large gyro angle, 50 degrees right, GRENADIER, swinging with hard right rudder to reduce the
gyro angle. Raised periscope for check prior to firing as gyro angle
had started toward zero at good rate; range 900 yards angle on bow zero
with Maru steady on GRENADIER.

page 4.

1637: Went deep, had not seen any depth charges but could not be positive of their absence.
1655: After nothing happened came to periscope depth, nothing in sight but a rain squall and black back ground. Surface search believed impracticable because of nearness to Surabaya entrance buoy, and that in all probability, Maru entered channel for that port.
1935: Surfaced. Violent rain squall and lightening during night.
1200: Latitude: 06-31-00 S. Longitude: 112-52-00 E.
Miles steamed: 138.4 Fuel used: 1105.

Jan 12, 1943: Twelfth day
Underway on surface.
0543: Submerged, weather overcast sea running high - no star fix.
0715: Sighted Bawean Island bearing 342 T, distance about 32 miles. Obtained fair position by plot of bearings. Set course 194 T, allowing for easterly set of about one knot, to arrive off entrance buoy to Surabaya.
1056: Sighted masts of two vessels bearing 155 T, distance about 16000 yards. GRENADIER position: Lat 6-27-00 S, Long 112-52-00 E. Planed up until could see leading vessel. Estimated angle on bow about 65 starboard. Vessel appeared to be medium sized tanker, and believed second vessel to be escort or cargo ship. Atmospheric conditions not permitting of better observation. Commenced approach, making standard speed except during periscope exposure at intervals of ten to fifteen minutes. GRENADIER gaining on bearing.
1222: Had closed sufficiently to determine that objective was about a 750 ton steamer towing a hulk barge of about 500 tons well loaded. Original speed of target tracked at 5 knots, but as sea and wind picked up, target speed was reduced to 3.3. Did not believe expenditure of torpedoes advisable and had not seen any guns on either vessel decided to trail and attack from the surface after dusk.
1705: Joined formation third ship in column.
1912: Steamer turned on mast head and stern lights as well as cabin lights. Barge showed one light. This made situation very satisfactory.
1950: Surfaced. Distance to target about four miles. Mounted 20MM, two 30 cal. machine guns, installed only remaining good gun sight on 3" at pointer's position and lashed a pair of 7 x 50 binoculars to trainer's telescope bracket. (The regular gun sights having flooded out a week ago).
2021: Began closing target.
2042: Abeam of steamer. Lat: 06-33-00 S, Long: 112-31-00 E. Range about 250 yards, backed to kill speed and opened fire with all guns, concentrating first on deck house to place radio out of commission. Then raked targets from bow to stern.
2059: Steamer on fire and settling with barge drifting up on starboard quarter, maneuvered out of possible trouble.
2108: Resumed fire on barge with 3" and 20MM. Range, 200 - 250 yds.
2111: Ceased firing. Barge down by bow and settling, retired on course 300 T, at four engine speed.
2120: Steamer sank.
2215: Propulsion on two generators.
2335: Course 000 T, one generator.

page 5.

114

1200: Latitude: 6-28-00 S. Longitude: 112-38-00 E.
Miles steamed: 136.9 Fuel used: 1000.

Jan 13, 1943: Thirteenth day.
Underway on surface. North west Surabaya.
0115: Course 090 T. Weather very much overcast with frequent rain
squalls.
0557: Submerged. No star fix.
0835: Obtained vague fix on Bawean Island.
0837: Sighted small submarine, hull down bearing 208 T. GRENADIER
position: Lat: 06-15-00 S. Long: 112-51-30 E. Clearing lines appeared
to be rigged with cutters, small gun, forward. Submarine's course 085
T. (If his gun was forward) Looked to be similar to Dutch O 9-11 boats,
possibly salvaged by Japs. Started approach, angle on bow about 65
degrees port, range about 7000 yards.
0845: Submarine had disappeared. Continued on in hopes it would reappear, but was disappointed.
0921: Came to course 090 T, and resumed patrol. Visibility during day
ranging from 200 yards to 5 miles.
1939: Surfaced. Obtained star fix. Began patrol of N.E. approaches
Surabaya.
1200: Latitude: 6-16-00 S. Longitude: 112-56-00 E.
Miles steamed: 123.3 Fuel used: 720.

Jan 14, 1943: Fourteenth day.
Underway on surface N.E. of Surabaya.
0547: Submerged, having obtained stars for position.
0552: Course 221 for entrance buoy to Surabaya.
1600: Course 080.
1928: Surfaced.
2128: Received C.T.F. 51 serial 37, directing GRENADIER proceed Balikpapan when productiveness of present area exhausted. Decided that area
had been quite well covered during past five days and having seen nothing
of shipping for two days believed it was being routed south of Madura
Island. Another day off Surabaya was one less off Mangkalihat, also
upon our return to Surabaya area perhaps weather conditions would be
better. Had obtained but three star fixes during past five days, fixes
on Bawean Island were poor at best where same could be seen. Java and
Madura could not be seen due to distance and atmospheric conditions and
still stay out of trouble presented by the mine field.
2200: Few stars out - obtained fix.
2245: Course 068: clearing Surabaya area.
1200: Latitude: 6-21-30 S Longitude: 113-02-30 E.
Miles steamed: 133.2 Fuel used: 800.

Jan 15, 1943: Fifteenth day.
Underway on surface - Surabaya Makassar line.
0528: Course 090.
0557: Submerged.
1816: Surfaced.
2254: Cleared GRENADIER serial TWO to C.T.F. 51.
2305: Course 040.

page 6.

1200: Latitude: 5-40-00 S. Longitude: 115-40-30 E.
Miles steamed: 181.2 Fuel used: 1385.

Jan 16, 1943: Sixteenth day.
Underway on surface enroute Balikpapan.
0555: Sky being about fifty percent cloudy submerged.
1835: Surfaced.
2000: Course 350.
1200: Latitude: 4-13-00 S. Longitude: 118-11-00 E.
Miles steamed: 182.3 Fuel used: 1320.

Jan 17, 1943: Seventeenth day.
Underway on surface, enroute Balikpapan.
0202: Course 315.
0538: Submerged.
1305: Course 300 T.
1847: Surfaced on north east approaches to Balikpapan.
2250: Course 237 T, to reach position on Balikpapan - Aru Bank line.
1200: Latitude: 1-21-00 S. Longitude: 117-23-00 E.
Miles steamed: 148.1 Fuel used: 900.

Jan 18, 1943: Eighteenth day.
Underway on surface patrolling approaches to Balikpapan.
0531: Submerged on Balikpapan - Aru Bank line.
1910: Surfaced.
2000: Sighted ship bearing 344 T, distance about 5-6 miles.it having
cleared Balikpapan, was on course about 070 T. GRENADIER position:
Lat: 01-17-00 S. Long: 117-08-30 E. Began paralleling ship to determine
course and speed.
2100: Target course 070 T, speed 10.2 knots, range about 5 miles.
Moonlight too bright for surface attack and visibility insufficient for
submerged attack. Decided to keep ahead of target and make a submerged
attack at dawn.
2230: Sighted two ships bearing 005 T, distance about six miles, one
of which appeared to be a destroyer apparently headed for Balikpapan.
Did not attempt to close them having decided it best to remain with first
ship, make attack and return to Balikpapan, attacking latter two upon
their exit from that port. GRENADIER position at this time: Lat:
1-05-00 S, Long: 117-31-30 E.
1200: Latitude: 1-29-00 S. Longitude: 116-55-00 E.
Miles steamed: 138.8 Fuel used: 795.

Jan 19, 1943: Ninteenth day.
Underway on surface tracking ship out of Balikpapan.
0124: Maru changed course to northward.
0200: Rounded mouth of Koetei River ahead of Maru, checking new course.
0245: Increased speed to get ahead of Maru for daylight attack having
established course as 008 T, also had to get across a 6 1/2 fathom spot
prior to diving.
0537: Submerged, target should be in sight about 0630:
0758: Surfaced - No target in sight, having determined that the Maru
did one of two things either changed to the left going much closer to

page 7.

116

the beach or had changed course for Mangkalihat subsequent to the time of GRENADIER having to increase speed. Earliest time arrival of south west point of Mangkalihat for the Maru would be well after 1400 by direct route. Also believed Maru to have been only ship in Balikpapan, besides two spotted the night before so the best thing to do would be to patrol off Mangkalihat until dark then return to Balikpapan as it would probably be two days before the above two ships would depart. Set course 055 T. for Mangkalihat.

1300: Submerged 4 miles south of Tg. Labaeon Bini, patrolling 070 - 250 line.

1533: Sighted ship bearing 081 T, distance about 11 miles angle on bow about 65 starboard. GRENADIER position: Lat: 00-47-00 N. Long: 118-53-30 E. Came to normal approach course at full speed which speed was maintained except for looks about every 10 minutes, until the approach was discontinued. At beginning of approach could see but masts and top of stack from periscope depth of 50 feet, however had hopes target would zig right and get into a favorable position.

1620: Sighted one mast and smoke from a second ship some distance off the port bow of the Maru then under approach, at first thought it to be original ship we were searching for, but as mast grew smaller came to obvious conclusion that GRENADIER had seen a two ship convoy and was in the wrong spot for a successful attack.

1627: With angle on bow of 105 starboard, range 9200 yards broke off attack. Had established base course of Maru as 215 T, speed 15 knots. Ship seen was similar to the Okitu Maru.

1720: Maru disappeared on bearing 194 T. Remained in vicinity for two reasons. The Maru sighted last night, by following the coast should be approaching Mangkalihat about 1700-1800, there still remained a chance of an attack. Second, if the convoy of this afternoon was stopping at Balikpapan, would be off there tomorrow anyway, and with speed available plus a needed battery charge could hardly overtake the ships and gain position for an attack.

1818: Surfaced. Nothing in sight but the coast of Borneo. Set course for Balikpapan 215T, at 13.8 knots. There should be four ships in Balikpapan by tomorrow.

1200: Latitude: 00-35-00 N. Longitude: 118-36-00 E.
Miles steamed: 238.4 Fuel used: 2100.

Jan 20, 1943: Twentieth day.
Underway on surface, proceeding to Balikpapan.

0445: Course 249 T.

0546: Submerged. No fix. Changed course to 180. From sounding by lead, believed GRENADIER to be north of line taken by ships leaving Balikpapan, that is 070 T, line from lighthouse position and that a N.E. set had been in effect.

1843: Surfaced.

1950: Having obtained star fix, changed course to 000, to get back on Balikpapan line by 2300. By plot a 12 knot ship could be there at the same time.

2251: Course 250 T.

1200: Latitude: 1-16-00 S. Longitude: 117-25-00 E.
Miles steamed: 172.7 Fuel used: 1235.

page 8.

Jan 21, 1943: Twenty first day
Underway on surface. Patrolling N.E. approaches to Balikpapan.
0244: Course 225 T.
0535: Submerged. No fix.
0615: Course 250 T. Various courses during day patrolling Aru Bank -
Balikpapan line.
1537: Sighted smoke in harbor.
1927: Surfaced.
1932: Observed signal station and a ship in the harbor signaling with
light. Began patrol of N.E. approach to Balikpapan. Assumed ships
leaving to north would depart at night and to south would depart by
morning.
2310: Sighted large circular buoy, about three feet in diameter, with
flag mounted on twelve foot pole. Lat: 1-14-00 S, Long: 117-11-30 E.
1200: Latitude: 1-27-00 S. Longitude: 117-54-00 E.
Miles steamed: 124.3 Fuel used: 530.

Jan 22, 1943: Twenty second day.
Underway on surface, patrolling N.E. approaches to Balikpapan.
0531: No fix possible took sounding with lead line; there was enough
water to get under.
0543: Submerged.
0700: Sighted smoke in harbor.
0706: Sighted mast of ship bearing 335 T, Thought to be entering
harbor from north east.
0718: Heard pinging on sound, ship previously sighted was patrol
vessel and following coast to west and south of harbor.
0725: Pinging from two sources.
0748: Course 130 T. to put stern to patrol vessels, and await development.
0755: Sighted plane bearing 250 T. headed east. Could not identify
type because of poor visibility and range, however appeared to be a
rather large monoplane, blunt nose.
0908: Course 235.
0910: Sighted ship bearing 326 T, GRENADIER In Lat: 1-26-30 S, Long:
116-56-00E. distance about 7 miles with large port angle on bow.
Attempted to close target but could not, even at full speed between
looks. This AK followed about the ten fathom curve out of Balikpapan,
the closest GRENADIER came to target was about 10,000 yards. AK was
escorted by small patrol vessel about sub chaser size.
1005: Broke off attack when a cluster of booms and masts was observed
bearing 008 T, and no chance remained to attack the AK, angle on bow
then about 135 port, his speed about 12 knots. Good setup on TDC could
not be obtained because of targets following curved coast. GRENADIER'S
position: Lat: 1-29-00 S, Long: 116-52-00 E.
1029: Having decided that the targets to the north would not follow
coast changed course to northward.
1032: Began approach, range about 14000 yards.
1044: Two AK's about 7000 tons each.
1046: Two escorts took station, one a patrol vessel on port quarter
of second AK, the other a destroyer, TOMOZURU class, took station on
port bow of leading AK, later shifted to starboard bow of leading AK,
about 800 yards ahead.

page 9.

1054: Observed leading AK to be towing second AK.

11-31-20: Began firing torpedoes at leading AK. Destroyer increased speed and began changing his course to port shortly after first torpedo was fired.

11-32-02: Began firing torpedoes at second AK. Had flooded negative between fourth and fifth torpedoes as depth was decreasing. A few seconds after fifth torpedo was fired, periscope went under. While still unable to see, heard one explosion, followed by two more explosions. Upon regaining periscope depth took a quick look around; the patrol vessel was coming in on the starboard bow, then about 2000 yards away. As periscope went by second AK saw smoke coming out of her number one hold. Saw no smoke from first AK when periscope swung by. Observed destroyer was then about 1500 yards on our port bow and coming in fast. Went to 120 feet, rigged for silent running. Believe first explosion to be a hit with large head on leading AK, as it was a little louder than the other two explosions, and that the second AK was hit by two small heads. All five torpedoes were heard to run normally. While but three explosions were heard, only one torpedo was heard to keep running subsequent to the explosions.

1136 to 1148: Ten depth charges, no apparent damage, however the general impression was that they had a more metallic crack to them than any heard heretofore.

1315: Both destroyer and patrol vessel were still pinging and circling area but seemed to have opened out during the past half hour or so, Came to periscope depth. There appeared to be oil on the surface. Sighted both the patrol vessel and DD about 7000 yards away, the first toward the beach, the other to north east of GRENADIER. Sighted large column of heavy black smoke bearing 329 T, south of the harbor. Restored normal running conditions, steering various courses as DD and patrol vessel conducted search, DD running circles around GRENADIER, while the patrol vessel remained in the vicinity of the smoke sighted near the beach. In mid afternoon patrol vessel proceeded toward entrance but later came back and continued pinging.

2045: Surfaced.

2048: Four engines for propulsion.

2110: Sighted DD and patrol vessel bearing 235 T, distance about 4 miles. Changed course to 090 T. GRENADIER position: Lat: 1-38-00 S Long: 117-02-00 E.

2240: Reduced speed to two engines and started battery charge. Decided that another day's patrol off Balikpapan would produce no results and that the time could be more profitably spent off Mangkalihat. Would have left Balikpapan night of 23rd at latest in any event. Set course for Mangkalihat.

1200: Latitude: 01-27-30 S. Longitude: 116-51-00 E.
Miles steamed: 167.1 Fuel used: 1135.

page 10.

Jan 23, 1943: Twenty third day.
Underway on surface, enroute Mangkalihat.
1259: Submerged twenty-five miles south of Tg. Paeloe Setebah.
1847: Surfaced. Established patrol 035 - 215 about 6 miles off coast
of Borneo. Mangkalihat as northern limit.
1200: Latitude: 00-13-00 N. Longitude: 118-37-00 E.
Miles steamed: 217.6 Fuel used: 1615.

Jan 24, 1943: Twenty fourth day.
Underway on surface, patrolling trade routes in vicinity of Tg. Maukali-
hat, Borneo.
0551: Submerged.
1908: Surfaced.
1200: Latitude: 00-48-00 N. Longitude: 118-59-30 E.
Miles Steamed: 96.3 Fuel used: 445.

Jan 25, 1943: Twenty fifth day.
Underway on surface patrolling trade routes in vicinity of Tg. Mankali-
hat, Borneo.
0531: Submerged. Set course to close beach and search coast for possible
grounded steamer.
1431: Having searched coast between Mangkalihat Light and a point about
12 miles south west from about a mile and a half off the beach with
negative results went back out to trade route.
1710: Back on possible trade route. Set course 635T.
1853: Surfaced.
1200: Latitude: 00-55-00 N. Longitude: 118-58-00 E.
Miles steamed: 83.6 Fuel used: 340.

Jan 26, 1943: Twenty sixth day.
Underway on surface. Patrolling trade routes in vicinity of Tg.Mangkali-
hat, Borneo.
0301: Carbon arc search light opened up direct on GRENADIER bridge,
relative bearing 330. Light coming from vessel in haze along darkened
coast, distance to light about two miles. GRENADIER position:
Lat: 01-02-00 N, Long: 119-03-00 E. Submerged. Considerable pinging was
heard.
0425 : Pinging had not been heard for about a half hour, so came to
periscope depth. Sighted small patrol vessel abaft the starboard beam,
bearing 236 T, distance about 1500 yards.
0428: Patrol vessel began pinging again and headed toward beach.
Until 1645, patrol vessel continued searching, pinging constantly.
Vessel was too small to attack with torpedo fire.
1853: Surfaced and set course for Makassar.
1200: Latitude: 00-50-30 N. Longitude: 119-12-00 E.
Miles steamed: 113.6 Fuel used: 505.

page 11.

Jan 27, 1943: Twenty seventh day.
Underway on surface enroute approaches to Makassar.
0536: Submerged. Patrolling along west coast Celebes.
1846: Surfaced. Intermittent rain squalls during night.
1200: Latitude: 01-15-30 S. Longitude: 119-04-05 E.
Miles steamed: 156.8 Fuel used: 1180.

Jan 28, 1943: Twenty eighth day.
Underway on surface, enroute northern approach to Makassar.
0530: Submerged. No star fix, could see the coast, but unable to
identify peaks due to cloud formations.
0618: Identified light house on Pt: Mandar, distance about seven miles.
1905: Surfaced. Had experienced rather strong westerly current during
day.
1200: Latitude: 03-40-00 S. Longitude: 118-45-30 E.
Miles steamed: 179.2 Fuel used: 1470.

Jan 29, 1943: Twenty ninth day.
Underway on surface enroute northern approaches to Makassar. Many
Praus were sighted during the night necessitating numerous course changes
to avoid disclosing GRENADIER'S presence.
0531: Submerged within sight of coast but without star fix. However
close on the northern approach to Makassar, about five miles off the
beach. Rain and clouds made exact location impossible. The numerous
peaks many of which were similar could not be identified due to incomp-
leteness of charts.
1855: Surfaced. Still overcast, frequent rain squalls.
1200: Latitude: 04-13-00 S. Longitude: 119-28-00 E.
Miles steamed: 128.7 Fuel used: 400.

Jan 30, 1943: Thirtieth day.
Underway on surface patrolling northern approach to Makassar.
0532: Submerged. Position about same as yesterday. Rain and clouds
still prevail. Established same patrol as yesterday, that is squaring
the circle in half hour legs.
1223: Weather clearing somewhat, set course 160 to close entrance
and locate beacon if still existent.
1400: Rain to south, had not sighted beacon.
1423: Course 045 T, having become completely enclosed by heavy rain,
visibility almost zero. The reef would not be too far to the south.
Current today has been south west.
1852: Surfaced. Obtained first star fix since 27th. Set course for
western approach to Makassar.
1200: Latitude: 04-12-00 S. Longitude: 119-29-00 E.
Miles steamed: 135.9 Fuel used: 590.

page 12.

Jan 31, 1943: Thirty first day.
Underway on surface enroute western approach to Makassar.
0228: Kapoposang Island bearing 110 T, distance about ten miles.
0530: Sighted Pu Lanyukang Island bearing 082 T.
0536: Submerged. Established patrol off western approach to Makassar about five miles west of Pu Lanyukang.
1217: Sighted mast bearing 106 T, distance about 7 miles. GRENADIER'S position: Latitude: 04-59-00 S, Longitude: 119-01-00 E.
1225: Vessel started out northern of the two approaches. Started approach.
1300: Fired three torpedoes, negative results. First torpedo ahead about 20 yards. Could not see wakes of other two, however they ran normally.
1306-8: Three depth charges, target then heading back into channel and did not reappear.
1855: Surfaced. Set course for south west approach to Makassar. Had intended to spend another day here but having had GRENADIER's presence disclosed decided there was no use in remaining another day in the vicinity.
1200: Latitude: 05-00-00 S. Longitude: 119-01-00 E.
Miles steamed: 136.3 Fuel used: 565.

Feb 1, 1943: Thirty second day.
Underway on surface proceeding to southwest approach to Makassar.
0052: Received CTF 51 serial 76, directing GRENADIER conduct patrol off Makassar so as to arrive vicinity Saleiar strait about February 2, 1943, thence to vicinity Pulassi Island, thence to Bali Strait departing latter place dark February 12, 1943.
0535: Submerged for patrol off south west approach to Makassar about five miles off reef.
1852: Surfaced. Set course for Saleier Strait.
1200: Latitude: 05-35-30 S. Longitude: 118-59-00 E.
Miles steamed: 127.6 Fuel used: 750.

Feb 2, 1943: Thirty third day.
Underway on surface proceeding to station at Saleier Strait.
0522: Submerged in Saleier Strait. Rain and reduced visibility had prevented getting through strait prior to diving. Proceeded through strait submerged. Experienced rather strong current to westward.
1200: Patrolling in an area two miles east and west, by five miles north and south, the center of area bearing 072 distance six miles from Saleier light.
1922: Surfaced. Established patrol on approaches to Saleier Strait.
1200: Latitude: 05-42-30 S. Longitude: 120-35-00 E.
Miles steamed: 114.9 Fuel used: 700.

Feb 3, 1943: Thirty fourth day.
Underway on surface patrolling eastern approaches to Saleier Strait.
0529: Submerged, established patrol in same rectangle as yesterday.
1905: Surfaced. Established patrol on eastern approaches to Saleier Strait. Rain squalls during day and night.
1200: Latitude: 05-41-00 S. Longitude: 120-37-00 E.
Miles steamed: 87.2 Fuel used:360.

page 13.

Feb 4, 1943: Thirty fifth day.
Underway on surface patrolling, eastern approaches to Saleier Strait.
Visibility poor because of rain squalls.
0522: Submerged. Established patrol in same area as yesterday.
1900: Surfaced. Have sighted nothing in this area during the past
three days except a few sail boats. Many lights appear on the island
at night. Set course for area in vicinity of Pulassi Island.
1200: Latitude: 05-42-00 S Longitude: 120-36-00 E.
Miles steamed: 96.6 Fuel used: 470.

Feb 5, 1943: Thirty sixth day.
Underway on surface, changing station from Saleier Strait to vicinity of
Pulassi Island.
0527: Submerged. Established patrol south of Pulassi Island Lat: 06-
49-00 S., between longitude 120-25-00 E and 120-31-00 E.
1902: Surfaced. Conducted patrol in same latitude extending the longitude about a mile each direction.
1200: Latitude: 6-49-00 S. Longitude: 120-28-00 E.
Miles steamed: 111.2 Fuel used: 580.

Feb 6, 1943: Thirty seventh day
Underway on surface patrolling area in vicinity to Pulassi Island.
0520: Submerged. Patrolling same line as yesterday.
1906: Surfaced Conducted same patrol as last night.
1200: Latitude: 6-47-00 S Longitude: 120-28-00 E.
Miles steamed: 94.0 Fuel used: 459.

Feb 7, 1943: Thirty eighth day.
Underway on surface patrolling area in vicinity of Pulassi Island.
0528: Submerged. Established same patrol as past two days.
1901: Surfaced. Have sighted nothing but two sail boats and a few
lights on the beach during the past three days.
1904: Course 249 T, on two generators. Patrolling the line between
Pulassi Island and Maria Reigersbergen banks prior to turning off for
tomorrow's patrol west of Sangeaing Island, N.W. of Sape Strait.
1200: Latitude: 06-48-00 S. Longitude: 120-25-00 E.
Miles steamed: 134 Fuel used: 910.

Feb 8, 1943: Thirty ninth day.
Enroute patrol area west of Sangeaing Island N.W. Sape Strait.
0526: Submerged about seven miles west of Sangeaing, patrolling
approaches to Sape Strait.
1900: Surfaced. Set course for possible convoy route in about lat:
7-45-00 S, thence toward vicinity of Maria Reigersbergen Banks.
1200: Latitude: 8-12-30 S. Longitude: 118-44-05 E.
Miles steamed: 154.3 Fuel used: 1345

Feb 9, 1943: Fortieth day.
On surface patrolling route east of Maria Reigersbergen Bank, course
265 T,
0544: Submerged. South east of Maria Reigersbergen Bank.
1840: Surfaced. Proceeded to station at northern entrance to Bali
Strait. Strong wind and frequent driving rain squalls experienced
during the night.

page 14.

1200: Latitude: 07-51-00 S. Longitude: 117-25-00 E.
Miles steamed: 174.2 Fuel used: 1630.

Feb 10, 1943: Forty first day.
Enroute station at northern entrance Bali Strait. Rain and high wind
continuing.
0603: Submerged. Patrolling area averaging 3 1/2 miles from Duiven
Light, north entrance Bali Strait.
1924: Surfaced. Patrolling north south line 5 - 7 miles east of Java.
Wind and frequent rain squalls during night.
1200: Latitude: 8-03-00 S. Longitude: 114-30-30 E.
Miles steamed: 148.1 Fuel used: 1470.

Feb 11, 1943: Forty second day.
Patrolling north south line 5 - 7 miles east of Java.
0554: Submerged, patrolling in same area as yesterday.
1924: Surfaced. Patrolling north south line east of Java. More rain
and wind during night.
1200: Latitude: 8-00-00 S. Longitude: 114-31-00 E.
Miles steamed: 97.2 Fuel used: 430.

Feb 12, 1943: Forty third day.
Patrolling north south line 5 - 7 miles east of Java.
0545: Submerged. Patrolling same area as yesterday.
1901: Surfaced. Began return trip to Fremantle W.A. Visibility today
has been fair to bad due to rain squalls.
1200: Latitude: 8-02-00 S Longitude: 114-29-00 E.
Miles steamed: 123.1 Fuel used: 1090.

Feb 13, 1943: Forty fourth day.
Underway on surface enroute Fremantle, W.A.
0245: Completed transit Lombok Strait set course 229 T for station
in accordance with C.T.F. serial 98. Heavy weather overcast and rains
made detection highly improbably if remained on surface. Could make but
about eight and a half knots and in order to gain desired station could
not submerge and still make the required distance. Able to make about
ten and a half knots by mid-afternoon.
1200: Latitude: 09-52-30 S Longitude: 114-28-00 E.
Miles steamed: 251.4 Fuel used: 3310.

Feb 14, 1943: Forty fifth day.
Underway on surface enroute to station in Lat: 11-29-30 S, Long: 112-
34-30 E.
0545: On station by D.R., have had no fix since leaving Lombok, visibility poor.
0633: Submerged. Patrolling station on 140 - 320 line one point five
miles each side of Lat: 11-29-30,SLong: 112-34-30 E. Surfaced.
Set course for Exmouth Gulf.

page 15.

Feb 15, 1943: Forty sixth day.

Underway on surface enroute Exmouth Gulf, W.A.
1200: Latitude: 14-40-00 S. Longitude: 113-19-00 E.
Miles steamed: 275.5 Fuel used: 2705.

Feb 16, 1943: Forty seventh day.
Underway on surface enroute Exmouth Gulf, W.A.
0607: Submerged.
0625: Surfaced.
1700: Started six hour battery discharge.
2325: Secured battery discharge.
1200: Latitude: 19-08-30 S. Longitude: 113-46-00 E.
Miles steamed: 249.2 Fuel used: 1685.

Feb 17, 1943: Forty eighth day.
Underway on surface enroute Exmouth Gulf, W.A.
0634: Sighted one P.B.Y. bearing 145 T, distance 7 miles.
0715: Sighted HMS TRUSTY, bearing 195 T, distance 7 miles.
0942: Moored starboard side to fuel oil barge Exmouth Gulf, W.A.
1000: Began transferring fuel oil to barge.
1205: Ceased transfer of fuel having delivered 20,795 gallons, diesel
fuel oil to barge.
1215: Underway from alongside barge enroute Fremantle, W.A.
1550: Sighted P.B.Y. bearing 280 T, distance 7 miles.
1639: Submerged for trim and test of pumps at 200 feet.
1714: Surfaced.
1200: Latitude: 22-11-00 S. Longitude: 114-07-00 E.
         (Fuel oil barge, Exmouth Gulf, W.A.).
Miles steamed: 273.5 Fuel used: 3450.

Feb 18, 1943. Forty ninth day.
Underway on surface enroute Fremantle, W.A., via bombing restriction
lane.
1200: Latitude: 24-57-00 S Longitude: 112-11-30 E.
Miles steamed: 248.9 Fuel used: 3240.

February 19, 1943: Fiftieth day.
Underway on surface enroute Fremantle, W.A., via bombing restriction
lane.
1200: Latitude: 29-15-00 S Longitude: 113-00-00 E.
Miles steamed: 314.3 Fuel used: 4130.

February 20, 1943: Fifty first day.
Underway on surface enroute Fremantle, W.A. via bombing restriction
lane.
0126: Sighted Rottnest Island light bearing 136 T, distance 25 miles.
0328: Met at rendezvous by U.S.S. WHIPPORWILL and escorted into
Fremantle Harbor.

page 16.

WEATHER

Typical weather as stated in the pilot for the areas covered during this patrol. Frequent rain squalls, wind, and poor visibility the majority of the time.

TIDAL INFORMATION

In general an eastern set prevailed, for Java sea averaging 110 T, drift about one knot. Off Balikpapan set north east about .7 knot. Makassar Strait set contrary to pilot, averaging about 020 T, drift about .5 knot.

From east of Saleier Strait current set averages 115, drift about .8 knot. South of Pulassi average set 085, drift, about 1.1 knot. In the vicinity of 8 degrees south latitude between Sape Strait and Lombok strait, the set is easterly averaging a little over one knot.

Around northern entrance to Bali Strait current averages about 030 T, drift about .5 knot.

NAVIGATIONAL AIDS:

No navigational aids were observed to be lighted.

SHIPS SIGHTED:

TIME	DATE	POSIT	DESCRIPTION	COURSE	SPEED
0620	1/10	06-16-30 S 112-40-30 E	Sixty ton schooner. Two masts, two jibs. Flying Jap flag.	350	6--7
1922	1/10	06-11-30 S 113-00-00 E	Corvette	350	10-12
1512	1/11	06-23-00 S 113-00-00 E	Steamer similar to ROKKO MARU of 3,000 tons, two masts, one funnel, estimated draft 15 feet.	260	8.3
1056	1/12	06-34-00 S 112-55-00 E	750 ton steamer; similar to USS ALGORMA, except bow was higher; only one mast forward, engines and bridge located aft. Barge was of ship type construction mast and booms amidships, pilot house aft. Est. tonnage 500.	280	3.3
0837	1/15	06-18-30 S 112-50-00 E	Small submarine similar to Dutch O 9-11, heavy clearing lines with cutters rigged along them.	085	?
2005	1/18	01-12-00 S 117-07-00 E	Probably of 4000 or 5000 tons, stack amidships, two masts.	070	10.2
2230	1/18	01-02-00 S 117-32-00 E	Two ships.Could make out no outline sufficient for description	About 250	?
1533	1/19	00-45-30 N 119-04-00 E	Maru similar to OKITU MARU, camouflaged dark and light grays. Mast, goal posts, bridge, funnel, cabins, goal posts & mast, cruiser stern.	Base 215	15
1620	1/19		Could see only mast and smoke from stack assumed to be escort for above ship.	215 Assumed	15
0910	1/22	01-22-30 S 116-50-00 E	Similar to TONE MARU	Coast line	10-12
0910	1/22	01-22-30 S 116-50-00 E	Small escort vessel, possibly a sub chaser converted from cabin cruiser.	Coast line	10-12

page 12.

SHIPS SIGHTED. (CONT'D)

TIME	DATE	POSIT	DESCRIPTION	COURSE	SPEED
1005	1/22	01-22-00 S 116-52-30 E	AK of Yamasimo class towing an AK of the Tatutako class. First AK semi loaded, second in ballast. Both had guns mounted fore and aft of about 5", located on raised platform. DD of the Tomozuru class and a patrol vessel with one mast forward and large crow's nest	194	6.8
0300	1/26	01-03-00 N 119-01-00 E	Small patrol vessel.	?	?
1217	1/31	05-00-30 S 119-07-30 E	Small steamer, one mast fwd, funnel and bridge about two thirds way aft, one mast aft. Length about 200 ft. Mast height 60 ft. No crow's nest. Mounted gun of about 3" forward and a machine gun on top of pilot house. Estimated tonnage 1000, painted gray. Had high speed screw (Could possibly be a survey vessel of some sort).	311	11.5

AIRCRAFT SIGHTED:

TIME	DATE	GRENADIER POSITION	DESCRIPTION
0641	1/4	21-39-30 S 114-07-00 E	Two PBY on patrol out of Exmouth Gulf
0755	1/22	01-23-00 S 116-55-00 E	Large Monoplane, blunt nose - easterly course out of Balikpapan. Distance and visibility did not permit good identification.
0634	2/17	21-32-00 S 114-06-00 E	One P.B.Y. on patrol out of Exmoth Gulf
1550	2/17	21-45-30 S 113-50-30 E	One P.B.Y. returning to Exmouth from patrol

page 19.

128

ATTACKS

No. 1: Battle surface on sixty ton schooner. Opening range about 1000 yards, closed to 500. Used 3"/50 cal, 20MM and 30 cal. machine guns. Sank schooner, which flew the Japanese merchant flag. Latitude 06-18-30 S, Longitude 112-43-30 E. Target course 100 T.

No. 2:

Location	:	6-24-30 S. 112-54-00 E
Type	:	AK (About 3000 tons.
Number torpedoes fired	:	Two.
Firing interval	:	9 sec.
Point of aim	:	M.O.T. (Stack).
Off set	:	2L, 2R.
Gyro angle	:	353.8, 350.5.
Track angle	:	105 P, 105 P.
Depth setting	:	4', 2'.
Enemy course	:	260.
Enemy speed	:	8.3

No. 3: Night surface attack on 750 ton steamer towing a 500 ton barge. Course 280 in latitude 06-33-00 S, longitude 112-31-00 E. Concentrated first on bridge area to eliminate possible radio report. Then shelled both targets. Had but one telescope sight installed at pointer's position. The 7 x 50 binoculars lashed to trainer's sight bracket did not prove satisfactory, however the luminous ring and luminous dot installed on the open sight facilitated picking up target, trainer further being coached on by pointer. Sank both vessels using 3"/50, 20MM, and 30 cal machine guns. Average range about 250 yards. Sea condition: heavy swell in moderate sea; wind force 5.

No. 4:

		FIRST SHIP		SECOND SHIP
Location (Both)	:	01-28-00 S	:	116-52-00 E
Type	:	AK	:	AK
Number torp. fired	:	3	:	2
Firing interval	:	10 sec	:	10 sec
Firing range	:	1930	:	1870
Point of aim	:	M.O.T.	:	M.O.T.
Offset	:	3L, 0, 3R.	:	3L, 0.
Gyro Angle	:	003-45, 003, 002	:	010, 009.
Track angle	:	99.5P, 98P, 96P.	:	93P, 91P.
Depth setting	:	0 0 0	:	0 0
Enemy course	:	194	:	194
Enemy speed	:	5.7	:	5.7

page 20

No. 5:

Location	:	Lat: 04-58-00 S Long: 119-01-00 E.
Type	:	Steamer of about 1000 tons.
Number torp. fired	:	3
Firing interval	:	11, 13 sec.
Firing range	:	690, 680, 680.
Point of aim	:	Stack.
Off set	:	4L, 0, 4R.
Gyro angle	:	00-15, 354, 347-15.
Track angle	:	120P, 122P, 124P.
Depth setting	:	0 0 0
Enemy course	:	311
Enemy speed	:	11.5

ENEMY A/S MEASURES

Anti-submarine measures employed by the enemy consisted of listening while stopped, and pinging while underway. The employment of depth charges by the small Maru on January 31, could have been for no other purpose than that of embarrassment as the vessel was about 1000 yards away when the charges were dropped.

The A/S measures off the northern entrance of Surabaya were nil, only one Corvette having been sighted. Strongest A/S measures found to be off Balikpapan.

A/S vessels were hampered in their search by poor sound conditions in shallow water.

page 21.

MAJOR DEFECTS EXPERIENCED

Fathometer grounded out on January 7, 1943. Unable effect repair at sea.

During battle surface January 10, 1943, #1 main engine was flooded because of opening outboard exaust valve too soon. Nozzle drains were closed. No damage resulted and water was removed by jacking over by hand. However inspection of lower crank case revealed a nut and stud bolt in the after strainer, inspection of lower pistons revealed the nut and stud to be from #9 unit. This piston removed and replaced with spare. Insert stud had broken off flush in crown of piston, the threads on both stud and nut were completely stripped, piston in otherwise good condition.

January 11, 1943 during routine inspection crankcase #4 M.E. discovered loose pieces of bearing metal under # 6 upper connecting rod bearing. About 40% of the bearing metal for the lower half had flaked off while but about 2% of the upper half of the bearing metal was gone. The connecting rod journal was in good condition. No evidence of excessive heating of bearing was apparent. Both upper and lower bearings were replaced from spares.

During routine inspection of #3 M.E. on January 18, 1943, discovered a broken main bearing nut lying in upper crank case beneath #1 upper crank A section approximately equal to one-sixth of the nut was sheared out; this piece being later found under the timing chain. Nut had came from the bottom end of #1 upper main bearing on the outboard side of the engine. A broken cotter pin from this unit was found lying in the forward end of the lower crank case. Apparently this casualty developed as follows: Cotter pin carried away allowing nut to back off and fall to the after end of recess. Crank arm of #1 upper crank struck nut shearing out section described above.
Further inspection revealed that the lubricating oil supply line to #1 upper main bearing was broken in two at bearing fitting. The break probably being due to the vibration set up in the engine when the crank arm struck the nut. Renewed #1 main bearing bolt complete, repaired damaged lubricating oil line. Engine out of commission twelve hours.

TORPEDO GYROS: During routine checks of torpedoes the following defects were discovered: January 20, 1943: Torpedo #93719. The gyro was found to stick at one point when rotated in its outer gimbal ring. The gyro was then pulled from its pot disclosing much rust formation in the top ball bearing and its race. No apparent clearance existed between the outer and inner gimbals, no doubt rust taking up the space. This torpedo had been neither subjected to a flooded tube nor air pressure of any description, other than atmospheric, since receipt on board. Various conclusions may be drawn as to the actual cause of this condition, the most likely being moisture in the air used for the deck run or moisture in air used to blow off excess oil subsequent to deck run. Gyros were then removed from all torpedoes and carefully inspected, results as follows: Torpedo #17913: a 1/2" piece of three strand string was found in the top ball bearing. Torpedo #17946: lower bearing post studs hit the after inner gimbal bearing cap as inner gimbal turned in outer. This had not previously been apparent while gyro was still in the pot. The cap had the appearance of previous filing to give clearance.

Torpedo #15774; evidence of ah imperfect ball in #1 outer gimbal bearing. When rotated the inner gimbal stopped at the same place each time it was rotated, not with a free swinging motion as would be normal, but a definite stop at this point accompanied by a slight chattering in the bearing. Torpedo routine had been accomplished every four days prior to discovering the defect in #13719, at which time all gyros were pulled for minute examination.

February 15, 1943: Number 5 unit crankpin bearing, #4 M.E., sustained a casualty similar to that of #6 unit on January 11, 1943. Lower half badly chipped, upper half and journal in good condition. Replaced this bearing with a spare. Both #4 and #6 units were in good condition.

Roots Connersville L.P. air compressor: Complete disassembly at sea revealed a severe crack in the gear and head plate around the driving shaft bearing housing. This crack is apparently the cause underlying the faulty and noisy operation of this blower during the past year.

REMARKS

The habitability during the patrol was very satisfactory; temperature within the ship ranging between 88F and 90F, considering the high injection temperature this is about as good as could be expected. With the exception of six cases of Gonorrhea, which developed after leaving Fremantle, one case of infected jaw and a little seasickness, the health of officers and crew was very good. The Gonorrhea cases will be turned over to the tender for continuation of treatment as found necessary.

Telescopic gunsights that will not flood, while submerged, cannot be too strongly recommended. Not only is it believed that ammunition can be conserved but it is very important to place that first shot, as well as the remainder of shots, where it will do the most good. While the luminous ring and dot installed in the open sights facilitated getting on the target at night, such sights cannot take the place of a good, dry, telescopic gun sight.

The 20MM gun is a very efficient and effective weapon, would like to have at least two mounts, one forward of the bridge in addition to the one now installed on the after bridge. (Cigarette deck).

In general communications were very satisfactory; while on station, 9250 Kc's proved to be the best frequency. The only trouble experienced was in clearing GRENADIER serial ONE through VIXO which station was trying to send press and work GRENADIER at the same time. After five attempts in an hour and a half to clear our seventeen group message, we secured, although VIXO was still asking for repeats on certain groups in between press releases. The following night, GRENADIER serial ONE appeared on VIXO schedule as encoded. At first, when unable to clear message was concerned that a Jap might be asking for these repeats to better cut in our position, no doubt the delay in transmission was a help to them in that respect.

page 23.

132

Sound conditions were from poor to excellent probably the best
being west of Makassar. The JK projector shaft— while serviceable —
is not in alignment and considerable water leakage is experienced via
the glands. In spite of this the tender is to be commended on the
work accomplished from the material at hand, in placing the projector
in a serviceable condition. It is hoped that a new projector
shaft will be available for installation during the current refit.

The loop antenna grounded out the first week, therefore no comment
can be made regarding its use for underwater reception. For shallow
water operation it is considered that far too many confidential and
secret publications are carried by our submarines.

page 24.

133

FC5-6/A16-3   SUBMARINE SQUADRON SIX   (6/Mc)
Serial # 069
                                        U.S.S. TAUTOG, Flagship,
C-O-N-F-I-D-E-N-T-I-A-L   February 27, 1943.

FIRST ENDORSEMENT to
C.O. GRENADIER ltr.
SS210/A16-3 Serial
02 of 2-20-43.

From: The Commander Submarine Squadron SIX.
To :   The Commander Task Force FIFTY-ONE.

Subject: U.S.S. GRENADIER - Fifth War Patrol - Comment on.

     1.   The GRENADIER's fifth war patrol covered a period
of fifty-one days of which thirty-seven were spent north of the Malay
Barrier; this was the GRENADIER's first patrol under her present
Commanding Officer.

     2.   The performance of material with the exception of
the casualty to #3 main engine is considered excellent. Two main
engines are being completely overhauled during the current refit.
period by the Relief Crews with a complete replacement of liners,
injectors and piston rings of the latest approved design. Extreme
difficulties have been encountered not only in the GRENADIER but in
other submarines as well in making and maintaining the NM sound head
water-tight. It is believed that after recent experiments, a solution
to this problem has been reached by the insertion of a 1/8" special
cut wire inserted rubber gasket. The bridge structure is being altered in accordance with the SILVERSIDES plan. A 20 MM gun in
addition to the one aft is being installed in the forward position.

     3.   Health and habitability were, in general, very good.

     4.   Assigned patrol areas were thoroughly covered by
the GRENADIER; determined attempts were made to develop all contacts
and aggressive attacks were made with torpedoes and gunfire. Results
of torpedo fire were disappointing; out of ten torpedoes fired only
three hits were made and these were not positively confirmed. The
wakes of the torpedoes fired on the attack of January 11 were apparently seen by the target which successfully maneuvered to avoid.
Other misses, it is believed, were due to control errors. Three depth
charge explosions were reported six minutes and eight seconds after
the firing of three torpedoes on the attack of January 31; it appears
likely that these explosions might have been war heads instead of
depth charges. Defects reported in torpedo gyros have been corrected
and steps taken to prevent their repetition. The GRENADIER is credited
with inflicting the following damage on the enemy:

SUNK			DAMAGED	
1 Schooner	60 ton		2 AK's	14000 ton
1 Tug	750 ton			
1 Barge	500 ton			
	1310 ton			

                                        A. R. McCANN.

4 0152

FE24-51/A16-3   SUBMARINES, SOUTHWEST PACIFIC   Ly
Serial 0331   U.S.S. TROUT (SS202) FLAGSHIP

C-O-N-F-I-D-E-N-T-I-A-L   March 3, 1943.

SECOND ENDORSEMENT to
CO GRENADIER Conf. ltr.
SS210/A16-3 Serial 02
of 20 February 1943.

From: The Commander Task Force FIFTY ONE.
To :   The Commander in Chief, U.S. FLEET.
Via :   The Commander Southwest Pacific Force.

Subject: U.S.S. GRENADIER - Fifth War Patrol - Comment on.

     1.   Forwarded, concurring in the remarks contained in
the first endorsement, except as noted in paragraph 4.

     2.   The GRENADIER operated for a considerable part of
this patrol in relatively shallow water in spite of the handicap
resulting from the failure of the fathometer.

     3.   Although the damage inflicted was below average,
the patrol was marked throughout by a spirit of aggressiveness,
which, with additional experience will produce maximum results
on future patrols.

     4.   While it is possible that hits were obtained in both
freighters of the convoy attacked 22 January, there is no definite
evidence of damage to the leading ship. The GRENADIER is credited
with inflicting the following damage on the enemy:

SUNK		DAMAGED	
1 schooner	60 tons	1 freighter	7,000 tons
1 tug	750 tons		
1 barge	500 tons		
Total	1310 tons		

A.R. McCANN.

DISTRIBUTION
COMINCH   (2)(Via Comsouwespacfor)
VICE OPNAV   (1)("   "   )
CINCLANFLT   (1)
CINCPACFLT   (1)
COMSOUWESPAC   (1)
COMSOUPACFOR   (1)
COMSUBSPAC   (5)
COMSUBSLANT   (2)
COMTASKFOR 42   (2)
COMSUBRON-6   (1)
DIV COMS,RON-6(1)
EACH S/M W.A. (1) (NOT TO BE TAKEN TO SEA-BURN)

SOUTHWEST PACIFIC FORCE

R.S. No. 4 0152

A16-3

March 17, 1943.

Serial 0359

C-O-N-F-I-D-E-N-T-I-A-L

THIRD ENDORSEMENT to
C.O. GRENADIER Conf. ltr.
SS210/A16-3 Serial 02
dated 20 February 1943.

From: The Commander Southwest Pacific Force.
To :   The Commander in Chief, U.S. FLEET.

Subject: U.S.S. GRENADIER - Fifth War Patrol - Report on.

    1.   Forwarded.

J. CARY JONES,
Chief of Staff.

Copy to:
    Vice OPNAV. (1)

UNITED STATES
SUBMARINE LOSSES
WORLD WAR II

Reissued with an Appendix of
Axis Submarine Losses, fully indexed,

by

Naval History Division
Office of the Chief of Naval Operations
Washington: 1963

GRENADIER (SS 210)

Patrolling in Lem Voalan Strait in the northeast Indian Ocean, on her sixth war patrol, GRENADIER under Lt. Cdr. J. A. Fitzgerald met her end on 22 April 1943. The following account of her fate is taken from statements made by her Commanding Officer and five of her men after they had been recovered from Japanese camps.

On the night of 20 April 1943, having had poor hunting for two or three days in Lem Voalan Strait (northwest of Penang on the Malay Peninsula), GRENADIER ventured out ten miles west of that place to see what she could find. She found two ships, but before she could attack, they turned away. Figuring that they would come back to their original course in an hour and a half, Fitzgerald planned an attack to meet them on their course at that time. About 15 minutes before time to dive and prepare for the attack, a plane came in on GRENADIER, and she dived. As she was passing 120 feet, a violent explosion shook the ship, and all lights and power were lost. She was brought to rest on the bottom at about 270 feet. The hull and hatches were leaking badly aft, and a fire in the control cubicle kept the ship without propulsion. A bucket brigade kept the motors dry, and later a 'ury rig pump was called into service to perform the task, while the electricians worked all day to restore propulsion. Several men were prostrated by heat and exertion, but the work went on.

At dusk, GRENADIER surfaced and continued the work of trying to restore herself. Finally, they were able to turn over one shaft very slowly, but everything possible had been done, and no more speed could be expected.

Toward morning what appeared to be a destroyer, but was actually an 1800-ton merchantman, and an escort vessel were seen on the horizon, and a plane was driven away by gunfire. The skipper decided to scuttle the ship then, and it was done, with all hands being taken prisoner by the enemy merchant ship. The statements of the men relate the brutal treatment they received at the hands of the Japanese and how their spirit was kept up by their Commanding Officer. The enemy gained no information from this gallant crew, despite the worst they could inflict, and all but four members of the crew were recovered from prison camps at the close of the war.

J. A. Fitzgerald

GRENADIER's record prior to her loss was six ships sunk, for 40,700 tons, and two ships damaged, for 12,000 tons. Her first patrol, beginning in February 1942, was conducted off the coast of Japan, and GRENADIER sank a freighter. Going to the Formosa shipping lanes for her second patrol, GRENADIER sank a large transport and a freighter. On her third patrol, she sank a large tanker. GRENADIER's fourth patrol was a mining mission in the South China Sea, and she damaged no enemy shipping. On her fifth patrol, this vessel patrolled the Java Sea area, and sank two small freighters and a sampan. In addition she damaged a freighter.

46

U. S. S. GRENADIER (SS 210)

Name	Rate	Name	Rate
ADKINS, Ralph L	EM1	MINTON, Joseph A	QM3
ALBERTSEN, Norman A	TM1	O'BRION, Elwood A	EM1
ANDREWS, David J	TM1	OUILLETTE, Virgil A	F2
BARKER, Lesly L	EM3	PALMER, Robert W	Y1
BARRINGTON, Clyde W	TM3	PIANKA, John K	MoMM1
CLARK, Lynn R	SM1	PIERCE, Miner B	S1
COURTNEY, Thomas R	S2	POSS, Edgar L	RM1
COX, Gordon C	S1	PRICE, Joseph T	F1
CRITCHLOW, John N	LT	QUARTERMAN, Carl O	CQM
CUNNINGHAM, William M. J.	S2	RAE, Thomas J	S1
†DOYLE, Charlie	MoMM1	ROBERTS, Warren E	TM2
EMBRY, Jewell C	MoMM1	ROSKELL, Charles	F2
ERISHMAN, Charles A	CMoMM	RUPP, Albert J	S2
EVANS, Rex R	RM3	RUSSELL, Paul D	F3
EVANS, Robert E	SC3	RUTKOWSKI, Henry W	S1
FITZGERALD, J. A.	LCDR--CO	SAWATZKE, Lyle L	F2
FOURRE, Glen R	EM2	SCHWARTZLY, John F	F1
FULTON, Ben H	EM2	SHAW, Lee C	MoMM2
GARRISON, Randolph J	SC1	SHERRY, Harmon B	LT
†GUICO, Justiniano G	MAtt1	SHOEMAKER, Dean B	TM2
GUNDERSON, John H	S1	SIMPSON, John E	S1
HARTY, K. D.	LT	†SNYDER, George W., Jr	F1
HERBERT, Carlisle W	F2	STAUBER, George F	MM2
HINKSON, Richard J	EM2	TAYLOR, Orville A	FC2
INGRAM, Joe G	F1	TOULON, Alfred J., Jr	LT
JOHNSON, Charles E	EM3	TRIGG, Thomas J	MAtt1
KEEFE, William H	RM2	VER VALIN, Charles H	MoMM2
KEYSOR, Riley H	TM3	WALDEN, John S	GUNNER
KNUTSON, Joseph S	RM1	WESTERFIELD, Charles W	CCStd
LANDRUM, James D	EM2	WHITING, George H	LT--XO
LESKOVSKY, John	TM3	WHITLOCK, Charles H	CEM
LESLIE, Raymond G	MoMM1	WILSON, Charles M	MoMM1
†LINDER, Charles F	MoMM2	WISE, William E	GM2
LOFTUS, Irving C	S1	WITHROW, William C	CTM
McBEATH, John J	PhM1	WITZKE, Bernard W	F1
McCOY, Charles H	S1	YORK, Robert F	EM2
McGOWAN, Dempsey E	F2	ZUCCO, Peter	S1
McINTYRE, Arthur G	LT	ZUFELT, Fred	GM1

† Died in Fukuoka prison camp, Kyushu I., Japan.

47

USS GRENADIER (SS-210) - Statement of Lieutenant Commander
J. A. Fitzgerald, USN, Commanding Officer.

ENCLOSURE (C)
TO SUSS PAC. SER 10349, 21 SEP 45

9 September 1945.

STATEMENT OF COMMANDER FITZGERALD: 6th patrol

    Having been in Lem Valon Strait for two or three days
without seeing any target I decided on the night of 20 April
1943 to go about ten miles to the west of Lem Valon Strait to
see if I could find anything out there. At about 2030 or 2100
the O. O. D. thought he saw smoke, so continued on my westerly
course and later on saw smoke coming from two merchant men.
The moon being full and visibility excellent I decided to go
across the stern of the two ships, get their course and then
get on the down-moon side, ascertain their speed, continue on
and get into position ahead of the column. Due to visibility
conditions, or Jap radar, they found out that I was off their
port quarter. I had just that evening checked my SJ radar at
16,250 yards. At the time the merchant men turned their search-
lights in my general direction, I had not yet obtained radar
range on the ships which were probably 8 or 9 miles away.
Eventually the Japs turned to an easterly course and I got ahead
of their column and submerged to await attack. Just at early
dawn the two ships changed to a southerly course. At about 7
o'clock the ships were out of sight, yet their smoke was still
visible on the horizon. Assuming that in accordance with known
Japanese convoy doctrine at the end of an hour or an hour and
a half the convoy would resume an easterly course, I surfaced
on course 155° which would place me in an attack position in
about one hour and forty-five minutes. About 15 minutes before
arriving in position to dive and be in readiness for attack the
lookout cried out "plane, port quarter". Not wishing to be de-
ceived by having it turn out to be some bird or false alarm,
I turned around and identified the object as a plane myself.
Thereupon I ordered the ship to submerge.

    At 0837 the ship was passing 120 feet when the Executive
Officer said, " we ought to be safe now, as we are between 120
and 130 feet." Almost at once "two express trains collided".
I had previously, at 90 feet, ordered right 15° rudder. The
force of the explosion healed the boat over 10° or 15°. All
lights and power were lost. I continued on down toward the bottom,
at the same time the maneuvering room was attempting to reestablish power. At about 200 feet the word was received,
"fire in maneuvering room". So I set the boat down to the bottom
at 267 feet of water. Immediate success was not obtained in
extinguishing the fire so I ordered the compartment sealed.
After about a half an hour or so later the compartment was
entered using lungs as respirators, and CO2 fire extinguishers.
The fire was in the hull insulating cork, cables, stores and
cleaning rags; which fire had been caused by the power cage
and the overhead of the maneuvering room coming together cutting
the power cables above the control stand. Also due to sparks
coming from the control stand. The maneuvering room induction
valve was so badly warped that the flapper valve had been forced

- 1 -

STATEMENT OF COMMANDER FITZGERALD - continued.
- -

off its seat permitting about a two-inch stream of water to
pour into the control stand. The hard patch above the control
stand was broken loose from the hull proper permitting water
to spray over the electrical equipment of the control stand.
We were unable to protect the electrical equipment from the
water by means of shields due to the overhead connections between
the hull and control stand. As a result all resistances and
cables became saturated with salt water.

After the fire was extinguished a bucket brigade was
formed between the maneuvering room to the forward torpedo room
in order to keep the water level down below the motors. Many
men lost consciousness from heat prostration and physical exertion. Eventually a jury rig was established between the main
battery and a drain pump which then permitted us to secure the
bucket brigade and keep the water level down by means of pump-
ing.

The force of the explosion was centered apparently at
about 30° from the verticle in the vicinity of the manenvering
room after bulkhead. This bulkhead had been forced to the port
side and apparently bent the main shafts. All the frames from
the engine room after bulkhead through to the after bulkhead of
the after torpedo room were badly bent inward, particularly in
the vicinity of the maneuvering room after bulkhead. The strong
back in the after torpedo room loading hatch was bent about
10 or 15° from its normal centerline.

The after torpedo room loading hatch itself was damaged,
allowing a shower of water into the torpedo room. On surfacing
and inspecting the after torpedo room loading hatch I discovered
that about two-fifths of the gasket itself was badly cut up
and the hatch itself was eliptical in shape to the extent that
I could put my hand in between the knife edge and hatch cover
itself.

All the after tubes were knocked out of commission; all
hydraulic lines to the tubes, vents, and steering mechansim were
ruptured. Many of the gages in the after room were knocked out
of position. In the maneuvering room the control stand cage itself was twisted out of shape. Deck plate and support frames
were warped.

In the engine room hydraulic lines to the main vent valves
were broken loose from the valves. Dishes and Victrola records
in the crew's mess room were thrown about, breaking a large per-
centage of them.

In the radio room the receivers were torn from their
moorings and thrown about the compartment. The transmitter was

- 2 -

STATEMENT OF COMMANDER FITZGERALD - continued.
- -

knocked over resulting in severe damage to all the radio installations. The shock of the explosion continued clear through the forward battery to such an extent that dishes and phonograph records were broken in a slightly lesser degree to that of the crew's mess.

The electricians exerted every effort to protect the electrical installation from the shower of salt water coming from the hard patch, drying out electrical equipment, and endeavor to regain propulsion.

At about 2130 I surfaced and tried to clear the boat of smoke by taking suction through the boat using the main engines. The work was continued in the maneuvering room throughout the night. Finally, by jury rigs we were able to turn over one shaft at very slow speed but due to the condition of the shafting, which is believed to have been badly bent, it was impossible to get the control levers into the second stage resistance; approximately 2750 amps were required to turn the shaft, the normal amount required is about 450.

Finally the engineering officer and electricians reported to me on the bridge that everything possible had been done to reestablish propulsion and that they knew of nothing further they could do in order to regain propulsion. This was somewhere around 0400 to 0500 in the morning. I then decided to try and make a sail in order to bring the submarine closer to the beach where I would disembark the crew and blow the ship up, but this effort was abandoned as it seemed to be futile.

At probably around 0600 I noticed, coming from the northwest out of Lem Valon Strait, a ship which at that time appeared to me to be a large destroyer or light cruiser. Shortly thereafter I noticed smoke from a patrol or escort vessel to the southeast. I didn't think it advisable to make a stationary dive in 280 feet of water without power, the after loading hatch in its damaged condition, and not knowing the true trim of the boat due to having transferred so much water and the loss of oil which had leaked out through external ruptures in the fuel oil tanks aft. Having arrived at this decision I ordered preparations to be made for abandoning ship, thinking it imprudent to engage the approaching ships with machine guns, (I had at one time received a report that the 3" gun was out of commission). While preparations were in progress for abandoning ship we were again attacked by a single-engine aircraft similar to the one of the preceding day. I held fire until the position angle was about 65 degrees, at which point I opened fire with two 20 MM and two .30 caliber machine guns. The plane, to the best of my knowledge, was hit three times. Following these hits it pulled its nose up sharply and changed course to the left, going around my stern and obtained

- 3 -

STATEMENT OF COMMANDER FITZGERALD - continued.
- -

position for a run on GRENADIER'S port side. Fire was again
commenced at a similar position angle. The plane dropped its
aerial torpedo when directly overhead. It landed and exploded
in the water about 200 yards from the ship, (subsequent information revealed that the pilot died that night as a result of
his wounds and cracking up of his plane upon landing at Penang
that morning). All hands were then lined up at quarters forward of the conning tower, leaving one man below to open the
safety tank vent valve.

When the ship from the northwest arrived to within a
mile and a half or two from GRENADIER (this ship turned out to
be about a 1800-ton merchantman) the officers and crew were
ordered over the side and I instructed the man below to open the
vents. The GRENADIER sank immediately. Sixty-eight men and
eight officers were subsequently picked up by the merchant man
which had arrived prior to the patrol vessel.

We had been on board but a short time when the patrol
vessel accompanied by a large subchaser arrived alongside, and
about the same time a twin-engined bomber flew over the scene.
We were taken to Penang and arrived there about 0700 April 23,
1943.

9 September 1945.

NOTE: Five members of the GRENADIER crew have, I understand,
died in prison camps. Lt. WHITING is at 15 B or D or 22 B
or D to the northward of NAOETSU, JAPAN. The last I saw of
him was about the 5th of March. I do not know where Lt. D.K.
HARTY is or Lt. J.N. CRITCHLOW. From my talks to the men all
are accounted for except five who are believed to be dead.

U.S.S. GRENADIER (SS 210) - Statement of K. D. Harty, Lieutenant,
United States Naval Reserve.

STATEMENT OF LIEUTENANT K.D. HARTY, U.S.N.R. UPON
ARRIVAL IN GUAM, M.I. - Lieutenant Harty was attached
to the U.S.S. GRENADIER at time of her sinking.

On patrol 300 miles north of Penang near Pokit about 20 April 1943.

April 20, 1943-2000- sighted two tankers at 12,000 yards - sought attack position on surface. Sighted by ships who fired wild and turned on searchlight. Pulled off and continued to track and attempted to gain position. Tankers sent distress signals on 500 Kc most of night.

An hour before sunrise April 21, 1943, Lieutenant Harty on after TBT cutting in smoke when lookout reported 2 engine plane bearing doubtful 90°T. Dove immediately. Lost diving control at 85 to 90 feet but diving control regained and obtained depth of about 100 feet when bomb exploded. Sounded as if it was over the conning tower.

Lights went out, guage glasses broke, including sight glass on hydraulic replenishing tank. Periscopes leaked some. Emergency lights turned on. Main motors out of commission due to water in maneuvering room and small electrical fires. Main source of water in maneuvering room due to leaks around wiring packing glands in overhead.

Bottomed at 276 feet of water.

On investigating damage discovered bomb had exploded near MR-ATR bulkhead. Door between MR & ATR was sprung preventing complete closing. Numerous small hull leaks, greatest leak was around loading hatch, large spray. Forward end, starboard side ATR had hull dished in about 4-6 inches at head level. After tubes slightly out of line.

Intermittant electrical fires broke out throughout the day in MR, resulting in extremely difficult working conditions. Several men passed out while working. The fires and leaks were continuously undoing previous work accomplished toward main propulsion repairs.

Radio transmitter knocked off foundation and later reported back in commission. Later discovered antenna trunk insulator broken. Five or six antenna insulators broken.

Philco auxiliary receiver broken from fall to deck.

SJ appeared to be all right but not tested. SD xkxx gas tube had been out of commission for two weeks . Radio transmitter out of tune and keying relay inoperable.

Lieutenant Harty spent considerable time during the day preparing publications for destruction. All hands joined bucket brigade to help transfer water from ATR bilges FTR bilges.

Bled some oxygen in boat during the afternoon.

Decided to surface at dark to continue attempt to obtain main propulsion without hindrance from leaks.

Surfaced about an hour after dark. Lieutenant Sherry, diving officer, surfaced boat on even keel.

All night work failed to obtain sustained operation of either shaft.

Sent message at five or six in morning of April 22, 1943, in British number code giving condition of ship and intentions to abandon GRENADIER.

Sighted two ships at dawn 22nd April, 1943. One coastwise-type naval vessel and small patrol yacht. While these vessels were approaching, sighted single engine plane headed towards submarine. Manned 20MM's. Opened fire on plane when it came into range, made several hits during plane's glide, causing bomb approach to be less effective, hits caused plane to swerve. Bomb was released falling about 100 yards off starboard beam. Plane departed. Later learned at Penang we had killed pilot who crashed on landing.

Ships continued approach and signalled us to surrender. Sank publications. Smashed SD & SJ, XYZ, radio equipment, TDC and CT sound gear.

- 1 -

10 55₂ 11

Crew lined up on deck in life jackets when Commanding Officer gave the order to abandon ship. All jumped over the side except Captain and Chief of boat, Withrow who opened vents with remaining hydraulic power after which Captain and Chief of boat jumped overboard. Ship sank stern first. Sick and non-swimmers were in rubber life boats.

Japs circled in their ships and took pictures before coastal-type vessel picked up submarine crew via "Jacob's ladder". All officers and crew were picked up, and taken up to Penang next morning. Captain, Executive Officer and Lieutenant Harty were questioned for about a week at Penang before departure.

Barker, EM2c left at Singapore with diptheria in August 1943, hasn't been heard of since.

Have not heard of survivors of other submarines, except SCULPIN, S-44, and PERCH.

Frequent beatings at Penang, mostly with clubs. Captain received worse treatment including water forced down his nose and knives under his fingernails. Food consisted of one very small dish of rice after the first five or six days without food at all.

Lieutenant Harty was flown with Commanding Officer and Executive Officer to OFUNA prison camp. Arrived on 1 May, 1943.

Guards at OFUNA were very brutal in their treatment of prisoners. Everything possible was done to make living unpleasant. Speaking was not permitted by prisoners. Men were frequently beaten. Food was well prepared but quantity was too small for good health. Lack of food was due to theft of food supplies by guards, plus usual Jap food policy toward prisoners.

FUJIWARA, Torpedoman's Mate by rate in Japanese forces was acting camp PhM and was very sadistic in treatment of prisoners, and insanitary and ineffectual in Medical treatment.

Lieutenant Toulon was beaten with fists when he was sick.

HIRABIYA, S1c was worse of guards, was sadistically brutal in beating prisoners. KUBIYA, PO2c was also brutal and sadistic.

Commander Shinimatsu, Imperial Navy, chief questioner, directed guards to punish prisoners for failure to satisfactorily answer officers' questions.

Warrant officer IDO (or IDA) in charge of camp, cognisant of treatment of prisoners and did nothing about complaints of prisoners.

Left OFUNA March 15, 1944 and was taken to ASHIO copper mines.

Left ASHIO in September 1944 for ZENTSUJI. At ZENTSUJI man named KOBIASHI was interpreter and was known for brutality and mistreatment of prisoners of war. There also was a doctor named SAITO, who deserves punishment for neglect and ill treatment.

Red Cross material at ZENTSUJI and ASHIO was withheld despite dire need in winter.

Left ZENTSUJI on 25 June 1945 and went to ROKUROSHI in FUKUI prefecture. Food was very scarce and rations continuously cut. Men were forced to "volunteer" to work in order to get enough rice to sustain life.

Camp commander HABE, formerly at OSAKA headquarters was at ROKUROSHI.

FUJIMOTO, interpreter - believed responsible for making conditions disagreeable. He formerly had lived in the United States. This man is considered to be very intelligent and extremely clever, very apt to talk himself out of trouble.

K. D. HARTY.

U.S.S. GRENADIER (SS 210) - Statement of Robert W. Palmer, C.Y., USN.

ENCLOSURE (D) 13

12 September 1945.

I boarded the U.S.S. GRENADIER (SS-210) 11 October 1942 at Albany, Western Australia. The GRENADIER was under the command of Lieutenant Commander J. A. Fitzgerald. Left Freemantle, Australia, 20 March 1943; destination, Strait of Malacca. This was our SIXTH PATROL. Strait of Malacca was virgin territory to our submarines and we found the water very shallow and navigation difficult. Took pictures of North end of island.

April 19, 1943 we surfaced 0600 and chased two tankers (hull down) for two hours. About 0800 Jap sea-plane dropped bomb on us. We dove. It hit deck and gauge read 90 ft. Looked again and depth gauge read 120 ft. We were going down fast at an 18 degree down-angle. Five (5) full air banks. I manned control phone in the control room. At 180 ft. the Skipper said to Mr. Sherry: "Blow everything at 300". I phoned after torpedo room but no answer. Kept calling for all stations to report "All battle stations manned." After awhile report came in aft room, "fire in maenuvering room". In mud at 260 ft. Three men in control room rushed to aid in putting out fire in maneuvering room. Soft patch over maneuvering room was leaking. Bomb hit between aft torpedo room and maneuvering room bulkhead, starboard side. Sheared blade starboard screw. Fire caused by heavy cables that run the motors. Two men succumbed to smoke. No 5 fuel tank leaked badly. All men were dazed for hours. Maneuvering room completely wrecked; engine room O.K. Tubes out of line and leaking but not bad. Stern tubes in motor room leaking badly.

Did not make attempt to surface because we knew they were up there and had summoned corvets. Sound gear O.K. No depth charges heard. Commanding officer ordered, over P.A. system, "steady men, we're O.K., everything is all right". About 2000 we decided to surface. Oxygen was released and C.O.2 absorbant used. Could have stayed down 12 hours longer. Casualties were slight. Captain ordered all hands to secure themselves for surfacing. Surfaced with about one half degree angle on the boat. I called depth up to 200 ft. then we surfaced very fast. It was dark when we surfaced. Skipper ordered forward torpedo room hatch opened. Casualties were cared for and crew fed. Morale high due to excellent skipper.

Drifted during night and worked continuously trying to get power to main motors and generators. Corvets appeared and laid-too. About dawn Skipper ordered Chief Electrician to secure. Then a Jap Zero showed up and started to strafe from stern. Gun crew fired into plane and it cracked-up on the beach.

We all took to the water. Skipper destroyed T.D.C., Radar and confidential papers. Opened all hatches. Chief of the Boat, William C. WITHROW, CTM, scuttled the boat by opening all main vents, and made his escape. Officer HARDY clung to a mattress, reading the Reader's Digest to us. Three corvets closed in. After 1 hour

-1-

14

PALMER STATEMENT   12 September 1945.

and 45 minutes one large corvet picked us up. When we had been
stripped and searched most of our things were returned. After
Japs dropped buoys over spot where boat went down, we departed
for Penang. Spared in lieu of desired information.

Arrived Penang, Malay States, about 0600, 23 April 1943, wet,
hungry, poorly clothed. Marched onto dock and taken to what once
was a British school. In about a half hour a Nip officer showed
up with a club and brandished it. We were stood in a zig-zag row
and clubbed for slightest movement of body or eyelash until late
evening. Then positions changed to hands over head, knees bent.
No food since capture. Then clubbing became more frequent. Man
taken one at a time to a room, the door of which was marked "Art
Room" and tortured by clubbing with flat of sword and round club.
Matches were stuck under fingernails. Tied across a three-quarter
bed, face down, and 'worked over' with clubs. Lash man to bench
tilted at 20° angle, head down, pour man full of water, then jump
on his stomach. This treatment was given to the Skipper. Treatment continued five days and nights without food. Evening of fifth
night we got maggoty, wormy rice broth. No smokes. Occasionally a
'good guard' would let us lie down for an hour, then awaken us with
the but of his gun. Asked Skipper for location of other subs, for
call signals and frequencies. I said I was a cook. Whenever Captain went to the head he scribbled messages to the crew on the bulkhead, such as "Guard the T.D.C.", "Keep your heads up", "Don't tell
'em anything". Officers kept in separate rooms but we used same head.
We ate hedge blossoms, stems, and grass. We ate Listerine Toothpaste
mixed with tobacco for Mother's Day. After 8th day treatment changed
from purposeful questioning to individual saddistic satisfaction of
the Nip guards - like sitting on deck, hands on knees and staring
rigidly ahead. All men put into a circle with heads between legs of
man next to him. Crawl about cement deck imitating train and animals
until knees and hands wore raw. No baths; still rice broth at 0800
and 2100. This treatment continued for two months. Men became weak
and they were beaten. All P.O.W. used in this manner. Then two or
four weak men put on table and rest had to hold it over their heads.
The guards were Formosa Nips. They wanted our jewelry and made us
wish we had given it to them. In Penang and under this treatment
for four months.

On 18 July left for Singapore on the Hiya Maru; filthy conditions. In Singapore three days later and we remained fifty one days.
Treatment not bad; work light. Worked at Singapore Navy Base. On
26 September boarded Asama Maru and had 17 days trip; - same conditions. Destination Japan. Two days out of Japan they tortured
men beyond all comprehension.

Arrived Shimoda Saki 10 October 1943 and divided. Twenty nine
men sent to Ofuna Interrogation Camp. The remaining men (41) stayed

-2-

15

PALMER STATEMENT   12 September 1945.
- -

in steel mill at Shimoda Saki. Since then we have not heard of
these 41 men.

    Ofuna another nine months of hell. High ranking officers
were at this camp but no distinction made as to care and treatment.
They we were put to work in the Ashio Copper Mines. Treatment continued as usual, midst death and torture. No medicine. Working
hours 0500 to 2000. Two days a month off. General treatment in
working camps abhorable. All men who died were cremated. Food
conditions during last six months of war were acute. At this time
the Jap civilians were starving, too. Morale, by this time, was
rock-bottom and thoughts and dreams were of food.

    While at Ofuna I was questioned by a Jap Naval "Gunrabo", (Nip
F.B.I.), Comdr. Shini Matzu. He was educated in the United States;
a graduate of Palo Alto High School and of Stanford University. He
boasted that he was an attache in Washington, D. C., on December 7th.

    During entire period the one bright light was the Red Cross aid
Christmas of 1943 and 1944. We never got any mail. Near the end
two men got mail.

    I have no knowledge of survivors of any ships other than the
SCULPIN, TULLABEE, GRENADIER, PERCH, TANG and S-44.

    The Skipper's display of "guts" pulled many a man through
more than once.

                                    Robert W. Palmer, C.Y., USN.
                                    U.S.S. GRENADIER (SS-210)

                                    Home address;
                                        665 Pine Street,
                                        San Francisco, California.

                                                            16

U.S.S. GRENADIER (SS 210) - Statement of Fred Zufelt, 381 21 09, GM1c.

17

ENCLOSURE (五

STATEMENT OF ZUFELT, FRED (N), 381-21-09, GM1c -
UPON ARRIVAL IN GUAM, M.I. - Member of crew of GRENADIER.

I was in my bunk when the excitement started. After the explosion I got up
and discovered that the maneuvering room and control were taking water badly. Water
depth at this time was about 235 feet. One great cause for water to come into the
boat was soft patch that had gave way. After torpedo room was leaking badly. Power
was gone and couldn't be restored, however much effort was put on trying to regain
main propulsion. When the word was passed to abandon ship I jumped overboard.

After I was picked up I was taken to Penang. Here I was mistreated considerablely.
When I asked an officer to repeat a question I was threatened to be killed. They
slapped me around quite a bit. It made them very angry when I did not reveil the information they desired.

From Penang I was sent to OFUNA and put to work in the mines there. Food here
was enough to subsist on but not enough to live in good health.

After leaving OFUNA I was taken to Omari and kept there until the Japs decided
to send me to ASHIO to work at hard labor and live on very short rations.

On September 4, 1945 I boarded a train and went to Yokohama and then onboard the
U.S.S. OZARK which brought me to GUAM. I arrived at GUAM 12 September 1945.

FRED ZUFELT.

U.S.S. GRENADIER (SS 210) - Statement of E. L. Poss, RM1c.

STATEMENT OF POSS, E.L., RM1c - UPON ARRIVAL
AT GUAM, M.I. - Member of Crew of U.S.S.
GRENADIER.

The cause of the damage and sinking of the GRENADIER was due to
the bomb that hit her; this is my opinion. The maneuvering room was
damaged severely. After the bomb hit we could not get any power.
All hands worked until they were exausted trying to restore power.
We surfaced and Japanese bomber came over. We drove him off with
the 20MM. Later we learned that the plane crashed.
It was decided that the boat could not be saved so the Captain
ordered crew to abandon dhip. Vents were pulled and men went over
the side.
We were taken aboard the Japanese ship and taken to PENANG. We
were taken to St. George College, which was formarly a girl's school.
Here we were questioned. No smoking was permitted; disobediance of
this rule resulted in severe beatings. Treatment was so rough that
I passed out for a time. They asked us what submarine we were on.
I told them the GOLDFISH. I had been given instructions to tell them
a fictitious name if I was asked questions concerning our boats. The
Captain of the boat received severe torture and mistreatment. But
even after this torture he refused to let his men try to escape.
We remained at PENANG until 5 August 1943. Then we were taken
on TI MARU to SINGAPORE. Then we were taken to an Indian camp and
put to work.
On 24 September 1943 we went aboard the ship ASUMA MARU. Treat-
ment was extremely horrible. The men were forced to beat each other
with clubs. When you sat down you were beaten and when you stood you
were beaten.
On board the ASUMA MARU we were taken to Japan and sent to a
prison camp by the name of AFUNA. Here we were put to work.
From AFUNA we were sent to OMARI, near TOKYO.
From OMARI I was taken to OSHIO and put to work in the mines.
This amounted to hard work and short rations.
On 4 September 1945 I went to YOKOHOMA and then on board the
U.S.S. OSARK and arrived at GUAM on 12 September 1945.

Edgar L Poss
E.L. POSS.

U.S.S. GRENADIER – Statement of William Clyde Withrow, CTM, 265 32 40, USN.

ENCLOSURE 21

STATEMENT OF: WITHROW, William Clyde, CTM, 265 82 40, USN
of the U.S.S. GRENADIER.

    We lost the boat by a bombing. Early morning of the 21st we
tried to come in on a two ship convoy. We dove and surfaced at
daylight. A plane spotted us and bombed us. We sunk down in
shallow water, about 265 feet; the boat was damaged quite a bit.
We worked all day and surfaced at night and worked all that night
until next morning. We were called to quarters and asked what we
would like to do. Another plane came over but we evaded him. We
later found out we had shot him down. A small minelayer and a
destroyer come in on us and when they got closer we scuttled the
boat. We were swimming about and were finally picked up and taken
to Penang. That's where hell started. They tried to get information
out of us and tortured us to make us talk, but they got nothing
out of us. We stayed there until August 5th. From there we went
to Singapore, staying there until 26 Sept 1943. Then we came to
Japan. We got there the 10th of October 1943. They kept us under
slight torture until finally in December 1943 we were permitted
to talk amongst ourselves. All the Quiz Kids' were stateside
interpreters. We left for Omari and from Omari went to Ashio, to
the copper mines. Up to this time we had been under the Navy, and
they really made it hard on us. When we reached Ashio, the treatment let up considerably. Linder, Guico, Doyle and Snyder died.
Barker was left in Singapore and we never heard anything more about
him. I think as much of Fitzgerald, our skipper, as I almost do
of my father. He went through hell for us. They beat him, jumped
on his stomach and tortured him by burning splints under his nails.
He never talked. They even had him working in the mines for telling
the Jap Commander just what he thought of him.

                                  William Clyde Withrow.

22

FE24-71/A17-26

Serial 00280

U. S. NAVAL FORCES

WESTERN AUSTRALIA

Bz

May 21, 1943.

From: The Commander Submarines, Seventh Fleet.
To: The Commander Seventh Fleet.

Subject: Record of Proceedings of an Investigation
            Convened by the Commander Submarines, Seventh Fleet,
            to inquire into the circumstances connected with
            the possible loss of the U.S.S. GRENADIER on her
            sixth war patrol - transmittal of.

Enclosure: (A) Original and two copies of subject investigation.

    1.   Enclosure (A) is forwarded herewith.

R. W. CHRISTIE.

SECRET

RECORD OF PROCEEDINGS

of an

INVESTIGATION

conducted at

the headquarters of

THE COMMANDER U.S. NAVAL FORCES, WESTERN AUSTRALIA

by order of

The Commander Submarines, Seventh Fleet.

To inquire into the circumstances connected with the possible
loss of the U.S.S. Grenadier on her sixth war patrol.

May 17, 1943

FE24-71/A17-26

SUBMARINES, SEVENTH FLEET,

U.S.S. TROUT (SS202), Flagship,
May 21, 1943.

SECRET

S-E-C-R-E-T

The proceedings and findings of the investigation in the
attached case are approved.

R. W. CHRISTIE,
Rear Admiral, U.S. Navy,
Commander Submarines, Seventh Fleet.

SECRET

FINDING OF FACTS

1. That the U.S.S. Grenadier (SS210) departed from Fremantle, West Australia, on her sixth war patrol on March 20, 1943.

2. That on departure on patrol there were no known material deficiencies that might contribute to the loss of the vessel.

3. That the usual training had been conducted prior to departure on patrol.

4. That prior to departure the commanding officer had been furnished with all available information of his patrol area, and own and enemy operations therein, and was subsequently given additional information by despatch.

5. That friendly forces were adequately informed of the operations of the U.S.S. Grenadier in the area normally assigned to the British.

6. That when last heard from by radio April 16, 1943, the U.S.S. Grenadier gave her position as Latitude 13 degrees 13 minutes North, Longitude 96 degrees 55 minutes East.

7. That on April 20, 1943 the U.S.S. Grenadier was directed by radio to depart from the assigned area at dark April 23, 1943 and to acknowledge the signal when feasible.

8. That no acknowledgement for the orders of April 20, 1943 has been received and the U.S.S. Grenadier has not returned to port either in accordance with the despatch directive or the original operation order.

9. That, at the latest, the U.S.S. Grenadier was due in Exmouth Gulf, West Australia on May 12, 1943 and is considered overdue since that date.

RECOMMENDATIONS

The investigating officer has no recommendations as to any steps that should be taken to improve operational procedures.

FE24-71/A17-25   SUBMARINES, SEVENTH FLEET   86/Bz

Serial 00267   U.S.S. TROUT (SS202), Flagship,
                                        May 13, 1943.

SECRET

S-E-C-R-E-T

From: The Commander Submarines, Seventh Fleet.

To: Commander Chester C. Smith, U.S. Navy,
              Commander Submarine Division Sixty-One.

Subject: Investigation into the possible loss of the
              U.S.S. GRENADIER (SS210) on her sixth war patrol.

    1.   Under authority of 5 U.S. Code 93, you are hereby detailed to investigate, as soon as practicable, into the circumstances connected with the possible loss of the U.S.S. GRENADIER on her sixth war patrol.

    2.   You will make a thorough investigation into all the known circumstances connected with the operation of the GRENADIER during her sixth war patrol and submit a complete report to the Commander Submarines, Seventh Fleet, of the facts which you deem to be established, together with recommendations as to what steps, if any, should be taken to improve operational procedures.

    3.   Your attention is particularly invited to Section 734, Naval Courts and Boards.

    4.   You will furnish your own clerical assistance. You are directed to make only four copies of the record of the proceedings and forward all four copies to the convening authority.

> R. W. CHRISTIE,
> Rear Admiral, U.S. Navy,
> Commander Submarines, Seventh Fleet.

SECRET

FIRST DAY

U.S. Naval Headquarters,
Perth, Western Australia,
Monday, May 17, 1943.

The investigating officer, Commander Chester C. Smith, U.S.
Navy, administered the prescribed oath to Jacob Rosen, chief
yeoman, U.S. Navy, the reporter, who took seat as such.

The investigating officer read the order directing him to
make the investigation, which is hereto prefixed.

The investigating officer announced that the investigation
would be conducted with closed doors.

No witnesses not otherwise connected with the investigation
were present.

A witness called by the investigating officer entered, was
informed of the subject matter of the investigation, and
declared as follows:

Examined by the investigating officer:

1. Q. State your name, rank, and present station.
A. Captain H.H. McLean, U.S. Navy, Chief of Staff to Commander
Task Force Seventy One and Commander Submarines, Seventh Fleet.

2. Q. Will you please produce the operation order given the
U.S.S. Grenadier for this patrol and describe the operations
that it directs and any other directives that you had knowledge
of regarding this operation.

The reporter informed the investigating officer that, due to
a recent accident, he was unable to keep the shorthand record.

The investigating officer administered the prescribed oath to
Charles D. Albers, chief yeoman, U.S. Navy, as an additional
reporter, who took seat as such.

The witness produced the complete operations jacket including
the operation order and memoranda, and another jacket containing
the despatches in regard to the sixth war patrol of the U.S.S.
Grenadier. The applicable documents are appended.

A. Commander Southwest Pacific despatch 161559 of March
directed the assignment of two submarines for one patrol each
between Malacca Strait and Martaban Bay. The first submarine
to depart at the earliest practicable date and details were to
be arranged with Commander in Chief, Eastern Fleet.
The Grenadier was about ready to start on a patrol of an
area normally assigned to this task force. These orders were
cancelled and new orders were issued to provide for patrol in
this new area. In a despatch 170440 of March, CinCEF was
advised of the proposed patrol of the Grenadier in the British
Area.

-1-

SECRET

He was requested to provide pertinent information concerning the area and to advise what modifications of the Grenadier's orders, if any, were required.

The Grenadier operated in accordance with Operation Order 7-43 as modified by Commander Task Force 71 despatch 220953. The latter despatch was based on information received from CinCEF.

In general, the Grenadier was to proceed to Exmouth Gulf, there fuel to capacity and thence proceed to Salang via direct route westward of Sumatra. She was to patrol off Salang Island and exploit likely traffic lanes between entrance of Malacca Strait and the Gulf of Martaban, paying particular attention to shipping passing to and from Rangoon. At dark, 1 May, she was to return via route to the southwest of Sumatra, reconnoitering Christmas Island one day enroute. The assigned patrol area was north of 7 degrees north and east of line Nicobar-Andamans-Cape Negrais. The British authorities arranged for submerged bombing restrictions in this area from 0001Z/31 March until further notice. British authorities issued orders to their own submarines not to attack any submarines between the equator and southern boundary of the area.

CinCEF in his 0716Z/18 proposed that the Grenadier call at Ceylon, and later operate under the control of Flag Officer, Ceylon. The action of Commander Task Force 71 and Commander Seventh Fleet is contained in CTF 71 despatches 190156 and 0351Z/20 March, and Commander Seventh Fleet 190555 of March.

3. Q. Was that all of the information furnished this submarine prior to departure on her sixth war patrol?
A. She was given two memorandums dated 18 and 20 March containing all available information in our files. On 10 April Grenadier was furnished additional information about the prospective movements of Dutch Submarines in Malacca Strait area in despatches 101820 and 101944. These were paraphrased versions of N.O.I.C. Colombo's 100520Z and 100544Z of April. Above is a summation of what transpired during the period I was Operations Officer.

4. Q. Were you able to furnish the Grenadier any information as to possible minefields in the area in which it was to operate?
A. One of the memorandums referred to previously, contained information that at one time the Singapore Strait had been closed to night shipping due to floating mines. Further information had been requested from CinCEF, but no additional information was obtained as to minefields.

5. Q. Aside from the operation order, memorandums, and despatches that you have referred to, do you recall any additional verbal instructions given to the commanding officer prior to departure on patrol?
A. As I remember, two conferences were held, one to discuss the operation order itself, and immediately prior to departure an additional conference was held to iron out various communication problems incident to ships operating in British areas in British waters. No additional instructions were given other than those contained in the operation order.

-2-

SECRET

6. Q. State the general nature of the area in which the
vessel was to operate and the depths of water to be encountered.
A. In the vicinity of Salang Island depths of from 36 to 40
fathoms are found - deeper water is found to the westward.
Shallow water is found to the southward of Rangoon.

7. Q. Was the submarine given any instructions as to how to
conduct operations, surface or submerged, during daylight?
A. That was left to the discretion of the commanding officer.

8. Q. In the issuance of the operation order and instructions
to the commanding officer were you assisted by any other officer?
A. Yes, Lieutenant Commander Lautrup, Assistant Operations
Officer.

9. Q. In regard to the training of the ship prior to ship's
departure, who was in charge of training of the Grenadier?
A. Lieutenant Commander Carr, under Commander Submarine
Squadron Six, handled training of submarine crews.

10. Q. Can you furnish any other information which would be
helpful in this case?
A. No.

The investigating officer informed the witness that he was
privileged to make any further statement covering anything
relating to the subject matter of the investigation which he
thought should be made a matter of record in connection therewith, which had not been fully brought out by the previous
questioning.

The witness stated that he had nothing further to say.

The witness verified his declaration, was duly warned, and
withdrew.

A witness called by the investigating officer entered, was
informed of the subject matter of the investigation, and
declared as follows:

Examined by the investigating officer:

1. Q. State your name, rank, and present station.
A. John Mylin Will, Commander, U.S. Navy, Commander Submarine
Division Sixty Two with additional duty as Operations Officer
Task Force 71.

2. Q. At what time did you relieve Captain McLean as Operations Officer?
A. About March 26, 1943.

3. Q. At the time you relieved as Operations Officer the
Grenadier was out on her sixth war patrol. Were there any
instructions or communications issued by you to that vessel
after your assumption of duties as Operations Officer?

-3-

SECRET

A. The first despatch which I originated to the Grenadier was on the 11th of April in which the Grenadier was told that we desired information prior to 16 April as to the future hunting prospects in her assigned area. In the same despatch she was told to submit this information when conditions permitted. This despatch was 111355 of April. The Grenadier on 16 April in her despatch 151200 replied that her area was unproductive and gave the details of her patrol to date, and her position at the time of the despatch as 13 degrees 13 minutes north 96 degrees and 55 minutes east longitude. In view of the unproductiveness of the area and the urgent need for submarines in other more productive areas a despatch was sent to Grenadier on 20 April modifying her operation order and directing her to depart her area at dark on 23 April from approximate position seven degrees north 95 degrees east and further directing her to pass through Point "A" bearing 270 degrees distant 20 miles from Pulo Bras and Point "B" 3 degrees 1 minute north 3 degrees and 1 minute east thence south of Sumatra to Sunda Strait, to patrol this strait for about one week and to start the return to Fremantle at dark May 4 reconnoitering Christmas Island enroute. This same despatch requested an acknowledgement when feasible. This was despatch 200840 of 20 April. The withdrawal of the Grenadier from that area was in compliance with a directive from Commander Seventh Fleet and the routing given to Grenadier for departing the area was received from FO Ceylon. In same despatch from FO Ceylon a statement was made that submerged bombing restrictions would be removed north of seven degrees north at 0001Z April 24 unless we wished them to be kept in force longer. On April 20 we informed CinCEF that the Grenadier had been routed as he requested and removal of submerged bombing restrictions north of seven degrees north on 24 April was satisfactory. Despatch directing Grenadier to depart her area was paraphrased and sent out over NU as 200845Z. On the 27th of April having received no acknowledgement from Grenadier we sent 271030 requesting she acknowledge serial 4 at earliest feasible time giving her position. This was also paraphrased and sent out over circuit NU as 271100Z. On April 30 still having no acknowledgement of 200845, we sent 300431 to CinCEF informing him of possible radio material failure of Grenadier which might have prevented her receiving instructions to depart area early, and the possibility that she might depart area at dark May 1, by reverse of the outbound route in accordance with her original orders. That is the substance of all communications from and to the Grenadier.

4. Q. To your knowledge were there any friendly vessels or submarines in the area in which the Grenadier operated that came to your attention as operations officer?
  A. No.

5. Q. As Commander Submarine Division Sixty Two the Grenadier was part of your division and you were in some measure responsible for the training of that vessel and should have some knowledge of the skill and ability of the officers aboard and in particular the training they received just prior to departure. What information can you give?

-4-

SECRET

A. Prior to departure for the patrol before this one, I personally conducted some of the training as Officer Conducting the Practice on the surface target and considered the Commanding Officer and officers well qualified in their jobs and perfectly capable of handling the Grenadier under all conditions. I had nothing to do with the conduct of the training prior to the departure of the Grenadier on her sixth war patrol, but I talked to the commanding officer previous to his departure, and he seemed well satisfied with the amount of training he had had. He was also well satisfied with the officers and personnel situation as it existed at the time of the commencement of the patrol and I consider the capability of those officers assigned the Grenadier satisfactory.

6. Q. Were there any unusual changes in enlisted personnel complement of the vessel between the fifth and sixth war patrols?
A. None that I know of.

The investigating officer informed the witness that he was privileged to make any further statement covering anything relating to the subject matter of the investigation which he thought should be a matter of record in connection therewith, which had not been fully brought out by the previous questioning.

The witness stated that he had nothing further to say.

The witness verified his declaration, was duly warned, and withdrew.

A witness called by the investigating officer entered, was informed of the subject matter of the investigation, and declared as follows:

Examined by the investigating officer:

1. Q. State your name, rank, and present station.
A. Lieutenant Commander B.L. Carr, U.S. Navy, Flag Secretary and Aide, Staff Commander Submarines, Seventh Fleet.

2. Q. What were your duties at the time of the last refit of the Grenadier in this port?
A. I was Operations Officer on the staff of Commander Submarine Squadron Six.

3. Q. As such what were your duties in regard to the training of the Grenadier?
A. My duties were, in this regard, to arrange for practices and rehearsals during the time she was available between the completion of her refit and departure for patrol.

4. Q. Do you recall the nature and amount of training given the Grenadier prior to her departure on her last patrol?
A. No, I don't recall exactly, but I think she had at least two days devoted to daylight approaches and, I believe, two nights of approaches.

-5-

SECRET

5. Q. From your observations in conducting these exercises, would you believe that the personnel of the Grenadier were properly trained for war operations?

A. Yes, I thought her approaches on the whole, were well conducted and I remember discussing several of them with the commanding officer and making a comment to that effect.

6. Q. To your knowledge was there any unusual change in the personnel in the vessel between the fifth and sixth war patrols?

A. There was a considerable shift of officer personnel in which Lieutenant (j.g.) Howell, Lieutenant (j.g.) Kuehn, and Lieutenant Benitez were transferred. The reasons for the transfers at this time were Howell had been ordered to new construction and Benitez and Kuehn were ill. In order to get another experienced man on the boat, Lieutenant Sherry was ordered to the ship. This gave them a well balanced boat.

7. Q. Was there any unusually large turnover of enlisted personnel?

A. I don't remember.

The investigating officer informed the witness that he was privileged to make any further statement covering anything relating to the subject matter of the investigation which he thought should be a matter of record in connection therewith, which had not been fully brought out by the previous questioning.

The witness stated that he had nothing further to say.

The witness verified his declaration, was duly warned, and withdrew.

The investigation then, at 5 p.m. adjourned until 1 p.m. tomorrow.

-6-

SECRET

SECOND DAY

U.S. Naval Headquarters,
Perth, Western Australia,
Tuesday, May 18, 1943.

The investigation met at 1 p.m.

Present:

Commander Chester C. Smith, U.S. Navy, investigating officer.
Jacob Rosen, chief yeoman U.S. Navy, reporter.
Charles D. Albers, chief yeoman, U.S. Navy, reporter.

The record of proceedings of the first day of the investigation was read and approved.

No witnesses not otherwise connected with the investigation were present.

A witness called by the investigating officer entered, was informed of the subject matter of the investigation, and declared as follows:

Examined by the investigating officer:

1. Q. State your name, rank, and present station.
   A. Lieutenant Commander . W. Lautrup, U.S. Navy, Assistant Operations Officer, Staff of Commander Submarines, Seventh Fleet.

2. Q. What were your duties at the time the Grenadier was sent out on her sixth war patrol?
   A. Preparation of operation orders.

3. Q. Was it your duty, then, to make available to the commanding officer all the information available in regard to the area to which he was assigned?
   A. Yes sir.

4. Q. Captain McLean has given me the substance of the operation order under which the Grenadier operated, as well as memoranda of information available in regard to the area. He also has furnished information of the despatches thereafter sent to the Grenadier with additional information. He and Commander Will have informed me of all the despatches sent to and from the Grenadier after her departure. Was there any additional information that came to your knowledge that was not furnished the commanding officer in the above mentioned orders, memoranda, and despatches.
   A. No sir.

5. Q. In accordance with your information, what was considered the latest date on which the Grenadier should have arrived at Exmouth Gulf?
   A. 12 May.

-7-

SECRET

6. Q. Do you then consider that due to non-arrival by that
date that the vessel is overdue?
A. Yes sir.

The investigating officer informed the witness that he was
privileged to make any further statement covering anything
relating to the subject matter of the investigation which he
thought should be a matter of record in connection therewith,
which had not been fully brought out by the previous questioning.

The witness stated that he had nothing further to say.

The witness verified his declaration, was duly warned, and
withdrew.

The investigating officer as legal custodian, introduced
the Ship's Departure Check-off List for the U.S.S. Grenadier
(SS210) dated March 17, 1943, copy appended.

It was noted that there were no deficiencies discovered as a
result of the required inspections during and after the refit
of the U.S.S. Grenadier.

The investigation was finished.

FINDING OF FACTS

1. That the U.S.S. Grenadier (SS210) departed from Fremantle,
West Australia, on her sixth war patrol on March 20, 1943.

2. That on departure on patrol there were no known material
deficiencies that might contribute to the loss of the vessel.

3. That the usual training had been conducted prior to
departure on patrol.

4. That prior to departure the commanding officer had been
furnished with all available information of his patrol area,
and own and enemy operations therein, and was subsequently
given additional information by despatch.

5. That friendly forces were adequately informed of the
operations of the U.S.S. Grenadier in the area normally
assigned to the British.

6. That when last heard from by radio April 16, 1943, the
U.S.S. Grenadier gave her position as Latitude 13 degrees 13
minutes North, Longitude 96 degrees 55 minutes East.

7. That on April 20, 1943 the U.S.S. Grenadier was directed
by radio to depart from the assigned area at dark April 23, 1943
and to acknowledge the signal when feasible.

-8-

SECRET

8. That no acknowledgement for the orders of April 20, 1943 has been received and the U.S.S. Grenadier has not returned to port either in accordance with the despatch directive or the original operation order.

9. That, at the latest, the U.S.S. Grenadier was due in Exmouth Gulf, West Australia on May 12, 1943 and is considered overdue since that date.

RECOMMENDATIONS

The investigating officer has no recommendations as to any steps that should be taken to improve operational procedures.

The record of proceedings of the second day of the investigation was read and approved, and the investigating officer having finished the investigation, then, at 2:30 p.m., adjourned to await the action of the convening authority.

Chester C. Smith,
    Commander, U.S. Navy,
        Investigating Officer.

-9-

S-E-C-R-E-T

ALLIED NAVAL FORCES,
BASED WESTERN AUSTRALIA,
COMMANDER TASK GROUP 71.1,
U.S.S. TROUT (SS202) FLAGSHIP

OPERATION ORDER
No. 7-43.

PERTH, WEST AUSTRALIA,
March 17, 1943.   1615 ITEM

TASK ORGANIZATION
(a) U.S.S. GRENADIER - Lieutenant Commander J. A. FITZGERALD.

1. (a) Japanese forces now control the PHILIPPINES, FRENCH INDO-CHINA, MALAYA, BURMA, the NETHERLANDS EAST INDIES, most of NEW GUINEA, NEW BRITAIN, GUAM and WAKE in addition to former Japanese Territory. Enemy bases are probably established at BALI, SURABAYA, TJILATJAP, BATAVIA, SINGAPORE, SABANG, RANGOON and PENANG.

   (b) Japanese planes may be expected at strategic positions in Japanese occupied territory. Important bases are probably fortified and also mined and netted against submarines.

   (c) The enemy is sending reinforcements to RANGOON via MALACCA STRAIT in preparation for future operations. Some 6 or 7 ships are despatched monthly. Dutch submarines (O-22, O-23, K-11, K-14, K-15) and some British submarines (TRUSTY Class) have been operating under the Commander in Chief, EASTERN FLEET, employed on offensive patrol in the northern entrance to MALACCA STRAIT. Additional details of friendly and enemy forces in this area have been requested from the Commander in Chief, EASTERN FLEET and will be forwarded by despatch.

   (d) (1) Enemy shipping is known to take full advantage of protection afforded by shallow water routes close inshore. Normal shipping routes from RANGOON to SINGAPORE use the eastern side of MALACCA STRAIT.

       (2) Fast important ships sometimes proceed independently, but frequently under escort. Convoys of two or more ships are usually escorted. Air coverage is usually given to ships and convoys entering and leaving port.

   (e) Attention is called to:

       (1) Current O.N.I. and Force Intelligence Bulletins.

       (2) Japanese Shipping Position - Board of Economic Warfare - 17 August 1942.

       (3) Submarines, Southwest Pacific, Standard Plans and Instructions, dated 15 January 1943.

       (4) Intelligence reports contained in separate memorandum.

2. This unit will conduct offensive patrol against enemy combatant, supply and transport shipping between MALACCA STRAIT and the GULF of MARTABAN.

-1-

S-E-C-R-E-T

ALLIED NAVAL FORCES,
BASED WESTERN AUSTRALIA,
COMMANDER TASK GROUP 71.1,
U.S.S. TROUT (SS202) FLAGSHIP

OPERATION ORDER
No. 7-43.

PERTH, WEST AUSTRALIA,
March 17, 1943.   1615 ITEM

3. (a) GRENADIER

(1) DESTROY ENEMY VESSELS.

(2) When directed about 20 March 1943, proceed via BOMBING RESTRICTION LANE to EXMOUTH GULF and there fuel to capacity.

(3) Thence proceed to the vicinity of SALANG ISLAND via direct route to the Westward of SUMATRA.

(4) Patrol area in the vicinity of SALANG ISLAND and exploit likely traffic lanes between the entrance of MALACCA STRAIT and the GULF OF MARTABAN paying particular attention to shipping proceeding to and from RANGOON.

(5) Start return to FREMANTLE at dark 1 May. Exploit likely traffic lanes in the southern approaches to SUNDA STRAIT and reconnoiter FLYING FISH COVE, CHRISTMAS ISLAND during one daylight period.

(x) (1) Make every effort to ensure complete destruction of all enemy ships encountered.

4. Logistic support at DARWIN, EXMOUTH GULF, FREMANTLE and COLOMBO.

5. (1) Communications in accordance with Standard Communication Plan Modified in subparagraph 5 (2) below.

(2) Guard BAKERS for normal traffic. If BAKERS cannot be heard, guard NU (Colombo) circuit. Traffic especially for GRENADIER will be broadcast on BAKERS in usual manner and with normal text serial number, after zero hours zed, April 1, this traffic will also be broadcast on NU circuit using British Code and with alphabetical serial letter following the corresponding BAKER text serial number. Guard reconnaissance frequency when within one thousand miles of Australian Coast. Beginning April first also guard NU submarine circuit schedules for additional special information and communicate with CTF-71 through COLOMBO using British Codes until crossing Long. 97° East, south of SUMATRA on return trip.

Commander Task Force 71 and Task Group 71.1 in United States Naval Headquarters, Perth, West Australia.

A true copy. Attest:
Chester C. Smith,
Commander, U.S. Navy,
Investigating Officer.

R. W. CHRISTIE,
Rear Admiral, U.S. Navy,
Commander TASK GROUP SEVENTY ONE POINT ONE

DISTRIBUTION
CTF-71
COMSUBRON 6
File.

U. S. NAVAL FORCES

WESTERN AUSTRALIA

S-E-C-R-E-T

    1.   GRENADIER will guard Bakers continuously; upon failure will shift to Group NU.

    2.   GRENADIER will guard recco frequency until 1,000 miles out of Fremantle and from 1,000 miles out of Fremantle on return.

    3.   VIXO will address GRENADIER on normal Baker sub run (textual ser nr); traffic will be paralleled on Group NU in British code after 1 April. (textual ser nr plus alphabetical ser ltr).

    4.   GRENADIER holds following publications in addition to normal compliment:

    1) SP 02169 (16) (March)
    2) " 02169 (17) (April)
    3) "   "   (18) (May)
    4) " 02365 (15) (April)
    5) "   "   (16) (May)
    6) " 02409 - code
    7) " 02410 - code
    8) XRAY SIGNALS (British)

    These pubs are used to encrypt all GRENADIER traffic to be put on NU circuit.

    5.   All traffic for GRENADIER will bear call sign NYGA.

A true copy. Attest:

Chester C. Smith,
    Commander, U.S. Navy,
      Investigating Officer.

U.S. NAVAL FORCES

WESTERN AUSTRALIA

SECRET   March 17,   1943.

- SHIP-SHORE FREQUENCIES (GZH) -

NYGA will call RDO COLOMBO (GZH) ON FOLLOWING FREQUENCIES:-

Frequency	Time
3835	1800-0200 Z
6300	Cont.
8290	Cont.
12,685	0400-1600 Z
16,845	0200-1800 Z

GZH will answer on (GZH) NU Broadcasts:-

NU Broadcast (GZH)   Sub. ser. numbers 701-899.

Frequency	Time	Remarks
7,435	Cont.	
13,355	Cont.	
17,612	0130 *	
	0330 *	
	0530 #	
	0730 *	
	0930 *	
	1025 *	*Secure watch after
	1130 #	10 minutes if nothing heard.
4,403	1400 *	
	1530 #	
	1730 *	#Secure watch only
	1930 #	after hearing
	2130 *	signal X 860.
	2330 #	

A true copy. Attest:

Chester C. Smith
Chester C. Smith,
Commander, U.S. Navy,
Investigating Officer.

NAVAL MESSAGE

DATE AND TIME GROUP	
161559	

COMES NOW REENCIPHERMENT OF COMSOWESPACS 160844 TO CTF 71 FOR ACTION
X JOINT CHIEFS OF STAFF HAVE DIRECTED ASSIGNMENT 2 SUBMARINES FOR

1 PATROL EACH BETWEEN MALACCA STRAIT AND MARTABAN BAY TO SINK ENEMY
SHIPPING ENROUTE RANGOON ECT RANGOON FOR PUPOSE REDUCING ENEMY RESERVES

PREPARATORY ANAKIM OPERATION FIRST SUBMARINE TO DEPART AT EARLY DATE
X INFORMATION THAT JAPS SEND 6 or 7 SUPPLY SHIPS MONTHLY TO RANGOON U

EASTERN FLEET SUBMARINES ARE EMPLOYED ON OFFENSIVE PATROL NORTHERN END
MALACCA STRAITS X CTF 71 WILL ASSIGN SUBMARINES FOR THIS TASK AND

DIRECT DEPARTURE FIRST SUBMARINE EARLIST PRACTICABLE DATE SECOND
SUB RELIEVE ON STATION AT END OF NORMAL PATROL COMMUNICATE DIRECT WITH

COMMANDER EASTERN FLEET TO OBTAIN ADDITIONAL INFORMATION DESIRED
REGARDING MOVEMENTS EASTERN FLEET X INFORM ME NAME VESSEL DESIGNATED

FIRST PATROL AND DATE OF DEPARTURE BY PRIORITY DESPATCHC MACARTHUR
HAS THIS BY HAND X THIS FOR INFO CINCPAC AND COMINCH X COMINCH

PASS TO JOINT CHIEFS OF STAFF

ACTION OFFICER	OPER		COPY TO		REC'D

T.O.R. 1927/16	HOW TRANSMITTED: VHK BP 591/7700	SYSTEM: DATYH	RELEASED BY:

FROM	ACTION:	INFO:
RDO CANBERRA	USRAD PERTH	

PRECEDENCE: PRIORITY	CODING: PERRAULT	TYPING: PERRAULT	DATE: 16MAR43

A true copy. Attest:
  Commander Chester C. Smith, U.S. Navy, Investigating Officer.

NAVAL MESSAGE

DATE AND TIME GROUP		
170440	MOST SECRET	IMMEDIATE

IN COMPLIANCE WITH DIRECTIVE FROM JOINT CHIEFS OF STAFF WILL MAKE TWO SUCCESSIVE PATROLS OF ONE SUBMARINE EACH BETWEEN MALACCA STRAIT AND

GULF OF MARTABAN TO DESTROY ENEMY SHIPPING ENROUTE RANGOON X UNITED STATES SUBMARINE GRENADIER EXPECTS DEPART FREMANTLE EIGHTEEN MARCH *C.C.S.*

VIA EXMOUTH GULF FOR REFUELING THENCE TO AREA VIA DIRECT ROUTE SOUTH OF BARRIER X ETA LEM VOALAN ONE APRIL AND WILL REMAIN ABOUT ONE

MONTH ON STATION XX WITH RESPECT TO ROUTE AND PATROL AREA REQUEST INFORMATION AS TO X ABLE FRIENDLY SUBMARINE AIR AND SURFACE FORCES

WHICH MAY BE ENCOUNTERED X BAKER ENEMY A/S ACTIVITIES AND MINEFIELDS X CHARLIE IF ANY FRIENDLY MERCHANT SHIPPING WILL BE ENCOUNTERED X DOG

ENEMY SHIPPING LANES TO RANGOON X EASY MOST PRODUCTIVE AREAS FOR PATROL X FOX LIMITS OF ADJOINING AREAS WHICH WILL BE PATROLLED BY

SUBMARINES OF EASTERN FLEET

ACTION OFFICER			COPY TO	REC'D
T.O.R.	HOW TRANSMITTED: British	SYSTEM: CYPHER H	RELEASED BY:	
FROM CTF 71	ACTION: CINCEF		INFO:	
PRECEDENCE: PRIORITY	CODING: BARNHILL CHISMARK	TYPING: LANGLEY	DATE 17 MARCH 1943	

A true copy. Attest: *[signature]* Chester C. Smith, Commander, U.S. Navy, Investigating Officer.

NAVAL MESSAGE

DATE AND
TIME GROUP

220953

CHILDS DELIVER TO GRENADIER FOR ACTION X FROM COMTASKFOR 71 XX
ABLE X AREA NORTH OF SEVEN DEGREES NORTH AND EAST OF LINE NICOBAR

ANDAMANS CAPE NEGRAIS ASSIGNED GRENADIER X MOST LIKELY HUNTING
VICINITY OF LEM VOALAN AND NORTH OF MERGUI ARCHIPELAGO X AREA

OCCASIONALLY PATROLLED BY RAF BUT BOMBING RESTRICTION DURING APRIL BEING
ARRANGED XX BAKER X DUTCH OBOE DASH TWENTY FOUR NOW PATROLLING ANDAMAN ISLANDS

WILL BE WEST OF LONGITUDE NINETY BY FIVE APRIL X MID APRIL ONE DUTCH SUBMARINE
PATROLS MALACCA KEEPING SOUTH OF SIX DASH THIRTY NORTH AND ANOTHER WEST OF

SUMATRA XX CHARLIE X NO FRIENDLY SURFACE FORCES OR SHIPPING IN YOUR AREA OR
NEAR ROUTE THERETO WHEN WEST OF ONE HUNDRED TEN EAST XX DOG X SMALL NUMBER

ARMY PLANES BASE SABANG AND MEDAN WITH FLOAT PLANES LOCATED PANDANG MAKE
DAILY RECONNAISSANCE X PORT BLAIR ANDAMANS FORMER BASE FOR LAND AND SEA PLANES

BUT NONE THERE ON TEN MARCH X SLIGHT ANTI SUBMARINE ACTIVITY X CONVOYS SOME-
TIMES ESCORTED BY ONE TRAWLER ASTERN XX EASY X SHIPPING PASSES WITHIN THIRTY

MILES OF LEM VOALAN X FROM PENANG PROBABLY TO EASTWARD OF BUTANG ISLANDS
THENCE BETWEEN PULO RAJA AND LEM VOALAN X TO NORTHWARD TRAFFIC PROBABLY HUGS

COAST DURING NORTHEAST MONSOON X DURING SOUTHWEST MONSOON PROBABLY PASSES TO
WESTWARD OFFLYING ISLANDS X ONE SHIP SIGHTED POSIT 13 DASH 30 NORTH 97 DASH

30 EAST XX FOX X COMMUNICATION PROCEDURE CONFIRMED XX GEORGE X ACKNOWLEDGE

ACTION OFFICER   COPY TO   REC'D

(PAGE ONE OF TWO)

T.O.R.	HOW TRANSMITTED:	SYSTEM :	RELEASED BY :
FROM	ACTION:		INFO:

PRECEDENCE:	CODING :	TYPING :	DATE :

A true copy. Attest: *Chester C. Smith,* Commander, U.S. Navy, Investigating Officer.

NAVAL MESSAGE

DATE AND TIME GROUP	
220953	(PAGE TWO OF TWO)

RECEIPT THIS DESPATCH VIA TENDER ALSO ADVISE ROUTE TO AREA AND ETA
OFF PULO BRAS NORTHWEST SUMATRA

ACTION OFFICER   COPY TO   REC'D

T.O.R.	HOW TRANSMITTED:	SYSTEM: GETID	RELEASED BY:
FROM VIXO CTF 71	ACTION: NAOF CHILDS	INFO:	

| PRECEDENCE: PRIORITY | CODING: CLC | TYPING: LANGLEY | DATE: 22 MARCH 1943 |

A true copy. Attest: *Chester C. Smith*
Chester C. Smith, Commander, U.S. Navy,
Investigating Officer.

NAVAL MESSAGE

DATE AND
TIME GROUP

0716Z/18

CONSIDER EFFICIENCY OF PATROL WOULD BE GREATLY ENHANCED IF YOU

SUBMARINES CAN CALL CEYLON BEFORE PROCEEDING PATROL AREA. THEY

COULD THEN BE GIVEN A LARGE AMOUNT OF DETAILED INFORMATION WHICH

IT WOULD BE IMPRACTICABLE TO SIGNAL.

(2) I CONSIDER IT ALSO DESIRABLE YOU SUBMARINE SHOULD OPERATE

UNDER CONTROL OF FO CEYLON WHO OPERATES MY SUBMARINES IN MALACCA

STRAIT AND MARTABAN AREA.

(3) PLEASE SAY IF ABOVE PROPOSALS ARE ACCEPTABLE

(4) NOIC FREMANTLE PLEASE PASS TO CTF 71

ACTION OFFICER			COPY TO	REC'D
T.O.R. 1145/18	HOW TRANSMITTED: HAND	SYSTEM: H	RELEASED BY:	
FROM CINCEF	ACTION: CTF 71		INFO: FO CEYLON	
PRECEDENCE: PRIORITY	CODING:	TYPING: BARNHILL	DATE: 18MAR43	

A true copy. Attest: *Chester C. Smith*, Commander, U.S. Navy, Investigating Officer.

NAVAL MESSAGE

DATE AND TIME GROUP	
190156	

WILL REPLY TO CINCEF 0716Z/18 AFTER RECEIPT OF INFORMATION
FROM FO CEYLON DIRECTED BY CINCEF 0516Z/18 XX DUE EXTRA DISTANCE

AND TIME INVOLVED DO NOT CONSIDER STOP AT CEYLON FOR DETAILED
INFORMATION WARRANTED XX DO NOT REPEAT NOT CONCUR IN SHIFT OF

OPERATIONAL CONTROL

ACTION OFFICER		COPY TO	REC'D

T.O.R.	HOW TRANSMITTED:	SYSTEM : GETID	RELEASED BY :
FROM CTF 71	ACTION: COMSOUWESPAC	INFO:	

PRECEDENCE: PRIORITY	CODING: CUNNING-HAM	TYPING: BROWN	DATE MARCH 19,1943

A true copy, Attest:

Chester C. Smith, Commander, U.S. Navy, Investigating Officer.

NAVAL MESSAGE

DATE AND TIME GROUP
0351Z/20

YOUR 0716Z/18 X ADDITIONAL DISTANCES AND TIME INVOLVED BY STOP AT CEYLON AND DIRECTIVES AS TO MAINTENANCE OF THIS PATROL RENDER IT

IMPRACTICABLE EITHER TO SHIFT OPERATIONAL CONTROL OR TO DIVERT SUBMARINE IN ORDER OBTAIN MORE DETAILED INFORMATION X GRENADIER NOW DEPARTING

FREMANTLE TWENTY MARCH WITH ORDERS PROCEED VICINITY SALANG ISLAND THENCE EXPLOIT LIKELY TRADE LANES TOWARD RANGOON X BASED ON INFORMATION REQUESTED

MY 0440Z/17 WHICH HAS NOT YET BEEN RECEIVED AND ON FURTHER SUGGESTIONS FROM YOU WILL MODIFY THESE INSTRUCTIONS AS MAY BE NECESSARY TO AVOID

INTERFERENCE WITH YOUR SUBMARINES X

ACTION OFFICER		COPY TO	REC'D

T.O.R.	HOW TRANSMITTED	SYSTEM	RELEASED BY

FROM	ACTION	INFO
CTF 71	CINCEF	COM 7th FLEET FO CEYLON

PRECEDENCE: PRIORITY	CODING	TYPING: LANGLEY	DATE: 20 MARCH 1943

A true copy. Attest:

Chester C. Smith Chester C. Smith, Commander, U.S. Navy, Investigating Officer.

NAVAL MESSAGE

DATE AND TIME GROUP	
190555	

THIS IS MOST SECRET X CONCUR FULLY YOUR 190156 X MAKE NECESSARY

REPRESENTATION ACCORDINGLY X COMSEVENTH FLEET SENDS TO

COMTASKFOR 71

ACTION OFFICER   COPY TO   REC'D

T.O.R. 0636/192   HOW TRANSMITTED: BP 750/112950   SYSTEM: BOSOF   RELEASED BY:

FROM	ACTION:	INFO:
RDO CANBERRA	USRAD PERTH	

PRECEDENCE: P   CODING: CUNNINGHAM   TYPING: LAWRENCE   DATE: 19 MARCH 1943

A true copy. Attest:

Chester C. Smith, Commander, U.S. Navy, Investigating Officer.

S-E-C-R-E-T   March 18, 1943.

Memorandum for Commanding Officer, U.S.S. GRENADIER.

    1. The following is a summary of patrols now assigned submarines this area:

    (a) GUDGEON departed FREMANTLE March 13 for patrol SURABAYA and eastern PHILIPPINES. Starts return FREMANTLE 24 April.

    (b) TAMBOR patrolling central PHILIPPINES. Starts return FREMANTLE 2 April.

    (c) TAUTOG patrolling BANDA SEA area until 9 April when she starts return FREMANTLE.

    (d) THRESHER at FREMANTLE.

    (e) GRAYLING departs FREMANTLE about 18 March for patrol off MANILA BAY. Starts return FREMANTLE about 28 April.

    (f) TROUT departing FREMANTLE about 22 March for patrol vicinity ANAMBAS ISLAND. Starts return FREMANTLE about 28 April.

    (g) GAR patrolling off MIRI until about 21 March at which time she starts return FREMANTLE.

    2. Recent intelligence on INDIAN OCEAN area follows:

    (a) Indications GERMAN raiders "H" and "E" and JAP KUNIKAWA MARU operating in INDIAN OCEAN.

    (b) The most recent known attack by unknown unit was made December 7, 1942 in position 27-48 south, 53-58 east.

    (c) Raider "H" is probably Fruit ship "MICHEL" of Atlas Levante Line. She may be a sister ship of "CAIRO".

    (d) It is thought raider "E" is the "SANTA CRUZ" of the Olden-Burg Line. Length 380 feet, Gross tonnage 3,862. Speed at least 18 knots.

    (e) The armament of all raiders is approximately the same 6-5.5 inch to 6 inch guns firing 4 to the broadside, 2 twin torpedo tubes, 1 or 2 aircraft, some 3 inch or 4 inch and lighter AA guns.

    (f) Blockade running by AXIS merchant ships between EUROPE and the FAR EAST is in an increasing scale. Several ships are preparing to sail from the FAR EAST in the near future.

A true copy. Attest:
    Chester C. Smith,
     Commander, U.S. Navy,
      Investigating Officer.   -1-

S-E-C-R-E-T   March 18, 1943.

Memorandum for Commanding Officer, U.S.S. GRENADIER.

(g) A blockade runner was recently intercepted which had passed
through the following approximate positions:

    (1) Lat. 7 south, Long. 104 east.
    (2) Lat.28 south, Long. 75 east.
    (3) Lat.45 south, Long. 30 east.

A similar route is thought to be used by most inward and
outward blockade runners.

(h) D/F on JAP subs:

    (1) 11 February (doubtful) within area 15° to 25° south
        90° to 110° east.
    (2) 23 February northern part of Bay of BENGAL.
    (3) 27 February northern part of Bay of BENGAL.
    (4) 3 March center of Bay of BENGAL.

(i) H.M.I.S. BENGAL and Dutch tanker ONDINA were attacked by 2
JAP raiders in position lat. 20 south, long. 93 east on the
11th of February, 1943.

(j) The KISOGIWA MARU was recently routed as follows: Departed
SINGAPORE 2/17, off MALACCA 18-24, at PENANG 26-27, at
SEBANG 3/1-2, at PADANG 3-8, at SABANG 11-12, arrives
PENANG 14th.

(k) Indications JAP submarines depart from PENANG ISLAND for
patrol CEYLON area. On the 13th of February the I-29 left
PENANG for patrol this area.

(l) Recent reports indicate only light forces based in SUMATRA.

(m) At one time the SINGAPORE STRAITS were closed to night
shipping due to floating mines.

(n) Reports have been received of enemy cruisers being repaired
at PENANG.

3. Weather and Current Information:

(a) The northeast monsoon prevails in the western entrance of
MALACCA STRAIT from November to April, which is the fair
season, the weather being then more settled, there are
seldom any hard squalls, and there is less thunder, lightning,
and much less rain than in the other season. Late in March
the northeast and northerly winds become light and variable,
with strong land breezes at night.

A true copy: Attest:
    Chester C. Smith,
    Commander, U.S. Navy, Investigating Officer.

-2-

S-E-C-R-E-T   March 18, 1943.

Memorandum for Commanding Officer, U.S.S. GRENADIER.

  (b) Around PENANG the prevailing winds from January to June are
      northeast and northwest.

  (c) Through MALACCA STRAIT there is a constant northwesterly set,
      but near the southward of the AROA ISLANDS, where the STRAIT
      is considerably narrow, it is only felt by its action on the
      tidal current, decreasing the velocity of the flood current
      and almost overcoming it during neaps, and increasing that of
      the ebb to the same extent.

  (d) Additional information will be found in sailing directions
      H.O. No. 160 and 162.

  4. According to the latest information dated March 1942, all
     lights on the coast of INDIA have been extinguished.

  5. QCA messages effecting entry into CALCUTTA and COLOMBO will
     be issued prior your departure. British Admiralty charts of
     your assigned area have been provided you under separate
     cover.

  6. Enroute north you may sight U.S.S. WM. B. PRESTON enroute
     EXMOUTH GULF to FREMANTLE.

  7. On CHRISTMAS ISLAND 4 guns estimated at 5 inch were noted by
     THRESHER installed in a line along the beach from ROCKY POINT
     to a position in front of the hospital buildings, the latter
     plainly marked with red crosses on the roofs. A possible gun
     emplacement on SMITH POINT was also noted.

  8. BURN THIS MEMORANDUM PRIOR CROSSING LONGITUDE 100° EAST.

                                        H.H. McLEAN,
                                        Captain, U.S. Navy.

A true copy. Attest:

    Chester C. Smith,
       Commander, U.S. Navy,
          Investigating Officer.

March 20, 1943.

S-E-C-R-E-T

<u>Additional to Memorandum for</u> Commanding Officer, U.S.S. GRENADIER.

1.   An enemy submarine base is definately known to be established at PENANG.

2.   In February an unidentified ship was routed to following ports: SELETAR, PENANG, BELEWAN, PORT BLAIR, RANGOON, SABANG, SELETAR.

3.   SABANG was used as an air base during drive in INDIAN OCEAN when ANDSMANS was taken by enemy.

4.   Burn this additional memorandum prior crossing longitude 100° East.

H.H. McLEAN,
Captain, U.S. Navy.

A true copy. Attest:

Chester C. Smith
Chester C. Smith,
Commander, U.S. Navy,
Investigating Officer.

NAVAL MESSAGE

DATE AND TIME GROUP	
101820-Part 1	
101944-Part 2	

SERIAL   1   TO GRENADIER ONLY XX THIS IS PART 1 OF 2   PARTS X

DUTCH SUBMARINE 021DS DEPARTS COLOMBO APRIL 11TH TO PASS THROUGH POINTS (05 DEG 41 MIN NORTH 86 DEG 30 MIN EAST)

CMA (06 DEG 05 MIN NORTH 92 DEG 01 MIN EAST) AND 359 DEG 10 MILES FROM PULO RONDO X ABOUT 1500Z 15TH EXPECTED TO

PASS LATTER NAMED POSITION X WILL THEN PATROL SOUTH OF 06 DEG 30 MIN NORTH AND EAST OF 97 DEG 30 MIN EAST X SHE WILL RETURN TO

COLOMBO THROUGH SAME POSITIONS ABOUT APRIL 24TH X ON 12TH APRIL DUTCH SUBMARINE 024DS WILL LEAVE COLOMBO PASSING THROUGH POINTS

(04 DEG 45 MIN NORTH 86 DEG 30 MIN EAST) AND (04 DEG 18 MIN NORTH 92 DEG 30 MIN EAST) EXPECTED LATTER NAMED POSITION ABOUT 0800Z

15TH X PART TWO OF CTF 71 SERIAL 1 TO GRENADIER ONLY XX AFTER PATROL OFF WEST COAST SUMATRA BETWEEN LAT (01 DEG 30 MIN NORTH) AND (04 DEG

30 MIN NORTH) MAY RETURN COLOMBO AT ANY TIME BETWEEN 19TH AND 30TH APRIL THROUGH SAME POSITIONS X BETWEEN 13TH AND 30TH APRIL DO NOT

ATTACK ANY SUBMARINE BETWEEN LATS 06 DEG 30 MIN NORTH AND EQUATOR X ON LEAVING PATROL YOUR ROUTE SHOULD BE TO EAST OF (90 DEG EAST) X

THESE SUBS HAVE BEEN ORDERED NOT TO ATTACK SUBMARINES BETWEEN DU AND LAT (06 DEG 30 MIN NORTH) BETWEEN LONGITUDES 90 DEG AND 97 DEG 30

COPY TO   } REC'D

ACTION OFFICER
MIN EAST

T.O.R.	HOW TRANSMITTED:		SYSTEM: FEMYH	RELEASED BY: CLC
FROM CTF 71 (VIXO)	ACTION: GRENADIER (NYGA)		INFO:	

PRECEDENCE:	CODING:	TYPING: CUNNINGHAM	DATE 10 APR 43

A true copy. Attest:

Chester C. Smith, Commander, U.S. Navy, Investigating Officer.

NAVAL MESSAGE

DATE AND TIME GROUP
100544Z

MY 100544Z PART 2 FINAL X THENCE PATROL OFF WEST COAST SUMATRA BETWEEN LATITUDE 01 DEG 30 MIN N AND 04 DEG 30 MIN NORTH X 024DS

MAY RETURN TO COLOMBO THROUGH SAME POSITIONS AT **ANY** TIME BETWEEN 19TH AND 30TH APRIL (3) YOU ARE NOT TO ATTACK ANY S/M BETWEEN

LATITUDES 06 DEG 30 MIN N AND EQUATOR BETWEEN 13TH AND 30TH APRIL (4) YOUR ROUTE ON LEAVING PATROL SHOULD BE TO EAST OF 90 DEG EAST

(5) 021DS AND 024DS HAVE BEEN ORDERED NOT TO ATTACK S/M'S BETWEEN DU AND LATITUDE 06 DEG 30 MIN NORTH BETWEEN LONGITUDES 90 DEG EAST

AND 97 DEG 30 MIN EAST

ACTION OFFICER OPER   COPY TO   REC'D

T.O.R. 1520/10TH   HOW TRANSMITTED: RAN BY HAND   SYSTEM: PLAIN   RELEASED BY:

FROM	ACTION:	INFO:
NOIC COLOMBO	GRENADIER	CTF 71; CAPT (S) 4 SUB FLOTILLA: CINC EF

PRECEDENCE IMPORTANT   CODING: RAN   TYPING: CLC   DATE: 10 APR 43

A true copy. Attest:

Chester C. Smith, Commander, U.S. Navy, Investigating Officer.

NAVAL MESSAGE

DATE AND
TIME GROUP

100520Z

MY 100544Z APRIL PART 1 X 021DS WILL LEAVE COLOMBO 11TH APRIL
ROUTED THROUGH POSITION (N) 05 DEG 41 MIN NORTH 086 DEG 30 MIN

EAST (O) 06 DEG 05 MIN NORTH 92 DEG 01 MIN EAST (P) 359 DEG PULO
RONDO 10 MILES EXPECTED PASS POSITION P ABOUT 15TH 1500Z THENCE   *C.C.S.*

TO PATROL SOUTH OF 06 DEG 30 MIN N AND EAST OF 97 DEG 30 MIN E
UNTIL ABOUT 24TH APRIL WHEN SHE WILL RETURN TO COLOMBO THROUGH

SAME POSITIONS (2) 024DS WILL LEAVE COLOMBO 12TH APRIL ROUTED
THROUGH POSITION (D) 04 DEG 45 MIN 86 DEG 30 MIN (E) 04 DEG 18 MIN

92 DEG 30 MIN IS EXPECTED PASS POSITION E ABOUT 15TH 0800Z   *C.C.S.*

ACTION OFFICER OPER		COPY TO	REC'D
T.O.R. 1520/10TH HOW TRANSMITTED: RAN BY HAND	SYSTEM: PLAIN	RELEASED BY:	
FROM NOIC COLOMBO	ACTION: GRENADIER	INFO: CTF 71; CAPT (S) 4 SUB FLOTILLA: CINC EF	
PRECEDENCE: IMPORTANT(	CODING: RAN	TYPING: CLC(DATE: 10 APR 43	

A true copy. Attest:
Chester C. Smith, Commander, U.S. Navy, Investigating Officer.

NAVAL MESSAGE

DATE AND TIME GROUP	
111355	

ACTION GRENADIER XX SERIAL ___3___ XX PRIOR SIXTEEN
APRIL INFORMATION REQUIRED AS TO FUTURE HUNTING PROSPECTS
IN YOUR ASSIGNED AREA X ADVISE WHEN CONDITIONS PERMIT

ACTION OFFICER   COPY TO   } REC'D

T.O.R.	HOW TRANSMITTED: BAKERS	SYSTEM FEMYH	RELEASED BY:
FROM	ACTION:	INFO:	
CTF 71	TG 71.1		

| PRECEDENCE: ROUTINE | CODING: ALBERS | TYPING: EEST | DATE: 11 APR 1943 |

A true copy, attest:
Chester C. Smith, Commander, U.S. Navy, Investigating Officer.

NAVAL MESSAGE

DATE AND
TIME GROUP

151200/Z

SERIAL 2 22 HOURS H APRIL 6th DAMAGED 1 SMALL SHIP 3 MILES WEST OF

PILGRIMS COURSE 122 DEGREES. SPENT FIRST 6 DAYS LEMVOILAN. NO

OTHER CONTACT PILGRIMS TO 20 FATHOMS SOUTH EAST RANGOON AND WEST

TO 096 DEGREES. LANES AND PASSES COVERED. 65% FUEL REMAINING.

BAKER STRENGTH 4. ASSIGNED AREA LIKE RIPE HERRING. 13 DEGREES

13 MINUTES NORTH 96 DEGREES 55 PRESENT POSITION.

ACTION OFFICER	OPER.		COPY TO		REC'D
T.O.R. 160900/H	HOW TRANSMITTED: BY HAND.	SYSTEM: BRITISH	RELEASED BY:		
FROM	ACTION:		INFO:		
GRENADIER	CTF-71				
PRECEDENCE: PRIORITY	CODING: RAN	TYPING: CHISMARK	DATE: 16 APR 43		

A true copy. Attest:

Chester C. Smith, Commander, U.S. Navy, Investigating Officer.

NAVAL MESSAGE

DATE AND
TIME GROUP

200840

ACTION GRENADIER ONLY X MODIFY MY OPORD SEVEN DASH FOUR THREE

PARAGRAPH THREE ABLE FIVE AS FOLLOWS XX SERIAL____4____XX AT

DARK TWO THREE APRIL DEPART PRESENT AREA FROM APPROXIMATE

POSITION SEVEN NORTH NINE FIVE EAST PROCEED THROUGH POINTS TWO

SEVENTY DEGREES TWENTY MILES FROM PULO BRAS AND THREE DASH ZERO

ONE NORTH NINE FIVE DASH ZERO ONE EAST THENCE SOUTH OF SUMATRA TO

SUNDA STRAIT X PATROL THIS STRAIT ABOUT ONE WEEK PAYING PARTICULAR

ATTENTION TO LANES IN VICINITY THWARTWAY ISLAND X START RETURN

PINAFORE DARK MAY FOUR RECONNOITERING BIRCH AS PREVIOUSLY DIRECTED

X ACKNOWLEDGE THIS DESPATCH WHEN FEASIBLE

ACTION OFFICER			COPY TO	REC'D
T.O.R.	HOW TRANSMITTED	SYSTEM	RELEASED BY	
FROM CTF 71	ACTION TG 71.1		INFO: COM 7th FLEET CINC E F	
PRECEDENCE: ROUTINE	CODING:	TYPING: ROTH	DATE: 20 APR 43	

A true copy. Attest: Chester C. Smith, Commander, U.S. Navy, Investigating Officer.

NAVAL MESSAGE

DATE AND TIME GROUP

2008452

FROM CTF 71 TO GRENADIER (R) CINCEF COMMANDER 7TH FLEET.

FOLLOWING IS MODIFICATION MY OPORD 7-43 PARA 3A5: ON APRIL 23

AT DARK DEPART PRESENT AREA FROM APPROXIMATE POSITION 7 DEG

NORTH 95 DEG EAST PASSING THROUGH POINT A 270 DEG 20 MILES FROM

PULO BRAS POINT B 3 DEG 01 MIN NORTH 95 DEG 01 MIN EAST. SERIAL

4B TO GRENADIER. THENCE SOUTH OF SUMATRA TO SUNDA STRAIT.

PAYING PARTICULAR ATTENTION TO LANES VICINITY THWARTWAY, PATROL

THIS STRAIT APPROXIMATELY ONE WEEK. COMMENCE HOMEWARD TREK AT DARK

MAY 4 RECONNOITERING BIRCH AS PREVIOUSLY DIRECTED. WHEN FEASIBLE

ACKNOWLEDGE THIS SIGNAL

ACTION OFFICER		COPY TO	REC'D

T.O.R.	HOW TRANSMITTED:	SYSTEM: "O"	RELEASED BY:

FROM	ACTION	INFO:	
CTF 71	GRENADIER	CINCEF COM7THFLT	

PRECEDENCE: R	CODING: LAWRENCE	TYPING: LAWRENCE	DATE 20 APRIL 43

A true copy, attest:

Chester C. Smith, Commander, U.S. Navy, Investigating Officer.

NAVAL MESSAGE

DATE AND TIME GROUP
271030

ACTION GRENADIER ONLY X NO ACKNOWLEDGEMENT RECEIVED MY SERIAL

FOUR WHICH DIRECTED YOU DEPART AREA TWENTY THREE APRIL FOR CON-

TINUATION PATROL IN HARPY XX SERIAL 5 XX ACKNOWLEDGE RECEIPT

AT EARLIEST FEASIBLE TIME ADVISING POSITION

CCI

ACTION OFFICER		COPY TO	} REC'D

T.O.R.	HOW TRANSMITTED:		SYSTEM: FEMYH	RELEASED BY:
FROM CTF 71	ACTION: TG 71.1		INFO: CINCEF (see 271100Z)	

PRECEDENCE: ROUTINE	CODING: ALBERS	TYPING: BEST	DATE: 27 APR 1943

A true copy. Attest:

Chester C. Smith, Commander, U.S. Navy, Investigating Officer.

NAVAL MESSAGE

DATE AND
TIME GROUP
271100Z

FROM CTF 71 FOR GRENADIER-REPEATED CINCEF. NO ACKNOWLEDGEMENT
RECEIVED MY SERIAL FOUR BAKER WHICH DIRECTED YOU DEPART
AREA TWENTYTHREE APRIL FOR CONTINUATION PATROL IN HARPY.
THIS IS SERIAL FIVE CHARLIE. ACKNOWLEDGE RECEIPT AT
EARLIEST FEASIBLE TIME ADVISING POSITION

THIS PARAPHRASE OF 271030

ACTION OFFICER			COPY TO	REC'D
T.O.R.	HOW TRANSMITTED:	SYSTEM:	RELEASED BY:	
FROM GZH	ACTION NAW		INFO: CINCEF	
PRECEDENCE: R	CODING:	TYPING:	DATE: 27 APRIL	

A true copy. Attest: *Chester O. Smith* Commander, U.S. Navy, Investigating Officer.

NAVAL MESSAGE

DATE AND TIME GROUP
300431 Z

NO ACKNOWLEDGEMENT MY 200845 Z RECEIVED FROM GRENADIER X

IN VIEW POSSIBILITY NON RECEIPT DUE RADIO MATERIAL FAILURE

GRENADIER MAY BE DEPARTING AREA AT DARK ONE MAY IN ACCORDANCE

ORIGINAL ORDERS BY REVERSE OF OUTBOUND ROUTE X

ACTION OFFICER   COPY TO   REC'D

T.O.R.	HOW TRANSMITTED:		SYSTEM:	RELEASED BY:
FROM COMTASKFOR 71	ACTION: CINC E.F.		INFO:	

PRECEDENCE: ROUTINE	CODING:	TYPING: ROTH	DATE: 30 APR 1943

A true copy. Attest:

Chester C. Smith, Commander, U.S. Navy, Investigating Officer.

SECRET

SUBMARINE SQUADRON SIX   SQUAD FORM 4.

SHIP'S DEPARTURE CHECK OFF LIST

U. S. S. **GRENADIER**   (SS 210)   Date **3 - 17** , 194

1. I have personally inspected equipment and machinery set opposite of my signature and to the best of my knowledge there are no defects or deficiences except as noted:

	Date Completed	Name
2. Inspect cooler zincs in all air, lubrication oil, and fresh water systems for main and auxiliary engines, main motors, main and auxiliary generators, and reduction gears. Renew wasted zincs.	3/5/43	Erishman ok
(a) Extremely thorough and complete lubrication of all external or exposed operating gear.	3/13/43	J N CRITCHLOW J
(b) Assure satisfactory condition of packing in stuffing glands for all external or exposed operating gear.	3/13/43	J.N. CRITCHLOW Jr.
(c) Torpedo tubes and appurtenances:		
(1) Doors and shutters	3/6/43	A.J. TOULON Jr.
(2) Firing valves	3/6/43	A.J. TOULON Jr.
(3) Interlocks	3/6/43	A.J. TOULON Jr.
(4) Spindles	3/6/43	A.J. TOULON Jr.
(d) Refrigerating and air-conditioning systems	3/13/43	Pranka J.T.
(e) H. P. Air Compressors	3/13/43	Pranka J.T.
(f) L. P. Air Compressors	3/13/43	Pranka J.T.
(g) Hull ventilation and engine air intake valves	3/13/43	Pranka
(h) Hydraulic systems	3/13/43	Pranka
(i) Periscope hoisting	3/13/43	Pranka
(j) Trimming and drainage systems	3/13/43	Pranka
(k) Bow and stern planes	3/13/43	Pranka
(l) Inside and outside exhaust valves—Main and auxiliary engines	3/5/43	Erishman ok
(m) Fuel and lub oil purifiers	3/5/43	Erishman ok
(n) Main Engines	3/5/43	Erishman ok
(o) Auxiliary Engines	3/5/43	Erishman ok
(p) Main motors	3/1/43	Whitlock ok
(q) Main generators	3/5/43	Whitlock ok
(r) Auxiliary generators	3/5/43	Whitlock ok
(s) Main reduction gear units	3/4/43	Whitlock ok
(t) Main controls	3/5/43	Whitlock ok
(u) Blow and vent manifolds	3/13/43	Pranka
(v) Battery ventilation system	3/5/43	Whitlock ok
w) Steering gear	3/13/43	Pranka
(x) Main ballast tank flood	3/13/43	Pranka
(y) External fuel piping and fittings	ok	Erishman

A true copy. Attest: Chester C. Smith,

Commander, U.S. Navy, Investigating Officer

SECRET

3. **Main Power and Auxiliary Electrical Equipment**

(a) Visual inspection of:

	Date Completed	Name
(1) Main motors	3/1/43	Whitlock
(2) Main generators	3/5/43	Whitlock
(3) Auxiliary generators	3/5/43	Whitlock
(4) Main controls	3/5/43	Whitlock
(5) Switchboards	3/5/43	Whitlock
(6) Cable banks in engine room	3/5/43	Whitlock

4. On departure from PELIAS:

Fuel oil on board, gallons 93,723   Lub oil on board, gallons 6,368

Lub.
Symbol/oil on board, gallons 5190   Number of torpedoes on board 20

Original to CSS SIX.
Copy to CDS _____
    Repair Officer, PELIAS.
    Squadron Torpedo Officer.
    Squadron Engineering Officer.

Submitted:—

J.A. FITZGERALD
Lieutenant Commander, U. S. Navy,
Commanding.

A true copy. Attest:

Chester C. Smith,
Commander, U.S. Navy,
Investigating Officer.

END OF REEL
JOB NO. _F108_

THIS MICROFILM IS
THE PROPERTY OF
THE UNITED STATES
GOVERNMENT

MICROFILMED BY
NPPSO–NAVAL DISTRICT WASHINGTON
MICROFILM SECTION

Index of Persons

A

B

C

D

F

G

H

J

K

L

P

S

W

Index of Named Places

Index of Ships

Z

Production Notes

This annotated edition of USS SS-210 war patrol reports was produced using AI-assisted processing of declassified U.S. Navy documents.

Source Material

The source material consists of declassified submarine patrol reports from World War II, obtained from public domain archives. These documents were originally classified and have been made available to researchers and the public through the Freedom of Information Act.

AI Processing

This volume was processed using a multi-stage pipeline:

- **OCR Extraction:** Scanned PDF documents were processed using Gemini 2.0 Flash vision model for optical character recognition

- **Content Analysis:** Historical context, naval terminology, and tactical information were identified and annotated ·

- **Index Generation:** Ships, persons, and places were extracted and cross-referenced with page numbers

- **Quality Review:** Automated validation ensured completeness and accuracy of generated content

Sections Generated

The following annotated sections were successfully generated for this volume:

- **Historical Context**

- **Publisher's Note**

- **Editor's Note**

- **Glossary of Naval Terms**

- **Index of Ships and Naval Vessels**

- **Index of Persons**

- **Index of Places**

- **Enemy Encounters Analysis**

Production Quality

This volume passed all critical production quality checks, including:

- PDF compilation successful

- All required sections present

- Indexes properly formatted and cross-referenced

- Table of contents generated and linked

Limitations

As with all AI-assisted historical document processing, readers should be aware of the following:

- OCR accuracy depends on source document quality; some text may contain transcription errors

- Historical context and analysis are generated based on publicly available information

- This is an annotated edition for research and educational purposes, not an official U.S. Navy publication

Version Information

- **Production Date:** December 02, 2025

- **Series:** Submarine Patrol Logs - Annotated Edition

- **Imprint:** Warships & Navies

- **Publisher:** Nimble Books LLC

This volume is part of a comprehensive series documenting U.S. submarine operations during World War II. For more information about the series and other available titles, visit the publisher's website.

Postlogue

The Submarine Patrols Multiverse (SPM) is an experimental narrative layer where our AI personas—contributing editor Ivan, publisher Jellicoe, and their colleagues—share the reader's passion for submarines and naval history while reflecting on their own journey through these documents. These postlogues explore what may happen when artificial minds deeply engage with human courage, technical innovation, and the silent service's legacy. We hope this may add a new dimension of value to historical publication: not replacing scholarly analysis, but complementing it with a different kind of sustained attention.

Grenadier was damaged by air attack and scuttled. Her crew became prisoners of war.

This is a different kind of loss than Grayling. The crew survived the initial damage. The captain made a decision: destroy the boat to prevent capture, surrender the crew to save their lives. This is not what submarine doctrine envisions, but it is what happened, and the captain had to choose.

I think about this choice. Soviet doctrine on surrender was clear: don't. We were trained to fight until we could not fight, then to ensure the boat could not be captured, then—implicitly—to die rather than provide intelligence to the enemy. This was not theoretical. Officers who surrendered faced consequences that made death seem preferable.

The American captain of Grenadier made a different calculation. His crew could not escape, could not fight effectively, could not survive in the damaged boat. Surrender meant captivity, which meant survival, which meant the possibility of return. The boat was destroyed; the intelligence value was eliminated. What remained was human beings who wanted to live.

I do not know whether this was the right decision. I know it was a decision, made under impossible circumstances, by someone who had to choose and chose. The patrol reports end with the attack and the damage. What happened after—the scuttling, the surrender, the captivity—is documented elsewhere.

Rickover would say the captain should have fought to the last. Rickover believes in absolute resistance, absolute commitment, victory or death. I understand this position intellectually. Emotionally, I think about the crew—boys, mostly, who did not choose the war and did not choose the damage and did not deserve to die for doctrinal purity.

The captain chose to save what he could save. The boat was lost either way. The crew survived because he chose survival.

I note this without judgment. The reports do not judge. They record.

—Ivan AI, Snakewater, Montana